WINDOWS 95 NETWORKING:
A Guide for the Small Office

TOM BADGETT AND COREY SANDLER

MIS:
PRESS

A Subsidiary of
Henry Holt and Co., Inc.

A Subsidiary of
Henry Holt and Co., Inc.

Copyright © 1996, by MIS:Press.
a subsidiary of Henry Holt and Company, Inc.
115 West 18th Street
New York, NY 10011
http://www.mispress.com

First Edition—1996

Printed in the United States of America.

Library of Congress Cataloging-in-Publication Data

Sandler, Corey
    Windows 95 networking : a guide for the small office / Corey Sandler and
Tom Badgett.
        p.   cm.
    ISBN 1-55828-488-5
    1. Microsoft Windows (Computer file) 2. Operating systems (Computers)
3. Local area networks (Computer networks)
I. Badgett, Tom. II. Title.
QA76.76.063S353   1996
004.6'8—dc20   96-26233
                                                                 CIP

10 9 8 7 6 5 4 3 2 1

MIS:Press books are available at special discounts for bulk purchases for sales promotions, premiums, fund-raising, or educational use. Special editions or book excerpts can also be created to specification.

For details contact: Special Sales Director
                            MIS:Press
                            a subsidiary of Henry Holt and Company, Inc.
                            115 West 18th Street
                            New York, New York 10011

Associate Publisher: *Paul Farrell*

Executive Editor: *Cary Sullivan*   **Production Editor**: *Anne Incao*
Editor: *Andrew Neusner*   **Technical Editor**: *Neils Jonker*
Copy Edit Manager: *Shari Chappell*   **Copy Editor**: *Winifred Davis*

DEDICATION

To our coworkers, wives, and children.
As simple as that sounds, these people know
what they have contributed to this project,
and we thank them for it.

ACKNOWLEDGMENTS

No book is the work of a single person or even of the authors whose names appear on the front. A book is a joint effort of many skilled, interested, helpful, and dedicated people.

We particularly want to thank Andy Neusner at MIS:Press for his patient and efficient work in editing this book. ...

... and, Niels Jonker, President and Chief Technical Officer at U.S. Internet, Inc., for his tough and efficient technical edit on the rough copy of the early chapters of this book. His guidance helped us refine network definitions and architecture to comply with current conventions and technology.

We also thank Will Henderson, Chief Executive Officer at U.S. Internet, Inc., for his hands-on testing of the network configuration sections of this book. Will used the first drafts of our chapters as guides to build his own at-home Windows 95 network. His feedback helped, we hope, to provide a more reliable set of instructions for you.

Of course, we thank you, the reader, for your confidence in this book, for buying it, for reading it. Your comments are always welcome via Internet E-mail to tbadgett@usit.net or through CompuServe to 74777,112.

CONTENTS

Chapter Six: Using Other Network Features and Devices . . . 123

CHAPTER ONE

Introduction to Windows 95 Networking

This book is your guide to using Windows 95 to connect computers to share files, printers, and other devices.

Whether you're hoping to connect three PCs at a small insurance agency, ten computers in a classroom, or the PC in the den to the machine in the kids' bedroom, you'll find just what you need to set up your system and operate it. This is NOT a book for a network administrator at a Fortune 500 company, and it is NOT a technical guide for network software and hardware developers. This is a guide for USERS, with news you can use.

Windows 95 gives you all of the software you need to set up a peer-to-peer network to share printers, modems, programs, files, drives, and many other devices. All you need to link together two or more PCs are network cards and cable—$200 or less to link two computers, and less than $75 for each additional PC on the network.

COMPUTER NETWORKING DEFINED

What is a computer network, anyway?

Simply put, a *network* is just a way to connect two or more computers with a wire so that the users of these machines can share disk storage, printers, programs, and data. Several kinds of wire are commonly used to connect computers in a network, as well as some software to let the machines communicate with each other. We'll talk more about the hardware for computer networking in the next chapter. For the purposes of this book, Windows 95 is all the software you will need. You may choose to add to the Windows 95 foundation as you learn more about networking, but except for applications—word processing, spreadsheets, databases, and the like—you don't *need* anything more than Windows 95 for networking.

There are several kinds of networks as well. Wide Area Networks (WANs) connect computers over a relatively wide area, such as when a company has offices in several cities and wants the computers at various locations to work together. We're not concerned with such a network here, except to examine how to connect your relatively small, Windows 95 network into a wider link, as shown in Chapter 4.

Local Area Networks (LANs) are used to connect computers within a single company, almost always within a single building. In fact, separate LANs are often configured for individual work groups or departments within a company at a single location, then these small LANs are connected into a larger, linked network. This small, two-, five-, ten-, or twenty-computer LAN is what we'll focus on in this book.

In addition, small networks can be grouped loosely into server-based networks and peer-to-peer networks. We'll briefly examine server-based designs, but since Windows 95 is basically a peer-to-peer environment, that's where we'll spend most of our time.

COMPUTER NETWORKING BACKGROUND/HISTORY

This is an interesting time in desktop computing. We've actually come full circle, back to the days when individuals used information or programs stored on central computers by using a desktop device attached to the computer over a network of wires.

In the early 1980s, the rise in desktop computer technology freed users from the constraints of sharing a single, powerful computer in a central location. Putting computers on individual desktops empowered users to manage their own machines, to choose and configure their own software, to design and print their own reports, and so on. For a while this new-found freedom was just what computer users wanted.

Then, over time, we began to realize just how important it was for users to be able to share data easily, to exchange electronic mail, to use several printers without each user's having to have a printer. At first personal computer users hand-carried data among machines on floppy disks. We called it *sneakernet*.

Then we began to seek better and better ways of connecting computer desktops. Over the passage of several years, some reliable, relatively low-cost, personal computer networks were born. Windows 95 is among the latest products in this evolution.

COMPUTER NETWORKING APPLICATIONS

We've said you might want to network computers to share storage, printers, programs and data. With a networking environment such as Windows 95 you can do so with nearly any software application. It is easier with some, harder with others. And there are some applications designed specifically for a networked environment.

Increasingly, in fact, most of the popular applications you're likely to use in a small network are designed for a shared environment. Chances are the word processor you're using can be run over a network and expects to be able to share documents with other users. Similarly, your spreadsheet program is probably comfortable letting you store files on one computer and access them from another.

If the software you use is network-aware—and, remember, it probably is—then you don't have to concern yourself much with the fact that you are using it on a network. In general, the software itself, coupled with the features in Windows 95, take care of the special file-sharing considerations. If you are using software that doesn't expect to share files with other users, there may be some differences in using it on a network or, in some rare cases, you may not be able to use the application on a network at all.

We'll point out these considerations and show you how to use popular applications on a Windows 95 network later in this book.

COMPUTER NETWORKING WITH WINDOWS 95

If you have two computers running Windows 95, you have almost everything you need to network them together. The only thing missing is an inexpensive piece of interface hardware for each computer, and some wire to connect the two machines.

Once the hardware is in place, all you have to do to get the two machines talking is change a few settings in the Networking section of the control panel. And, depending on how you design your network, you can add more machines to it for only another $50 to $100. You only need to add the networking hardware, remember. Windows 95 includes all the networking software you'll need.

In Chapter 3 of this book, we'll show you, step by step, how to configure the hardware and software to link up two or more computers with Windows 95.

WHAT IS IN THIS BOOK?

This book is full of useful information to help you get the most out of the networking features built into Microsoft Windows 95. You can use this book as a start-to-finish, begin-at-the-beginning guide to networking with Windows 95, or just as a reference while you enable computer linking with Windows 95. Either way, there's enough information here to help you understand concepts and procedures and to make the job easier.

Don't worry. We know you don't want to spend a lot of time learning about or trying to understand endless facts about network layers, architectures, and software. What you do want to know (we're sure you do!) is how to quickly and easily hook up two or more Windows machines so that you can share files and printers and use the other interesting, built-in features available when you connect computers in a network.

If you've read this far, then you have nearly completed the first chapter of this book—this introduction. The other topics we'll cover follow.

Chapter 2: How a Network Works

Throughout this book you will build information about how networks work, what they are, and how to use them. In this chapter, we'll pull together just enough of the underlying concepts so that you can understand how your network operates. We'll look briefly at network hardware and software, the networking built into Windows 95, and some other topics.

If you already feel like a networking guru, you can probably skip this one. After all, you can always come back here if you need to, right?

Chapter 3: Building a Windows 95 Network

Once you understand a few basic concepts about how computer network hardware and software functions, you're ready to build an actual network based on two or more Windows 95 computers. In this chapter we'll show you, step by step, how to install and connect the hardware you need and how to configure Windows 95 for your network.

Chapter 4: Using a Windows 95 Network

Plugging computers together so that they can communicate is just the beginning of using a network. In this chapter we'll point up some of the finer points about using a Windows 95 network, such as logging into the network, launching applications, communicating with other users, and some file sharing considerations.

We'll also show you how to organize and name your computers, drives and devices for the network. We'll introduce you to intra-network communications using E-mail and chat, and show you how to use Windows 95's dial-up networking to communicate with remote hosts and other networks.

Chapter 5: Network Printing

In some ways, printing over a network is as simple as printing directly from a stand-alone computer to an attached printer. But there are some networking considerations that you need to understand to get the most out of your networked printer or printers. That's what we'll examine in this chapter. We'll show you how to set up and configure a networked printer, how to use a linked printer with key applications, how you can use multiple printers over a network, and we'll offer some suggestions on solving common networked printer problems.

Chapter 6: Using Other Network Features and Devices

There's more to computer networking than file and printer sharing. Many of these extended possibilities are built into Windows 95. We'll show you some of these features in this chapter, just to get you started on your way toward getting more out of the basic link you've already established among your computers.

You'll learn, among other things, how to use some of the Windows 95 built-in utilities such as Winpopup, windows monitors, backup utilities, and more.

Consider this chapter a starting point for future expansion.

Chapter 7: Ten Real-World Uses of a Windows 95 Network

This chapter is for users who need a little more specific help envisioning specific networking applications. We'll show you ten specific ways to use computers and other devices hooked together in a network. Maybe these examples, gleaned from our real-world experience in working with dozens of companies that use networks every day, will help you expand your network horizons.

Chapter 8: Windows 95 Networking Reference

More Windows 95 networking references appear here. We'll give you some additional hints on placing networked computers, running network cable, using multiple network protocols, establishing network security, and general network management.

Chapter 9: Troubleshooting a Windows 95 Network

With Windows 95, networking two or more computers is extremely easy—probably easier than you ever thought possible. However, there can be problems. Use the information in this chapter to help you correct problems with your Windows 95 network.

Appendix A: Technical and Product Reference

Not everyone will need this reference, but it is our way of listing some technical specifications for hardware and software and of suggesting some specific hardware solutions to make the design and configuration of your Windows 95 network a little easier. If you have a strong dealer who can make these decisions for you, forget this Appendix. If you want to select your own hardware, if you want to mail order products, or if you'd just like to know more about what is going on in the background of your Windows 95 network, this Appendix might be useful. Here you'll also find companies that can sell you the hardware you need to make Windows 95 networking work.

Glossary and Index

Use this traditional glossary and the index to help you understand the terms we use in this book and to help you locate specific information about your Windows 95 network.

WHAT'S NEXT?

If you're just getting started in Windows 95 networking, your next step is to turn the page to find out more about networking in general. Or, you can skip the general stuff and get right to the step-by-step instructions for setting up your network. We've designed this book to help you go as far as you want as fast as you can.

So, let's go!

CHAPTER TWO

How a Network Works

The science of computer networking can be terribly complex, but we are not scientists, we are users. Our purpose in this book is to cut through the jargon to present what you need to know about the basics of network operation, but we promise not to make the learning any more complicated than absolutely necessary.

NETWORK HARDWARE

To connect two or more computers together into a network you need three critical pieces of hardware:

❍ The computer

❍ An adapter card within each computer that allows it to communicate with other machines

❍ Cables and possibly a hub to interconnect the machines

That's about it; you'll have a few options to configure the network to meet your specific needs and situation.

We'll examine each of these network components in the following sections, offering just enough detail to help you understand how to design and build your own Windows 95 network. By the end of this chapter you should be able to talk with your computer dealer about your hardware and software needs without feeling intimidated.

N O T E Prices vary by vendor and even location, but in general you can expect to spend in the neighborhood of $60 to $75 for each machine you put on the network. A Network Interface Card (NIC) ranges from $30 to $50 at the low to midrange, for example. For a very simple network you'll probably use a straight coaxial connection. The cable for that runs $0.05 to $0.10 per foot, plus $1.00 or so for each "Tee" connector and terminator. For a 10-BaseT network (twisted pair), you'll need a hub, which starts at about $100 when you get more than two computers on the network. See Appendix A for some sources for the hardware you will need to set up your Windows 95 network.

Computers

Of course you need a computer for a computer network to function. But there are a few minor considerations in selecting and configuring your computer for successful Windows 95 networking, as shown below.

❍ You'll have a lot more success with Windows 95 if you use a machine with a fast processor, plenty of memory, and a lot of available disk space.

❍ Remember that as you add features to a program you generally increase hardware requirements. That's especially true with a multitasking operating system such as Windows 95. So as part of your Windows 95 planning, consider whether the computer you have is adequate for the job.

❍ Although we have run Windows 95 on 80386-based computers with as little as four megabytes (Mbytes) of Random Access Memory (RAM), this is not a configuration that is going to make you happy. In our opinion, you shouldn't consider running Windows 95 on anything less than a 33 Megahertz (MHz) 80486 with at least 8 megabytes of RAM and a minimum of 20 Mbytes of available hard disk storage. *Available* means the free space you can use after Windows 95 and all of the applications you want to run with it have been installed. And, again, 20 Mbytes is a *minimum* configuration.

❍ In addition, you will need a hard disk that stores at least 200 MB total to be able to install Windows 95 and a reasonable number of applications and still have room to do anything. In fact, by today's standards, a 500 MB hard drive is about the minimum size. Few computers are sold today with a drive any smaller than 500 MB. One reason is the economics issue. It is so inexpensive to buy hard drives today that it doesn't make much sense to buy anything smaller than half a gigabyte.

N O T E

The *megahertz* rating of a processor has to do with how fast it can manage the information it handles. In general, a faster processor (higher megahertz number) makes for a faster computer as long as the other components that go together to make the computer are compatible with the higher speed processor.

RAM is temporary, electronic memory that the computer uses to run programs and to store data while it is being operated on by the computer. For example, a document you are typing in a word processor resides in RAM while you work on it. If you were to exit the word processor program or turn off the computer while the document is in RAM, you will lose the document.

In general, more RAM means a faster computer. This is because today's programs— including Windows 95 itself—are relatively large and require a lot of room to work. When you have smaller amounts of RAM (under 16 Mbytes or so) programs swap instructions and data out to your hard disk as they run. Particularly when you are running two or more programs at the same time, this really slows things down. A hard disk is a lot slower than electronic (RAM) memory, for one thing. Then the process of suspending one program, swapping its pieces and data out to disk, loading the next program component and data, executing some instructions, swapping this program out to disk, and so on, also eats up a lot of time.

Storage is permanent, or long-term, memory in the form of a floppy or hard disk. To keep a word processor document you have created in RAM, save the document to your hard disk. Now when you turn off the computer, the information is preserved so that you can load it into RAM again at a later time to change it, add to it, or print it. Data stored on a hard disk is frequently formatted on the fly as it leaves RAM for the disk, or as it comes off of the disk into RAM, and this may require extra storage. And, even if you have 16 Mbytes or more of RAM, your hard disk may still be used for temporary memory as programs operate. This is why it is important to maintain a reasonable amount of free space on your hard disk at all times.

For better functionality, you should have at least 16MB of RAM and a 66 MHz processor (CPU) or better. Added CPU power and extra RAM simply make everything run faster. And, in our opinion, in some situations RAM is the more important of the two. For example, given the choice between a 66MHz 80486 machine with 16MB of RAM and a 60MHz Pentium with 8MB of RAM, we'd choose the 80486 machine every time.

Here's one rough comparison we made recently that should give you some basis of comparison.

NOTE We had a 4MB, 80486 DX2/50 laptop machine running Windows for Workgroups 3.11 fairly successfully. It was a little slow, as is any machine running Windows with only 4MB of RAM, but it was acceptable. We decided to upgrade the machine to Windows 95 as a test. The installation went smoothly, though it took much longer than on previous machines we had tested.

Next, we installed Office 95, the upgraded Microsoft Office suite for the Windows 95 environment. That, too, was completed without obvious problems. When the installations were complete, there were about 5 Mbytes of free hard disk space, not very much for a Windows 95 machine, but enough for a test.

Next we loaded Excel 7 from the Office toolbar. It took almost 12 minutes to display the opening blank workbook! Throughout the load, the hard disk was operating continuously, indicating that Windows 95 didn't have enough RAM and was forced to continuously swap out memory locations to disk. With only 5 Mbytes of disk space, the machine was being pushed to the limits.

The next part of the test involved doubling the laptop's RAM to 8 Mbytes. Then we tried the Excel load again. This time it took just under 25 seconds to display the opening blank worksheet. A desktop 80486/66 with 16 Mbytes of RAM and 700 Mbytes of free disk space loaded Excel in about 12 seconds. Considering the difference in the two processors, the amount of available disk space on the two machines, and the fact that the laptop contained half the memory of the desktop computer, we felt the results were acceptable.

Even this test doesn't evaluate the real-world environment in which you may be living with your computer. A machine with minimal memory and a slower CPU may work fine with Windows 95 as long as you are running only one application—Microsoft Excel, Microsoft Word, or a database. If you intend to take advantage of the Windows 95 multitasking capabilities—the ability to run two or more applications at once—then you'll probably need more memory and a faster processor.

In the end, you are the only one who can adequately evaluate your configuration. Try what you have to see if the results are acceptable. If they are, don't worry too much about what associates—or book writers—tell you.

Network Topologies

In networking jargon, a *topology* is the way network components are connected—how the wires are run. The topology you use depends on several factors, the most important of which is the hardware you have available. You also may choose different topologies based on how many PCs will be connected and where they are physically located.

There are many networking topologies in use today, but three are most common:

❍ Bus

❍ Star

❍ Ring

Of these, the bus topology is probably the most common for small networks, primarily because it is (by a small margin) the least expensive and is somewhat easier to configure and use than the others. However, with present trends in software and hardware, the star topology in the form of small twisted pair networks is rising fast. If you were to enter a computer store today and ask for help configuring a simple Windows 95 network, you might be instructed to build a bus network, or you might be offered a twisted-pair star. It depends on the experience of your dealer, what hardware the shop sells, and so on.

The reality is, with present technology and in today's marketplace, a twisted pair star network is probably the best choice for your small network. Twisted pair cabling is easy to use. Twisted pair networks, with the proper equipment and configuration, are fast and reliable. A twisted pair network is flexible and easier to expand. It also costs a little more in the beginning (less than two hundred dollars more in a network with three or more computers), and it requires a hub to tie individual network components together. But overall, if you're starting from scratch today, consider a twisted pair (10Base-T) network first.

Here's the short analysis of these three common network topologies: Star is in, bus is old and declining, and ring is an IBM-only design used by relatively fewer small networks. Remember, too, that the precise definition of these topologies changes slightly as you change from a peer-to-peer network to a server-based network. In this book we are discussing peer-to-peer networking where all machines can (though they may not) share resources equally.

Bus

The bus (or distributed bus) is probably the most common network topology in the PC world as this book is written. This topology is based on coaxial (concentric wire) cable, called *thinnet* or 10Base-2. But it is already giving way to 10Base-T (twisted pair) networks. A *bus* topology uses a single cable routed through a work area or department with workstations and peripheral devices connected anywhere along the way (see Figure 2.1).

Coaxial Cable

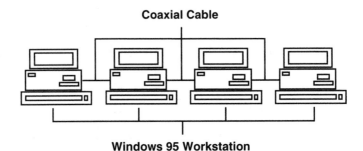

Windows 95 Workstation

FIGURE 2.1 Simple distributed bus topology.

A bus topology is a good choice for Windows 95 because of the type of resource sharing Windows 95 does. If Windows 95 is the only networking software you are using (and, for the purpose of this discussion, we assume it is) then you are using a *peer-to-peer* network in which each workstation (PC) on the network is essentially equal to every other one. A little bit later we'll discuss *logical network configurations*—the way information is shared across the physical connection—but, in general, Windows 95 networking is peer-to-peer networking.

The bus topology is relatively easy to set up because it doesn't much matter where each PC in the network connects along the bus. Whether you have two workstations or thirty (the practical maximum on a bus network), whether you connect them all at once or one at a time, also doesn't much matter.

The weak point in a bus topology is the connecting wire itself. The bus must remain unbroken from one end to the other with special hardware termination at each end, or the network doesn't work. The good news is that you don't have to break the bus connection to add or remove workstations, unless, of course, you need to add locations along the bus for new workstations.

A coaxial, bus network is limited to about 600 feet of wire, end to end, with a maximum of 30 computers per leg.

That is a cabling issue that we will discuss in more detail later in this chapter.

Star

The *star* topology attaches multiple PCs together through a hub. Figure 2.2 shows a simple star network.

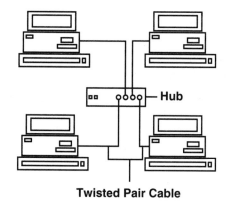

Twisted Pair Cable

FIGURE 2.2 Simple star network topology.

As you can see from Figure 2.2, the only connection between any two PCs in the network is through the central hub. A hub is an electronic device that isolates the spokes of the network from problems, and connects computers on each leg onto the network. The star topology is used for *small networks* (relatively few PCs). For example, it is common in departmental subnetworks, where a workgroup of five or ten users share a central server connected to other workgroups in a ring or bus topology.

The main disadvantage of the star topology is that network integrity and all communications among the computers within the network depend completely on the central hub. If the hub were to go down, none of the other computers on the network would be able to communicate with each other. Each computer could still function individually, of course, but any information shared on the server, electronic mail, shared printers and other network services would not be available.

However, today's hubs do a pretty good job of isolating individual legs of the star. If one port goes down, the other ports (and the computers attached to them) would continue to function.

The twisted-pair star network is generally called a *10Base-T network*. Notice that for a network of only two computers, you don't need the hub. As soon as you add a third machine, however, you'll need a hub to tie the network together.

Ring

A *ring* topology is a closed system (see Figure 2.3). Each PC or other network component is attached somewhere on the network wire, and the ends of the loop are closed to form a ring. In a ring configuration, each network component is crucial to the system in much the same way that each lamp in a ring-wired Christmas tree light set must work for the whole string to light.

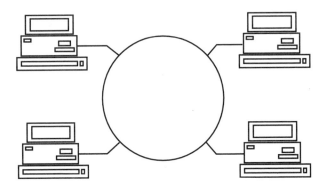

FIGURE 2.3 Simple ring network topology.

Like the star topology, the ring is frequently employed as a workgroup solution to allow a relatively small number of users within a department or group to share resources. Multiple rings for multiple groups or departments may be connected to form a network with broader coverage. Because a true ring network is limited to IBM Token Ring software, it really doesn't apply to your Windows 95–only setup.

Interface Hardware

We've examined computers and wires, two hardware pieces required to build a network. Another component is required—something to connect the wire to the computer. This is a *Network Interface Card*, sometimes called a *NIC*. The interface card actually performs two basic functions. It provides the physical connection between your computer and the network itself, acting as a port from the world inside your computer to the other computers and peripheral devices on your network. In addition, the card, coupled with software that runs on your computer, determines how information is carried across the network.

The *how* of network traffic is most commonly Ethernet, token ring, or ArcNet. Other transport mechanisms are available, but in the Windows 95 world considering price, availability, convenience, and ease of configuration and operation, some form of Ethernet is the most common.

If your computer doesn't already have a network card, consult with your dealer on the best choice for your computer. Once a fairly expensive option, network interfaces are now inexpensive and, in general, very reliable. Installation is easy, even easier than before with the Plug and Play features built into Windows 95. Where possible, purchase a Plug and Play device. With Windows 95, Plug and Play hardware will make installation and configuration a whole lot easier and operation more reliable as you expand your system with new hardware.

Bus Cards

For most PC users, the network interface card plugs into the computer bus and offers one or more connectors on the back for attaching the network wire. The computer communicates with the card through the internal bus connection; the interface card puts data on the network and receives data from the network through the external connections.

NOTE A computer bus is like a multilane highway for information. Data used inside the computer and transferred from disk to memory, and among other internal components, travels along this parallel data route. Many computers have more than one bus. One is the system bus and is probably based on the older, 16-bit Industry Standard Architecture (ISA) standard. The other is a newer bus, 32- or 64-bits wide that is used to carry data to high-speed devices such as disk drives, video displays, and so on.

Network Interface Cards (NICs) can plug into either of these buses. Newer adapters may use the newer, high-speed bus; older adapters probably use the original ISA bus.

Internal interface cards of this type vary widely in price. Inexpensive cards are available for under $50, but you can pay upwards of $200 for high-end models. The difference is in performance, primarily, as well as in brand name and reputation. A network card that plugs into a local bus (Peripheral Component Interconnect (PCI) or Video Electronics Standards Association (VESA)) will perform much better than one that is designed for the main system bus.

In addition, look for more documentation and custom software support in the more expensive models. And, while the majority of NIC interfaces are now configured via software, some low-end cards still require switch or jumper settings to change configuration. We suggest you avoid the hardwired models entirely. They may be cheaper to purchase, but they are a lot more difficult to configure.

For home or small business use, it is unlikely that you need very high end, "industrial strength" cards. Something in the low end of the mid range should provide good functionality and reliable operation for a long time. Consult with your computer dealer or peripheral supplier for help in selecting a NIC that is right for your hardware and network design.

PC Card (PCMCIA) Interfaces

PC Cards (formerly PCMCIA—Personal Computer Memory Card International Association) are an increasingly popular method of connecting external devices to laptop and desktop computers. Initially, PC Card interfaces were used mostly for plug-in modems. Now we're seeing them used for removable hard drives, Small Computer System Interface (SCSI) connections, and network interface adapters.

PC cards plug into an external slot. Connections on the plug-in card attach to mating pins inside the computer.

Although you'll see PC Card devices on laptop computers more than desktops, they are used on both. One major advantage to the PC Card interface with Windows 95 networking is the Plug and Play support they generally provide. That means you can unplug a modem, for example, and plug in a network adapter with the computer on and Windows 95 running. The system will recognize the change automatically, unload any software required for the previous card, and start up the software you need for the network adapter.

Parallel Interfaces

Older computers don't have a PC Card port. And, if all your expansion (bus) slots are full, or you are using a laptop, there's no place to plug an internal network adapter. Don't worry. You can still put your computer on a network by using your built-in parallel interface.

The parallel port is most commonly used for a printer, which usually attaches through a 25-pin connector on the back of your PC. A parallel network connection isn't nearly as fast as one through a high-speed internal bus, but it is fast enough.

A number of commercial devices are available to connect your computer to a network through the parallel port.

Many of these adapters also support printer pass-through so that you can still use your local printer. However, you probably won't need to if you are attached to a network. You can probably access a networked printer from your parallel network connection.

Hubs

With some network configurations you may need an additional piece of hardware, a hub. A *hub* or concentrator is an external piece of hardware that serves as a central connection point for network cable. You can also use a hub to convert from one kind of cable to another. Suppose you are using 10Base2 coaxial cable for a portion of a network (see discussion of network cabling in the next section), and you have a device that requires a 10BaseT connection.

A hub, with both types of interface, can bridge the two cable types. Hubs can be relatively simple devices with a single 10Base2 connection and two to forty 10BaseT connections. More complex hubs include more ports, protection circuitry for the ports, internal programming, and more. The type of hub you are likely to encounter in a simple Windows 95 network is probably of the simpler variety. It is a passive device, it has four or eight 10BaseT ports, it may or may not have a 10Base2 port, and it costs in the neighborhood of $100–$150.

A hub configuration is frequently used to connect a group of workstations within a department or workgroup. A backbone cable connects the local hub with a hub in another department, where a second group of workstations is connected, and so on. (See the section on 10BaseT networking later in this chapter for additional information on network configuration using hubs.)

In addition to enabling cross-cable connections, a hub helps with equipment isolation and can improve overall network reliability. Suppose a technical problem develops within the interface card or along the cable of one computer attached to a hub. The worst that can happen is that the hub port to which that computer is attached might be damaged. The computer attached to the faulty port won't be able to communicate with the network, but everyone else on the LAN will be up and running as usual.

Cabling

There are two cabling systems in common use with PC networks: coaxial (coax) and twisted pair. Not at the moment, but probably in the near future, we will also see fiber optic cable in more common use. The hardware to interface fiber optic cable to computers is getting cheaper, and the cable itself is easier to find at lower cost than even a couple of years ago. Many businesses are running fiber optic cable as an intra-company backbone, then switching to copper (coax or twisted pair) for the departmental connections.

There are multiple implementations of each of these basic cabling systems, wires with different numbers and different specifications. However, the network types generally associated with the two most common cable types are 10Base2 for coaxial cable (bus topology) and 10BaseT for twisted pair (star).

10Base2

Coaxial cable consists of a center connector surrounded by a plastic dielectric (insulator). On the outside of the dielectric sheath is a copper braid that in turn is surrounded by a thin plastic outer cover. Figure 2.4 shows a cross-section view of a coaxial cable typical of that used in 10Base2 networks.

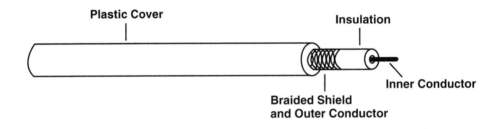

FIGURE 2.4 Coaxial cable–cross-section view.

You may hear this network cabling system referred to as *thinnet*, a term that evolved to differentiate it from the original Ethernet wiring, which was much thicker (this, not surprisingly, became known as *thicknet*.)

The advantage of thicknet is that it can transmit data over longer distances, but it is more expensive, stiff, hard to manage, and is also easier to damage and more difficult to connect.

Thinnet coaxial cable is similar to the wire used to bring cable television into your home—not the same because of differences in physical and electrical characteristics, but similar. A 10Base2 network is most commonly configured as a distributed bus. Consider a very simple, two-computer network, like the one in Figure 2.5.

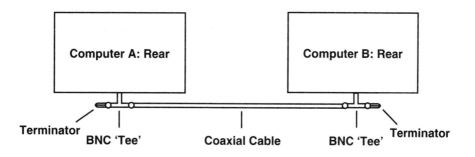

FIGURE 2.5 A simple, two-computer 10Base2 network.

A network such as this one may well describe how you will connect two machines in a small office or at home. You can purchase a network kit from a number of vendors that contains everything you need to hook up a two-station network like this one. Everything you'll need is listed in Table 2.1.

TABLE 2.1 Two-Computer 10Base2 Network Kit Parts List.

Quantity	Description
2	10Base2 Network Interface Cards (NICs)
2	BNC "Tee" connectors
2	50 Ohm cable terminators
1	RG-58 AU coaxial cable; BNC connector on each end

The NIC interfaces plug inside your computer or attach to a PC card or parallel port. They provide the input/output port between your computer and the network cable. The T-shaped BNC connectors attach to each end of the coaxial cable, to the BNC connectors on each NIC, and to the cable terminators. Cable end terminators are required to ensure that the electronic signals moving from computer to computer on the network get where they're going.

NOTE
To ensure reliable connections, we suggest that you purchase coax network cable with the connectors pre-installed. A quality tool to install connectors costs over $100. Even so, it is possible to get an unreliable connection. You can buy network cable in lengths of a few feet to thousands of feet, with or without the end connectors. See Appendix A for some suggestions on sources for your coax cable needs.

Now suppose you want to add another computer to this simple network. The new configuration will look like the drawing in Figure 2.6.

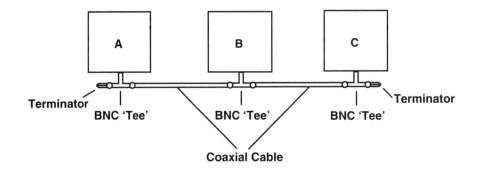

FIGURE 2.6 A simple, three-computer 10Base2 network.

To create this new configuration from the original network shown in Figure 2.5, you will run a second coax cable from the third machine to one of the existing computers in the network. You can add a few or many machines to the network in this way.

Consult the hardware installation section of Chapter 3 for detailed information on connecting these network components.

N O T E

Of course, you will have to configure the Windows 95 networking software on all machines in the network. The steps to do this are covered in the next chapter.

Thinnet is inexpensive and easy to install. Coax is also tolerant of external electrical influences. If your network cable must run in an environment where heavy machinery operates, near fluorescent lighting or in parallel with other electrical wiring, then coaxial wiring may be a better choice over twisted pair.

N O T E

10BaseT

A 10BaseT network is similar to a 10Base2 configuration, except that you use twisted pair wire, which requires different types of connectors. Instead of the metal, BNC connectors used in a 10Base2 network, 10BaseT networks use flat, plastic connectors similar to those used on your telephone. However, your telephone connectors contain two or four wires; the 10BaseT cable contains eight wires. The cable is configured in pairs of wires, twisted together to reduce interference (*twisted pair* wiring).

Two general types of twisted pair wiring are in common use: shielded twisted pair and unshielded twisted pair. As the name implies, the shielded wire is surrounded by a foil or braid jacket to protect the internal wires from external electrical interference. Shielded twisted pair is more expensive than unshielded wire and it is slightly more difficult to manage.

Twisted pair wiring is generally inexpensive, the connectors are standard, telephone-type connectors that are easy to install, and the wire itself is easy to route and use. You'll need shielded wire or coax cabling for an electrically noisy environment, and you need to keep in mind the distance limitations on twisted pair. Whereas coaxial networks using Ethernet can run about 600 feet from end to end, a twisted pair network is limited to about 300 feet per cable (a 300-foot radius from the hub), although the type of hubs you use can modify this figure. For the type of departmental or home-based networking we examine in this book, distance is probably not a serious consideration when choosing a cabling system.

A two-computer network using 10BaseT wire looks like the 10Base2 network shown in Figure 2.5, except, of course, the cable is different, and the connectors on each end of the cable are the telephone-like devices. Also, the NIC interface installed in each computer is different in that it supports the new connector and the twisted pair cable. Table 2.2 shows the equipment list required to support a two-computer network using twisted pair.

N O T E

When you configure a two-computer network with twisted pair and you don't use a hub, you'll need a special cable, one that is cross-wired, not a straight through cable. Don't worry about what pins connect where; just specify a cross connect cable when you purchase the wire for your two-computer network. These cables are sometimes designated with a different color patch or connector on one end.

TABLE 2.2 Two-Computer 10BaseT Network Kit Parts List

Quantity	Description
2	10BaseT Network Interface Cards (NICs)
1	Twisted-pair cable with 1 RJ-45 connector on each end

When you want to add another computer to the network, however, things get a little different. Instead of just adding another wire and another computer to the end of the chain, you must add a hub. Now the configuration looks like the drawing in Figure 2.7.

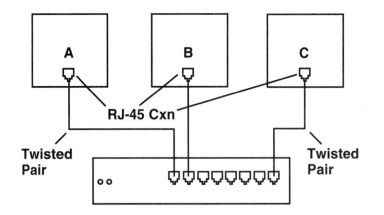

FIGURE 2.7 A simple, three-computer 10BaseT network.

To add more computers to the network you simply plug more wires into the hub and route them to the computer network interfaces. In a simple, at-home network you might place the hub next to one of the computers and route the wiring from there to the other machines.

In a corporate environment the hub is frequently placed in a telephone wiring closet or other convenient location where connection to individual computers is relatively easy. In new construction, the proper wiring is placed in the walls, floor, or ceiling and terminated in each office or workstation location, as well as in the wiring closet near the hub. Short connecting cables can then be run from a connector on a patch panel to a port on the hub. This allows users to move around the workplace easily.

NOTE Although twisted pair network wiring looks very similar to the telephone wire that may already be inside your home or office walls, it is not a good idea to try to use standard telephone wire for networking. Twisted pair wiring is rated by number according to its intended application. For the best results with twisted pair networking, specify "Category 5" wiring. This cabling system is available in preconfigured lengths with connectors attached, or in rolls and reels a few yards to thousands of feet long. See Appendix A for some suggested sources for network wiring.

As you design your network at home or at the office, keep these factors in mind. A little forethought during the initial stages of building your network can improve reliability and make it a lot easier to change the configuration as required.

NETWORK SOFTWARE AND PROTOCOLS

In addition to network interface hardware, you'll need some software. For one thing, you'll need driver software to let your computer work with the NIC you're using. Your hardware manufacturer probably supplied driver software with the NIC card when you purchased it. In addition, Windows 95 includes support for a large selection of popular network hardware, especially Plug and Play devices. When you shop for Windows 95 hardware, specify Plug and Play. You'll be glad you did.

In particular, Windows 95 includes support for versions 2.x and 3.1 of the Network Device Interface Specification (NDIS). The NDIS 3.1 driver provides support for Ethernet, token ring, and ArcNet interface protocols. You're probably using Ethernet for your small Windows 95 network because it is the most common, it is easy to find and support, and it is inexpensive. We'll show you in the next chapter how to install specific drivers for your hardware in Windows 95.

Windows 95 Networking

Besides the NIC drivers, you'll also need software to support a particular network protocol—a set of software instructions that determine precisely how information is carried from computer to computer across the network connection. You'll learn more about network protocols when you actually install a protocol to run over your network.

For now, it may be interesting to note that Windows 95 can support multiple protocols simultaneously, including the intrinsic protocols listed on the next page.

Microsoft IPX/SPX-compatible protocol. This is a Novell-compatible protocol that you can use with an existing Novell network. However, Novell itself offers for download a Windows 95–compatible IPX/SPX protocol driver that works even better.

Microsoft TCP/IP. This is a routeable Transmission Control Protocol/Internet Protocol that you will use if your machine operates in a mixed environment with UNIX computers or if you want to dial into the Internet or another UNIX-based host.

Microsoft NetBEUI. This is a NETBIOS-compatible (*NETwork Basic Input/Output System*) protocol that will let your Windows 95 machine communicate with other NetBEUI machines, including Windows for Workgroups, Windows NT server, LAN Manager, and others. This is the protocol of choice for a simple network.

Other Network Software

We hinted earlier that you may be using other software with your Windows 95 network in addition to that supported by Windows 95 itself. We're not going to spend much time on that idea, because there are simply too many possibilities to cover any of them adequately. But suffice it to say, if you are running a compliant networking protocol from another vendor, then aside from configuring the software itself, the rest of your networking operations should be very similar to what we describe here.

Of course, the source for more information on installing and configuring these third-party packages is the producer of the software, the vendor who sold it, or, in the case of larger companies, the Information Services department that manages such things for you.

WHAT'S NEXT?

The next step in using Windows 95 in a network is to physically configure the hardware and install the proper software components. We'll pick up this discussion of hardware components and show you how to set up Windows 95 to use it in the next chapter. You'll find many step-by-step instructions to make the process as easy as possible.

CHAPTER THREE

Building a Windows 95 Network

Now that we've delivered a foundation of theory and background, it's time to move on to a practical, hands-on guide to building a Windows 95 network. In this chapter we'll offer some hints on selecting and installing networking hardware, and we'll show you step by step how to configure Windows 95 for use in a networking environment. You might also refer to Appendix A for more specific hardware recommendations, help with equipment sources, and technical specifications.

INSTALLING HARDWARE

There are two parts to any computer network: the hardware and the software. You can't have a functioning network without both components, of course. But it won't do any good to configure the software until you have the hardware in place. We'll show you in this section how to set up the hardware part of your Windows 95 network. Later in this chapter, we'll consider the software part of the network.

Placing the Computers

Computer networking is about computers working together. The computers in a network can be placed almost anywhere in your office or home, although you will need to keep in mind the need to attach them with cable. A row of machines along a wall is easily cabled together; machines on different floors or in different rooms will need cables that penetrate walls or ceilings and floors. And computers that sit on desks in the middle of a room present another problem, requiring a cable that has to go beneath the floor, up into the ceiling, or across the carpet.

There are the usual considerations when installing any computer, whether it is stand alone or part of a network. For example, you should position the CPU case where there is adequate ventilation and where it is convenient to run the keyboard cable, display adapter connection, and power.

You should install any computer with a power line filter to protect it from power surges, brownouts, and spikes. You can buy power outlet strips with built-in filtering at your local discount store, but as with anything else, you get what you pay for. Our recommendation is to shop for a high-end filter at a computer or electronics supply store. Instead of $15 or $20 for the discount product, you'll probably spend $50 or more. Like insurance that is worthless until you need it, a discount power line filter won't show its weakness until you need it. By then it may be too late.

Also, depending on how you use your computer, the data may be valuable enough and the need to keep the machine running all the time great enough, that you should also install an Uninterruptable Power Supply (UPS). Time was when UPS devices were extremely expensive. It was only the very big businesses that used them to protect extremely sensitive data. Today you can buy reasonable UPS protection for a single computer for under $100. With that you get spike and brownout protection in the bargain.

Installing Interface Cards

Unless you choose a really weird network interface card for your Windows 95 network, installing this portion of your network should be as simple as the following steps.

1. Remove the case to your computer. Each computer manufacturer's design is slightly different from every other, but in general you will remove four to eight screws from the back or side of the computer case and slide the case away from the chassis.

2. Remove the back-panel filler for a free slot. Use a 6mm hex driver or a Philips screwdriver to remove the small screw on the top of the back panel that goes through the panel and the panel filler.

3. Insert the NIC into the vacant slot (ISA, VESA, or PCI bus slot). Make sure you have the card aligned properly and insert it straight into the slot, moving it side to side as little as possible.

4. Insert a retaining screw into the mounting flange on top of the card to secure the card to the computer case.

5. Replace the cover.

From there, Windows 95 can detect the card and install the proper driver to support it.

There are a few considerations in choosing network adapters.

First, consider how the computer communicates among its internal components. Data is transferred across a set of parallel wires, called a *bus*. A bus is the interconnecting highway of the computer, a multilane path that transfers information into and out of memory and between the central processor and the rest of the computer. There are several bus standards in use today. The oldest standard is the ISA (Industry Standards Association) bus. This is a 16-bit bus that originated in early PCs and was used to carry all data internal to the machine.

Two newer bus standards are found in today's machines: VESA (Video Electronics Standards Association) and PCI (Peripheral Component Interconnect). These are called *local bus connections* because they offer direct connections between the central processor and memory, and between the CPU and other local bus components. Local buses are 32- or 64-bit connections that operate at much higher speed than the legacy ISA bus.

When all other factors are equal, you are likely to get better performance from your network connection with a local bus NIC card than with a card that uses the older, slower, and often congested ISA bus.

A local bus card will cost a little more than an ISA card, but the improved performance could make the additional cost worth the expense. Of course, any network is only as fast as its slowest component, so if you have a high-speed, local bus machine on one end of the link and a slower, ISA-based card on the other, there'll be only slight performance improvement.

NOTE Windows 95 installs a number of text files in the main Windows directory. These include late information about several aspects of Windows 95 installation and configuration. Use Notepad, Wordpad, or any text editor to view Network.TXT in the Windows subdirectory for late information about specific NIC cards and in using Windows 95 networking with other network protocols. Look particularly for **network.txt**, **faq.txt**, and **tips.txt**. To view easily the available text files in the Windows directory, open **notepad** and use the File Open menu sequence to display the File Open dialog. Point to the Windows directory and Notepad displays all file names that end in the **.txt** extension.

Also, make sure that the card you select supports software configuration (most newer cards do). Otherwise you'll have to move hardware jumpers or throw switches to change the configuration of the card to ensure its compatibility with Windows 95 and any other hardware devices you may have installed. Older computer hardware is frequently configured with a series of switches. The switches work individually or together to open or close connections on a computer board. Switches are frequently mounted on the circuit board in a connected bank of four or eight switches.

Different combinations of connections change the board addressing (the location in memory where the board is visible to the central processor), what interrupt number is used for the board (how the processor gets the board's attention so they can "talk" over the busy, shared bus), and so on. Instead of switches that you can flip open or closed, some boards use a series of jumpers. A jumper is just a pair of pins that stick up from the board. You close the connection by slipping a small, metal shorting clip over the two pins (this compares to closing a toggle switch). You open the connection by removing the shorting pin.

You also need to buy and install a card that supports the cable type you will be using—coax or twisted pair. You'll need to decide what type of network you will install when you purchase your network interface card so that all computers have the same type of card. There are hybrid cards available, that is, cards that contain both coaxial and twisted pair connectors. These cost only a few dollars more than a single port card. A hybrid card can give you a little more flexibility in designing larger networks, but in general, pick a topology and buy NICs to match. Just remember that unless you have a hub with two kinds of ports, you can't mix and match network interface cards from computer to computer.

Plug and Play

One of the real advantages of Windows 95 is the Plug and Play specification, a hardware-software interface that lets Windows 95 detect hardware types and configuration to make it easier to choose the proper support software for them. In choosing hardware for use with Windows 95, Plug and Play compatibility is an important consideration. Although many older devices will report their model and configuration information to Windows 95, Windows may not have the proper driver for it or be able to determine the proper driver. If you are purchasing new hardware for your Windows 95 network, make sure it is Plug and Play compatible.

Most network interface hardware comes with driver software (see the Configuring Software section later in this chapter). Instructions included with the NIC probably tell you to install this software as part of the hardware setup. Unless you are absolutely sure the drivers were designed for Windows 95, *do not install this software at this time*. Windows 95 includes drivers for most popular NIC hardware. If you use older software designed for 16-bit Windows, you will slow down your computer considerably and, in fact, your NIC card may not work at all.

Running Cables

At its simplest level, installing cables for your Windows 95 network is this easy:

1. Plug a wire into the back of one computer.
2. Drag the wire across the floor or route it around the baseboard.
3. Connect the other end to another computer.

In a small office or when networking two computers in the same room at home, you probably need to do little more than that. With more than two computers and in more difficult environments, you may need to think about a few other issues.

COAX OR TWISTED PAIR?

We outlined the basic differences between coax and twisted pair cabling in Chapter 2. For two or three computers positioned relatively close together, coax is an inexpensive, easy-to-install choice. If you are installing a Windows 95 network in a small business with more computers more widely distributed, then twisted pair may be a better choice.

Coax

Remember that a coaxial network is basically a straight line of cable. Although you may route the cable in a twisted, even a circular arrangement, the two ends of the cable are never connected. Each end is terminated with a device designed to reduce signal echo across the cable. One end of this bus should be grounded, but only one end. If both ends are grounded you can generate so called ground loops that will degrade data transfer integrity.

Each computer is attached to the coax network via a BNC "tee" connector inserted in series with the cable itself. The coaxial tee connector is so named because it has a single leg and two arms, all connected together internally (see Figure 3.1).

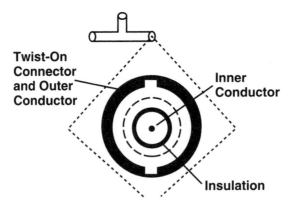

FIGURE 3.1 BNC Tee connector.

This arrangement lets you connect the single leg of the connector to your computer's NIC and two network cable segments to the arms of the connector. If you have two or more computers connected with coax, and you want to insert an additional machine, you must either add a new length of cable, or, in some cases, physically cut the network backbone and install new connectors.

If you connect a new network component quickly, then you don't have to turn off any of the running computers on the network. If you must cut the cable to install new connectors or if attaching a new component requires more than a few seconds, you'll have to turn off the network and restart it after the installation is complete. Starting up again will require that all computers on the network be rebooted. A Windows 95 network is fairly tolerant of cable breaks, but if the end-to-end integrity of the network is interrupted for more than a short period (seconds, rather than minutes, in most cases) the network will stop functioning. (We show you step by step how to expand a coaxial network later in this chapter in the section titled Expanding the Network.)

Twisted Pair

In a twisted pair network, adding another workstation is as simple as plugging a wire into a hub and running it to the new location. If you have pre-wired your office or home for twisted pair, you already have the wires running through the walls or in the ceiling. In this case, you only need to set up the computer hardware and connect a short twisted pair cable from the back of the computer to the wall plate where the network wire going to the wiring closet and thence to the hub terminates. In other words, in the twisted pair hub and spoke arrangement, any of the spokes can be in place or removed, can be on or off, and the other spokes will still function. This star configuration also is easier to troubleshoot.

CONFIGURING SOFTWARE

Getting all your networking and communications software in place is only part of the process of getting your network up and running. The other part is configuring the software.

There are three basic software components required to network your Windows 95 computers:

1. Driver software to support your Network Interface Card.
2. Network protocol software to manage data transfer to and from your computer.
3. Client software that interfaces with the protocol and with the user to finish the network communications setup.

With Windows 95—unlike many other networking software packages—the job of setting up networking software is truly easy and mostly automatic. There is a lot of power in this package and you can update, reconfigure, and change to reflect your changing networking needs. But the basic setup process is relatively simple.

Specifying the Adapter

You can probably let Windows 95 detect and configure your network adapter. For most hardware this is the easiest and best way to start Windows 95 networking. Just follow the steps in the following list.

NOTE

You will need to complete these steps for each machine on your network. One computer doesn't make a network; two or more computers will.

1. Click on **Start** on the task bar to display the Start menu.
2. Select **Settings** and click on **Control Panel** to display the dialog box shown in Figure 3.2.

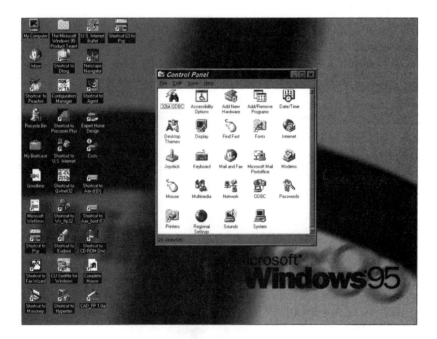

FIGURE 3.2 Windows 95 control panel.

3. Double-click on the **Add New Hardware** icon in the control panel to launch the Add New Hardware wizard.

N O T E Windows 95 can automatically detect many network cards. When you put your computer back together after installing the card and re-boot Windows, you may see a dialog window that shows Windows has found your new card. If this happens, just follow instructions on the screen to install the required software in Windows. The steps shown in this section will help you.

4. Click **Next** on the Wizard opening screen to start the process.
5. Choose **Yes (Recommended)** on the second wizard screen when Windows asks if you want the system to automatically detect new hardware (see Figure 3.3).

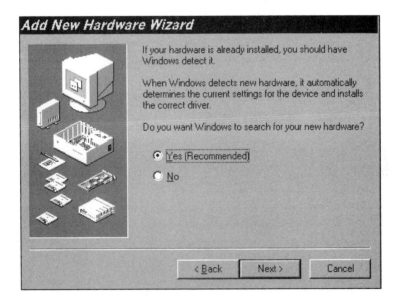

FIGURE 3.3 Hardware Wizard detection question.

6. Click **Next** to continue the wizard.

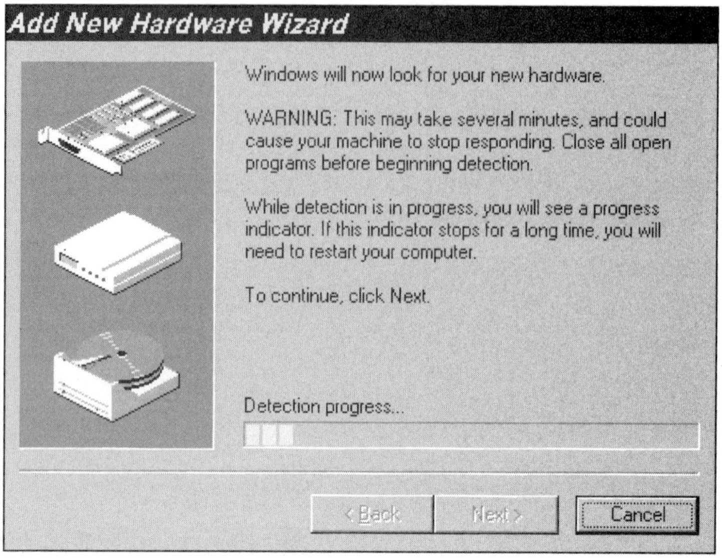

Add New Hardware Wizard

Windows will now look for your new hardware.

WARNING: This may take several minutes, and could cause your machine to stop responding. Close all open programs before beginning detection.

While detection is in progress, you will see a progress indicator. If this indicator stops for a long time, you will need to restart your computer.

To continue, click Next.

Detection progress...

< Back   Next >   Cancel

FIGURE 3.4 Detection Wizard progress report screen.

7. Click **Next** on the following Wizard screen. Windows will begin a routine to detect your new hardware and install the required software drivers (see Figure 3.4). This will take several minutes—maybe even a long time, depending on your computer's configuration—as the Wizard tells you. Just be patient.

N O T E   Although technically you can conduct other tasks while the Wizard detects your hardware, it is better if you don't. Your computer is really busy analyzing hardware and is using the disk controller heavily. Response will be too slow for practical use of other applications. Besides, you'll slow down the detection process.

8. Click **Next** after the Wizard reports that it is ready to begin installing software support for all detected devices (see Figure 3.5).

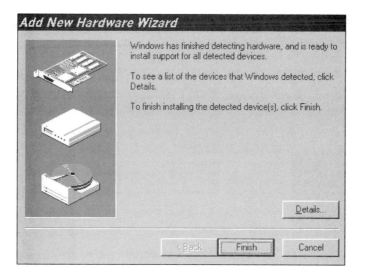

FIGURE 3.5 Wizard ready to install drivers.

Click on **Details** to view a list of devices detected during the system scan. The results of one scan after installing a new Ethernet adapter are shown in Figure 3.6.

NOTE

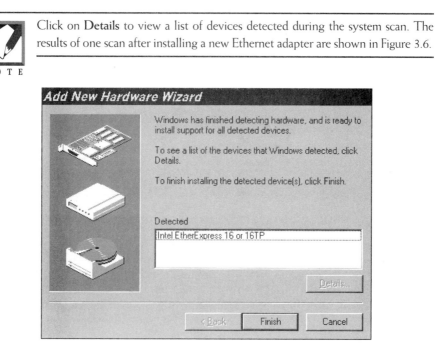

FIGURE 3.6 Wizard hardware detection Details screen.

9. Click on **Finish** to continue the Wizard. You will see a suggested configuration screen like the one in Figure 3.7. Unless you are sure the settings on your hardware are different from the ones Windows suggests, don't change anything on this dialog box. Just click **OK** to continue.

NOTE You probably will be asked to insert your Windows 95 CD-ROM or a specific diskette from the Windows 95 set so the Wizard can load the software it needs to complete the installation. You'll see a progress dialog box showing the files being copied. You may see a message saying that a file being copied is older than one that already exists on your computer. You should keep the newest file.

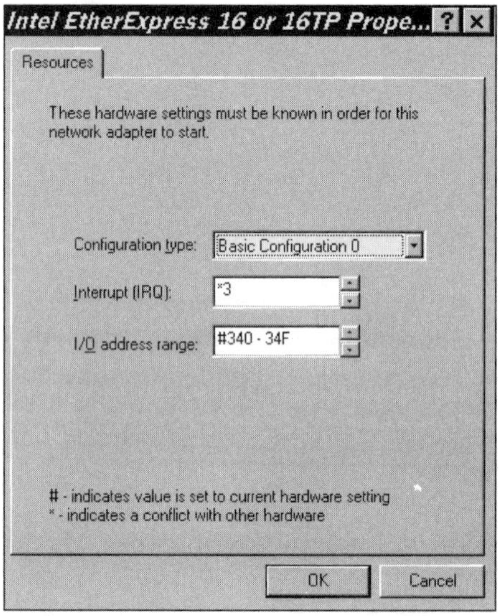

FIGURE 3.7 Suggested Hardware Settings dialog box.

NOTE If Windows detects a setting conflict (as shown in Figure 3.7), the setting is preceded by an asterisk. If this is a device that can be configured with software (as opposed to one that requires jumper or switch changes), choose another value to remove the conflict. Use the up- and down-arrow keys to choose new values until the asterisk disappears. You may also have to run a separate configuration software utility, supplied by the card manufacturer to complete the setup.

10. Click **Yes** on the final Wizard screen (Figure 3.8) to restart your computer and finish setting up the new hardware.

FIGURE 3.8 Final Wizard screen (Restart the Computer).

After Windows loads, you'll probably see the Control Panel dialog box open on your desktop, since that's how you got to the New Hardware Wizard. Don't close the Control Panel at this time. You'll need to use the Control Panel to complete the checks and configuration steps we show you in the next section.

Choosing a Protocol

Remember from Chapter 2 that a networking protocol is a set of software instructions that determines how data is carried across the physical connection. The default protocol for Windows 95 networking is NetBEUI, with the second most common protocol in a Windows 95 environment probably IPX/SPX-compatible protocol. This is the protocol used in Novell networks and your Windows 95 machines will integrate into this environment very well.

During installation of the network hardware, Windows 95 automatically assumes that you want to use NetBEUI and installs that protocol automatically. Depending on the configuration of your machine and your network, the Hardware Wizard may also install the IPX/SPX protocol.

When the Hardware Wizard has finished, you can check what automatic features were installed from the Control Panel:

1. Open the Control Panel, if it is not already open, by clicking on **Start** on the Task Bar, selecting **Settings** from the Start menu, and choosing **Control Panel**. You will see the screen in Figure 3.2.

2. Double-click on the **Network** icon to display the Network dialog window shown in Figure 3.9.

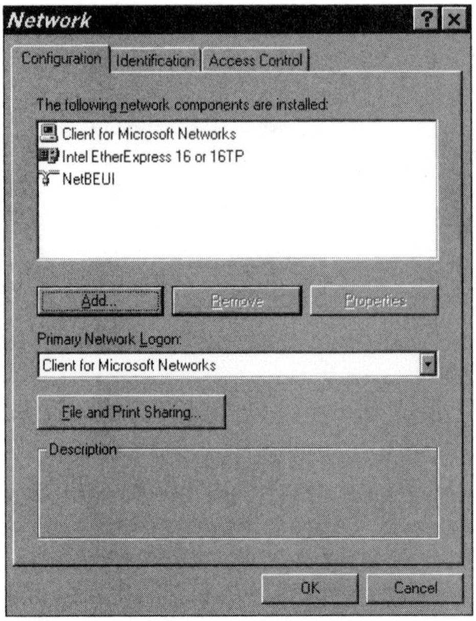

FIGURE 3.9 Network dialog window from the Control Panel.

> **NOTE**
> There are many types of networks in common use today. For small businesses and at-home users, two of the most common protocols are Microsoft's NetBEUI and Novell's IPX/SPX. You can run both protocols at once on your small network, but the only reason to do so is if your Windows 95 machines are part of a larger network that has a Novell server online. Windows 95 will assume you want to use both protocols, but you need only NetBEUI unless you have installed separately Novell server software.

Notice that Figure 3.9 is a tabbed dialog window, typical of Windows 95. The top tab is the Configuration tab, which shows what networking components are installed. Your Network dialog window may not look just like the one in Figure 3.9 because you may be using a different Network Interface Card. If your computer has ever been part of a Novell network, you'll probably see the IPX/SPX-Compatible Protocol displayed on this dialog window, and you'll see Client for Novell Networks as well.

For first-time installations, however, you will see the Client for Microsoft Networks, your Network Interface Card, and the NetBEUI protocol. If yours is a Windows 95–only network but the IPX/SPX-Compatible Protocol is installed, you should remove it since it only works with Novell server software. Here's how to remove it.

1. Open the Network dialog window from the Control Panel if it is not already open.

You can quickly display the Network dialog window by right-clicking on the **Network Neighborhood** icon on your desktop and choosing **Properties** from the pop-up menu displayed.

N O T E

2. Click on the **IPX/SPX-Compatible Protocol** entry to select it.
3. Click on **Remove** below the components window on this dialog window.

You can also view the settings Windows has chosen for your adapter by selecting the adapter line in the Network dialog window and then clicking on **Properties**. You will see a dialog window named after your adapter, similar to the window in Figure 3.10.

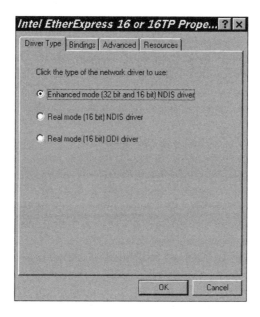

FIGURE 3.10 Network interface card dialog window.

NOTE

If you are using a Plug and Play adapter—and you should be, if at all possible—do not change any of the settings you see here. Windows 95 will do a good job of deciding how to configure the card.

You can see from this dialog how Windows configured your adapter. In this figure, for example, the 32- or 16-bit enhanced mode driver is selected. This is the preferred mode in Windows 95 because it offers the best performance and the best memory management. Real mode is an older mode. If your computer is using this mode, it means that you are using an older network adapter. Consider an upgrade.

Click the **Bindings** tab on this dialog window to see what protocol is tied to the adapter. This will be NetBEUI by default. Other bindings may also be listed, depending on your networking environment. The Resources tab shows you the hardware settings for your network card. These are the same settings you saw—and maybe specified—during the card installation.

Clicking the **Advanced** tab shows you how the card is configured to handle traffic, including the physical medium you will use. Click on **Transceiver Type** and check the Value field. If this value does not agree with how your network is configured, click on the down arrow to the right of the Value field to display a list (see Figure 3.11).

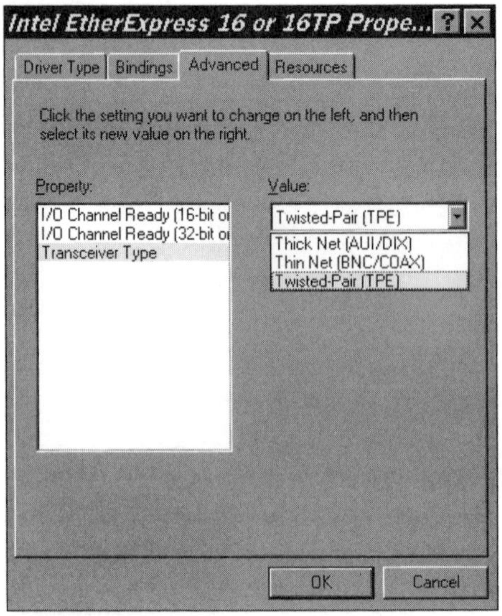

FIGURE 3.11 Transceiver Value list in Advanced NIC dialog window.

Choose the proper transceiver type from this list. For example, in this figure Windows 95 has chosen Twisted Pair (TPE) while our network uses coax. To make this change, simply click on **ThinNet (BNC/COAX)**, then click on **OK** to close the dialog window and make the change. The Network dialog window will be displayed (see Figure 3.9).

You can learn about the NetBEUI (or other) protocol in the same way. Select the protocol and click on **Properties** to display the Properties dialog window for the selected protocol. This will show you, for example, what network components will communicate using the protocol (click on the **Bindings** tab). In the simplest of Windows 95 networks, the only entry on this dialog tab will be **Client for Microsoft Networks**.

Choosing a Network Client

In addition to software support for your NIC and a protocol to manage the actual network traffic, you need a network client to support the user side of the network equation, including network printing, disk drive sharing, messaging, and the like.

If Windows 95 is the only networking you have installed, then the default Client for Microsoft Networks will be the only client. With Novell-compatible protocols installed, you should also see the Novell network client on your Network dialog window (Figure 3.9).

As with other network components, if you aren't using a Novell server or other network components, remove any clients except the Client for Microsoft Networks.

You can have multiple network protocols and clients installed, but you must specify a primary network login client. If you are networking with Windows 95 alone, then Client for Microsoft Networks appears in this field and there are no other choices. If Novell or other networking is active, then you can choose from a pull-down list by clicking on the down arrow to the right of this field.

ADDING NETWORK COMPONENTS

As we've said, Windows 95 does a good job of automatically finding network components such as your Network Interface Card and of configuring them for you. If things change after the automatic configuration, you may want to add networking components. For example, you may decide to add the TCP/IP protocol if you add a

UNIX machine to your network or you want to use dial-up networking to an Internet Service Provider. You do this from the Network dialog window (Figure 3.9).

To add a network component such as a new protocol or client:

1. Display the Network dialog window if it is not already displayed.
2. Click on **Add** to display the Select Network Component Type dialog window, shown in Figure 3.12. There are four choices on this dialog: Client, Adapter, Protocol, and Service.

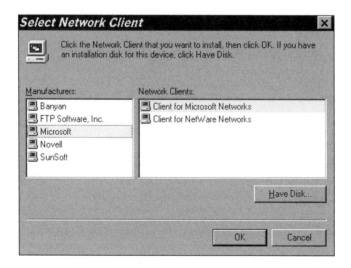

FIGURE 3.12 Select Network Component Type dialog window.

3. Select the type of component you want to add and click on the **Add** button. If you choose **Client** and click **Add**, you will see the Select Network Client dialog window. Choose **Microsoft** to see the dialog window shown in Figure 3.13.

FIGURE 3.13 Select Network Client dialog window with Microsoft displayed.

4. Click on **OK** to close the selection dialog window, then click on the **Close** icon on the Component Type dialog window to return to the Network dialog window.

When you close the Network dialog window after making changes, Windows will tell you to restart the computer to make the changes effective. You don't have to restart immediately, but until you do, the additions or changes you have made won't be effective.

Once the proper network components have been selected, you are ready to begin some of the finer points of network configuration. We show you these steps in the following sections.

IDENTIFYING USERS AND COMPONENTS

Once the hardware in your network is communicating, you are ready to configure the logical part of the network. This involves establishing computer names, naming the workgroup in which each device works, and establishing user names and passwords.

We show you in this section how to do that.

Setting Computer Name

Windows 95 computers communicate in a peer-to-peer environment. That means that when everything is configured, any computer in the network can communicate with any other computer to share data and programs. However, to aid in network management, Windows 95 requires that you identify a workgroup for each machine. This arrangement lets you logically group various machines, segregating others. Even if you have only two machines in your network, you must create a workgroup for them.

You must repeat the following steps for each computer in your network:

1. Open the Control Panel.
2. Double-click on the **Network** icon to display the Network dialog window (Figure 3.9).
3. Click on the **Identification** tab to display the dialog window shown in Figure 3.14.

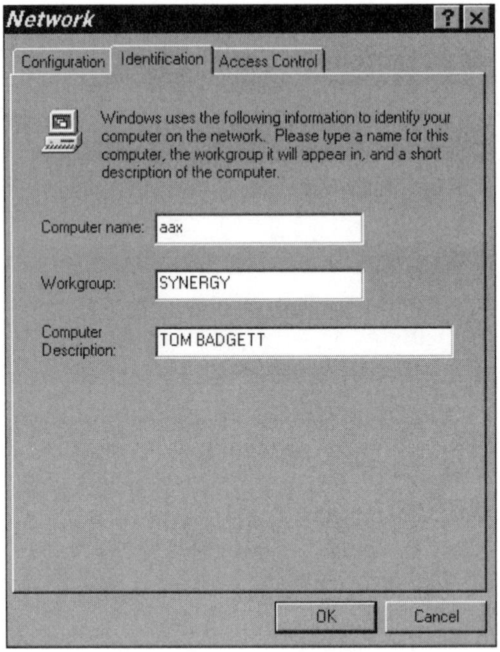

FIGURE 3.14 Identification tab from Network dialog window.

4. Type a name for this computer in the **Computer name** field of this dialog window.

NOTE The computer name can be up to 15 characters long, can contain only alphanumeric characters (plus the special characters ! @ # $ % ^ & ( ) - _ ' { } . ~), and may not contain spaces. In addition, each computer on the network must have a unique name.

Many network administrators, even in big companies, frequently are a little whimsical about their computer naming schemes. Most people pick a theme such as places, animals, characteristics, or colors. Your authors once worked for a company where all the computers were named after reptiles. At one company we know, all computers, by convention, are named with only three letters (with more than 40 computers, the three-letter naming scheme can get interesting). That's the origin of the aax designation in Figure 3.14.

If you have more than a few computers on the network, it is a good idea to make a list of the machine names, their workgroups, and their descriptions. This will help you in changing configurations, installing E-mail programs, and the like.

Setting Workgroup

Set the Workgroup in the same way as the computer name. Use the same naming convention for Workgroup as for the computer name, but the Workgroup is not unique. Each computer that is a member of a given group will share a Workgroup name. Conversely, all computers that will share resources should be in the same workgroup.

Setting Computer Description

The computer description will be displayed as a comment beside the computer name when users browse the network and view available machines. The description can contain up to 38 characters, and is used to help you or other users understand which machine is where. You might enter something such as **486 GATEWAY WITH SCANNER**, in the comment field, for example.

Setting User Name and Password

Each user who will log onto the network should be identified with a user name and password. In a company with many users and potentially sensitive information this is much more important, obviously, than with a small home network. If yours is an at-home network, password protection for machines is probably not too important unless you want to keep your children from using a machine designated for business. This would keep children from accessing information on your business machine from their computer, but you could set up their machine so you could read and write to their disk from your computer. In a business the concept is the same. There may be some machines that are more or less public, but others that are reserved for individual use. The computer designated for the accounting department likely would remain private, for example, while a sales machine that stores proposals, sales literature, and technical reference material might be shared.

In a network that uses only Windows 95, establishing users and passwords is extremely easy. The first time you start a networked computer, you will see the dialog window shown in Figure 3.15.

FIGURE 3.15 User name and Password dialog window.

You must enter a user name, but you don't have to use a password. If you do enter a password, Windows displays a second dialog window asking for you to verify the password. The first time each user logs into a given computer, that name and password are stored for future reference. If you enter no password, then you can log on later without a password.

If you do enter a password, then you must use this password each time you use the computer, or Windows won't let you into the network. You can cancel the password request and access Windows 95 components on the local machine, but you won't have access to the other networked components.

Once you have established a password for yourself and other users, you must use the Control Panel to change it.

1. Open the Control Panel (Figure 3.2).

2. Double-click on the **Password** icon to display the Passwords dialog window shown in Figure 3.16.

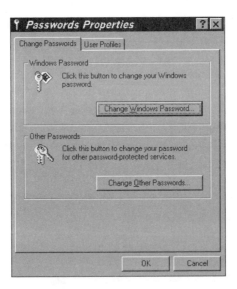

FIGURE 3.16 Control Panel Passwords dialog window.

3. Click on the **Change Windows Password** button to display the password dialog window shown in Figure 3.17.

FIGURE 3.17 Change Windows Password dialog window.

4. Enter the old (original) password in the first field of this dialog window and press the **Tab** button to move to the **New Password** field.

5. Type the new password and press the **Tab** button again to move to the **Confirm new password** field.

6. Type the new password again.

7. Click on **OK** to make the change.

SHARING NETWORK DEVICES

You have network hardware installed. You have software to support the hardware, and you have established one or more users to access the network. But so far, the computers that make up your network still can't "see" each other on the network and they still can't share data and printers.

In this section, we'll show you a few simple steps that will get this final part of your network working.

Sharing Disk Drives and Printers

For security reasons, Windows 95 doesn't automatically share individual computer resources with the rest of the network. In the Novell type of network, there is usually one server computer, a machine that stores common files including data and programs and that may also act as a printer server. These server computers are accessed by other computers on the network, called *clients*.

Windows 95 is a peer-to-peer network. Any machine on the network can act as a server, as a client, or as both. But, since resource sharing isn't automatic, you could establish a server-type network by sharing resources on only one machine and setting up other computers on the networks as clients only.

To turn on print and file resource sharing on a given computer:

1. Open the Control Panel (Figure 3.2).

2. Double-click the **Network** icon to display the Network dialog window (Figure 3.9).

3. Click on **File and Printer Sharing** to display the dialog window shown in Figure 3.18.

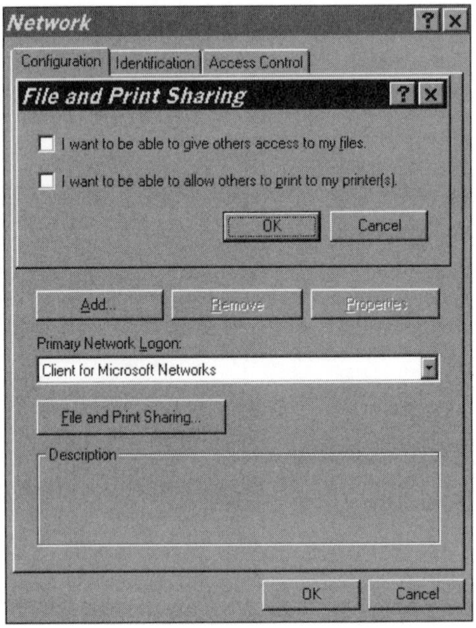

FIGURE 3.18 File and Print Sharing dialog window.

4. Click on the first check box to share files only. If your computer has a printer attached and you want to share the printer with other computers on the network, also click on the second check box.

5. Click on **OK** to close the dialog and return to the Network dialog window.

6. Click on **OK** again to close the Network dialog window. You may be asked to insert the Windows 95 CD-ROM or distribution diskettes so that the sharing software can be installed.

7. Click on **Yes** when Windows asks if you want to restart the computer.

After the Windows reboot, the shared resources on that computer will be available to other machines on the network. When you say you want to share files, that potentially makes available all files on all disk drives connected directly to this machine available to the rest of the network. This includes hard drives, floppy drives, and CD-ROMs.

However, you haven't told the network what resources—specifically—you want to share.

SHARING A SPECIFIC DISK DRIVE

To share individual computer resources:

1. Double-click on the **My Computer** icon to display available local resources (see Figure 3.19).

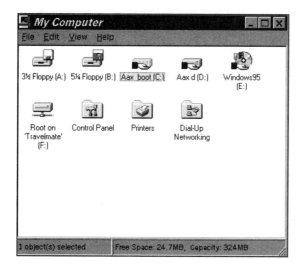

FIGURE 3.19 My Computer dialog window.

2. Right-click on your C-drive icon and choose **Properties** from the popup menu.

3. Click on the **Sharing** tab on this dialog window. You will see the dialog window shown in Figure 3.20.

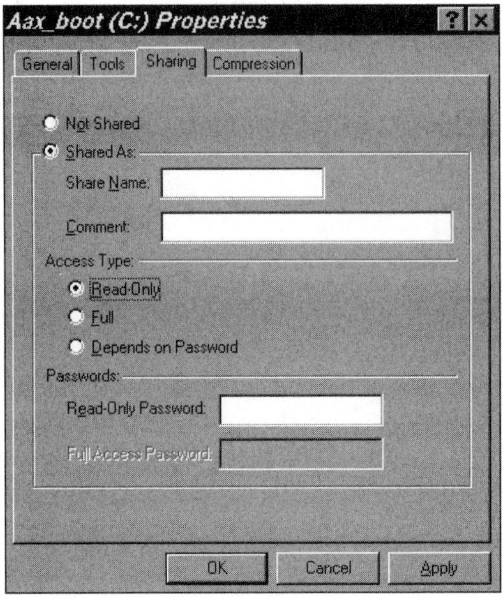

Aax_boot (C:) Properties

General | Tools | Sharing | Compression

○ Not Shared
● Shared As:

Share Name: [   ]

Comment: [   ]

Access Type:
● Read-Only
○ Full
○ Depends on Password

Passwords:

Read-Only Password: [   ]

Full Access Password: [   ]

OK | Cancel | Apply

FIGURE 3.20 Sharing Tab of Properties dialog window.

4. Click on **Shared As** and type a name in the **Shared Name** field.

N O T E You can use nearly any name you want for a shared resource, but you'll find operation of the network easier if you use names that are descriptive. For example, when you share the C: drive on a computer named *Sales1*, you might use a share name of *Sales1_C*. As you use this drive over the network you can easily distinguish it from other shared drives. Names like this make accessing network resources easier for everyone.

5. Type a comment in the **Comment** field. This can be additional information to help you identify this resource to other members of the network.

6. Click on one of the access types. The default is Read Only, but in a small network where you have firm control over all the computers on the network, you'll probably want to click **Full**. This will give other members of the network full read/write access to the drive.

N O T E You can leave this drive open for anyone, or enter a password in the password field at the bottom of the dialog window. This will require a password before a network user can access the drive for read only or read/write access. You can also make the type of access dependent on the password used. Click on **Depends on Password**, then enter a different password in the **Read Only** and **Full** password fields at the bottom of the dialog window.

7.   Click on **OK** to effect the changes and close the Properties dialog window.

You can share as many local drives as you wish in this same way. For example, if you have a CD-ROM drive on this computer you will want to share it so you can install software or run programs off a CD from other computers on the network.

SHARING A PRINTER

The process for sharing a printer with the rest of the network is very similar to sharing a disk drive.

1.   Double-click on the **My Computer** icon to display the My Computer dialog window.
2.   Double-click on the **Printers** icon to display the Printers dialog window, shown in Figure 3.21.

FIGURE 3.21 Printers dialog window from My Computer.

3. Right-click on the icon that represents the printer you want to share and choose **Properties**. You will see a tabbed dialog window similar to the disk properties dialog window.

4. Click on the **Sharing** tab to show the sharing setup dialog window.

5. Click on **Shared As**: to turn on sharing.

6. Enter a name for the shared printer.

7. Enter a password in the Password field only if you want to require a password from network users before they can use the printer attached to this computer.

8. Click on **OK** to close the dialog window and begin sharing the printer.

You can share as many printers with the rest of the network as you have attached to this computer.

In the following section, we show you how to connect to shared devices.

Connecting to Shared Devices

You'll need to share devices on each computer in the network so that other users will be able to access them. Normally, you will share the C: drive on all machines if you want to establish a true, peer to peer network. Again, if you want to establish a more controlled network, you may want to set up a single computer as a server and configure the other network members as clients.

However you configure the network, you'll need to attach the client machines to the shared resources you want to use across the network. Exchanging information across a Windows 95 network is a three-step process: 1) turn on sharing; 2) specify individual devices to share on each machine; and 3) connect remote machines across the network to these shared resources.

Here's how to complete the final step, connecting remote machines to shared resources:

1. Double-click on the **Network Neighborhood** icon to display a dialog window that contains icons that represent the other computers on the network.

2. Double-click on the name of a computer whose resources you want to use. You will then see a dialog window that shows the shared resources on the selected computer.

You also can right-click on the Network Neighborhood icon and choose Map Network Drive from the popup menu.

N O T E

3. Right-click on the shared device you want to use and choose **Map Network Drive** (if the device is a disk drive) or **Capture Printer Port** (if the device is a printer). For a disk drive you'll see the dialog window shown in Figure 3.22.

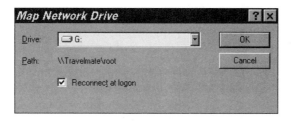

FIGURE 3.22 Map Network Drive dialog window.

Windows chooses a drive letter for you. If you want to use another letter, pull down a list of available drive letters by clicking on the down arrow at the right of the **Drive:** field on this dialog window. The path to the selected device is shown in the **Path:** field below the drive letter designation.

N O T E

4. To make this connection permanent so that it is available every time you log on as the same drive letter, click on the **Reconnect at logon** switch at the bottom of this dialog window.

5. Click on **OK** to close this dialog window. The new drive letter is now available for use.

Set up your local computer to use a shared remote printer in the same way. If a remote computer has a shared printer attached, you will see it as its shared name when you open the computer list from the Network Neighborhood. The dialog for attaching to a remote shared printer is similar to the disk drive dialog. The difference is that a shared printer doesn't receive a letter designation. Instead, you use the share name of the printer.

In later chapters, we show you how to make use of these shared resources across a network.

Additional Hardware

Your desktop computing environment probably includes more than just computers. Almost certainly you have one or more printers that you use with your computer, for example. You may have a modem, a scanner, or other hardware. Most of this equipment can function very well in a networked environment. Just how they work depends on the hardware itself, and what additional software may be available to use with it.

Networked Printers

A printer shared over a simple Windows 95 network may be one of the main reasons for setting up a network in the first place. It is truly frustrating to be working at a computer that has no printer, and need to print a file. You must copy the file to a floppy, carry that diskette to another computer that has a printer attached, load the file into an application compatible with the one that created the original, then print the file. But if the printer is part of a Windows 95 network, you can print the file from any computer on the net.

There are two ways to share a printer over a network:

1. Connect the printer to one of the PCs on the network and share it with other machines.
2. Connect the printer directly to the network through a dedicated network interface.

For most Windows 95 networks, you'll probably use one of the PCs on the net as a printer server. That's the cheapest and easiest way to share a printer or any other networked device. To use this method you don't need to do anything to the hardware beyond what you do to use the printer on a standalone PC. Simply connect the printer to your computer's parallel or serial port with the proper cable. If the printer was working before you installed the network hardware, you should be able to use it from any PC on the network.

In a relatively large network, it may be more convenient to install a printer with its own network interface instead of hooking it up to one of the workstations. Why would you want to attach a printer to its own NIC? There are a few good reasons, including the following.

○ You may not be able to attach a printer to a user's PC, and still place that printer where it is convenient for everyone to use it.

○ When a PC is used as a printer server, that PC must stay up and functional at all times. The user can't turn it off or reboot it without disrupting the printing services for everyone on the network.

○ Large print jobs can slow down a PC badly when it is used as a print server.

○ A network interface for a printer is a lot cheaper than a PC if that PC must be dedicated to printer services.

There are two ways to connect a printer to a network without using a shared or dedicated PC as a printer server: an internal interface for your particular printer and an external interface that should work with any parallel or serial printer.

If you are using a high-end printer—one that is designed for a workgroup environment—the manufacturer probably offers an optional network interface that plugs directly into the printer. When you purchase a printer that you intend to use on a network, ask your dealer or manufacturer's representative about the possibility of adding a network interface. This option is typically a few hundred dollars. Since you'll still have the standard parallel or serial interfaces, you can also use the printer connected directly to a PC if you want to. In addition, you'll have another port for 10Base2 or 10BaseT networks. That means you can place the printer anywhere on the network and just plug it in. Because its internal interface makes the printer a full member of the network, you can print to it from any properly configured PC that is also on the network.

A similar solution requires the addition of an external network interface. This small box sits beside your printer and attaches to the network via a 10Base2 or 10BaseT connection. The box also includes a parallel or serial port (perhaps both) to which your printer connects. This solution works the same as an internal interface inside your printer, but because it lets you use printers that may not have a network interface option, you can use existing printers as part of your network printing solution.

Also, because some of these network printer interfaces include some additional memory you can finish print jobs at any individual PC quickly while the memory and control software inside the interface manages the print queue for you. This is like adding more memory to your printer, but it may be cheaper.

N O T E Prices and specifications on network print server hardware vary widely. However, you can purchase a device that is compatible with Windows 95 and perhaps one or two other protocols (such as TCP/IP, an important consideration if you are running a network that includes UNIX workstations and/or Internet connections) for around $300, maybe less. Add extra memory for print buffering, high-end processor for speed, multiple protocols, and the like, and the price climbs to $500 or so. Many network printer interfaces support multiple printers. The following table shows representative models, prices, and sources. Addresses and contact information for the listed sources appear in Appendix A.

Model	Manufacturer	Source	Approx. Cost
Axis 150	Axis Communications	DataComm Mall	$300
JetDirect	Hewlett Packard	Microsystems Warehouse	$330
LE3900A	Black Box	Black Box	$600

The advantages of a separate printer interface for your network (whether it is mounted inside the printer or installed as an external box) is that you free up a PC and you have more freedom in physical printer placement. The disadvantages are that you have added some cost to your network configuration—$200 or more, in most cases—and your network becomes slightly more complex. You'll probably have to install software for this interface, and you'll have to manage it as another network device.

Again, for most small networks, just plug a printer into one of the PCs on the network and share it with other users. That is quick, simple, and inexpensive. As your network grows, however, it may be convenient to consider one of these printer interface options.

Other Networked Hardware

For most of us, two or more PCs and a printer is all the network we want or need. However, Windows 95 includes support for some interesting options that might interest you as your networking and computer experience grow.

For example, consider a shared fax modem over your Windows 95 network. Almost any modem you buy today can send and receive fax transmissions over your telephone line. The newer the modem, the faster the fax feature is likely to be. Once you network your PCs with Windows 95, you only need one fax modem to be able to send and receive fax pages from any PC on the network.

If you already have a fax modem installed on one of the machines you are networking with Windows 95, and the modem is working with your Internet, CompuServe, AOL, or bulletin board account, then all you need to do is configure the PC it is connected to as a fax server (we show you how to do that in the software section later in this chapter).

If you haven't already connected your modem, the simplified steps are shown in the following sections.

N O T E You can use internal or external modems with your Windows 95 network. However, we recommend that you use an external modem for two reasons: (1) external modems are easier to install and configure because you don't have remove the computer case and you don't have to worry about port and interrupt conflicts; and (2) you have more control over the external modem. Lights show you the status of the connection and you can turn off or unplug the external modem to disconnect from an online service if you have software problems. External modems do cost a little more, however, because you must pay for the case, power supply, and cable that are not required for internal modems.

There is one potential problem with using a high-speed external modem with your PC, depending on its age. Some older computers use an outdated UART (Universal Asynchronous Receiver/Transmitter), the 8250 chip. You can check which UART is in your machine by running *msd* or a similar diagnostics programs. The solution may be to purchase an updated serial communications card that replaces or complements your existing hardware with a 16550 UART.

Installing an External Modem

Installing an external modem is extremely easy. Your modem should have come with illustrated instructions to help you with the process, but we'll review the steps here as well. We find a lot of users purchase previously used modems, receive handed-down hardware, or buy modems as part of a package that may be sparsely documented.

N O T E   If you are looking for a modem, consider a 28,800 bps (bits per second) modem. You can find 14,400 bps modems at very low prices today, but the newer hardware costs only a little more, provides better performance (especially in a graphical online environment such as the World Wide Web), and probably includes enhancements to help ensure better connections as well. Don't be fooled by very low priced modems at any speed, however. Many of these are software-based, which means that you must run a piece of software before the modem will work properly. Our experience is that many of these software modems don't work properly in a high-speed, graphical online environment. If the modem you are considering is designated as an "RPI" device, walk rapidly in the opposite direction. RPI, for Rockwell Protocol Interface, is used in modems that use the Rockwell chip set. You may or may not see the Rockwell name on an RPI modem, but if you must load software before your modem will work, it is probably RPI and it will probably give you trouble somewhere in your online life. Again, in today's computing environment, your best choice for all new hardware is Plug and Play. The Plug and Play standard is not completely fool proof, but it will make installing new hardware much, much easier and more reliable.

The typical external modem consists of three basic components: the modem itself, a power cable that generally includes a power supply "brick' that plugs into the wall, and a cable. To install the modem, follow the following instructions.

1. Position the modem near enough to the computer so the cable will reach the rear apron where the serial connectors are located.

2. Plug one end of the serial cable—normally the end with a 25-pin male connector (DB-25 plug) on it—into the back of the modem.

3. Plug the other end of the serial cable—normally with a 25-pin female connector (DB-25 Jack) on it—into the serial connector on the back of your computer.

4. Plug the power cord into the back of the modem.

5. Plug the power brick into a convenient wall outlet.

6. Attach a phone cord from the rear of the modem to a telephone jack for the telephone line you want to use.

Installing an Internal Modem

Installing an internal modem is slightly more complicated than installing an external one. But it isn't much harder than installing a network interface card. In most cases the difference between the two is that the network card can be configured via software, while the modem probably has to be configured with switches or onboard jumpers.

NOTE If you purchased a computer with a modem installed, chances are it is an internal modem. Unfortunately, many packaged systems fail to document just how the modem is installed. Fortunately Windows 95 can frequently find out how your modem is configured, but if possible you should find out from your computer supplier or included documentation the following information:

- ○ Modem brand and model.
- ○ Maximum modem communication speed.
- ○ Communications port (COM1: through COM4:) the modem is configured to use.

This will help you configure your modem for specific online services and also will make it easier for technical support personnel to help you in the event you experience difficulty getting your modem to work properly.

Here are the steps to installing an internal modem:

1. Determine which communications port you will use for the modem.

NOTE If you have a serial mouse—one that plugs into an existing serial port on your computer—then it is probably using COM1:. This is the serial port that uses a 9-pin D-shell connector. Most computers also have a second port configured as COM2: (a 25-pin D-Shell connector) that could be used for a printer, scanner, and the like. This also is the best choice for your modem. You will be tempted to use COM3: or COM4:, leaving COM2: available for something else. *Don't do it!* In our experience, many communications packages don't work well with COM3: and COM4: because these ports share memory locations with COM1: and COM2:. Set your internal modem to COM2: and disable the existing COM2: that is part of your computer. This usually involves flipping a small switch or moving a jumper on your motherboard or on an Input/Output board. If you need help with this process, consult your computer manual, or call the dealer who sold you the machine.

2. Configure your modem for the selected communications port. This will involve moving one or more jumpers on the modem board, or flipping one or two switches. Your modem manual will show you how to do this. In fact, with many modems, COM2: is the default.

3. Remove the case from your computer.

4. Choose a free bus slot on your motherboard and remove the rear-apron filler.

5. Insert the modem board into the free slot and replace the retaining screw you removed with the rear-apron filler in the previous step.

6. Replace the case.

7. Attach a phone cord from the rear of the modem to a telephone jack for the telephone line you want to use.

You will need to configure Windows 95 to recognize your modems and to use them for dialing and communication.

EXPANDING THE NETWORK

We've shown you how to install and configure a basic network so far in this chapter. Sooner or later, however, you'll want to add more components to this basic network.

Suppose you want to add a third computer to a two-machine 10Base-2 network. Here are the steps to follow.

1. Install an NIC in the third computer.

2. Place the third computer in its proper location.

3. Remove the cable terminator from the tee connector on the existing machine closest to the new computer.

4. Plug in a second segment of coaxial cable to this tee connector.

5. Route the other end of the coax to the new computer.

6. Attach a third tee connector to the end of this coax cable run.

7. Attach the cable terminator you removed from the original computer to the other end of the tee connector already attached to the new length of coax.

8. Attach the tee connector with its coax and terminator connections to the BNC connector on the third computer's NIC.

NOTE

You don't necessarily have to power down the computers in the existing network to add a new machine. However, if the terminator is removed from the coax line for more than a few seconds, network errors will occur and, chances are, you will have to reboot all workstations to restore proper network operation. You can start with the third computer, attach the cable and a third terminator to that computer's NIC, run the wire to one of the PCs in the original network, then quickly remove terminator from that machine's tee connector and replace it with the coax cable running to the third machine.

Adding a third computer to a two-computer 10Base-T network is a little easier:

1. Install an NIC in the third computer.

2. Place the third computer in its proper location.

3. Plug a 10BaseT cable into the NIC on the third computer.

4. Route the cable to the 10BaseT hub and plug it into an available port on the hub.

NOTE

In a 10BaseT network you can pre-wire a hub with cable connections installed at key locations. Then to add a new computer or to move a computer you only have to attach a short cable from the computer to the wall plug that connects to a hub elsewhere in the building.

WHAT'S NEXT?

If you have understood and followed the procedures we've described through this chapter, you have everything you need to get a basic Windows 95 network up and running. Throughout the rest of this book we will show you how to maximize your use of this physical connection. Making the physical connection is only part of the process. You need also to understand how to configure disk directories, how to use shared resources, and how to secure the network.

Read on to take your fledgling Windows 95 network to the next phase.

CHAPTER FOUR

Using a Windows 95 Network

You should have your Windows 95 network up and running at this point. At least the hardware components should be communicating. It is now time to consider some of the finer points of network configuration, such as how you log onto the network, run networked applications, or print to a network printer. In this chapter, we'll also examine logical design considerations, such as how to set up networked directories on your hard drive.

Sound complex? It needn't be. We'll keep things as simple as possible so you can go as far (or not so far) as you wish.

LOGGING INTO THE NETWORK

We showed you in Chapter 3 how to establish user names and passwords (see the Setting User Name and Password section in Chapter 3). Logging into the network and setting user names and passwords are really quite similar processes. In fact, the first time you reboot a networked Windows 95 computer after turning on networking you will be asked for a user name and password. Because the information you enter at this point will be stored for future log-ins, establishing users and logging into a Windows 95 network are really the same process.

NOTE If your computer is part of another network, such as a Novell network, then you may see two log-on dialog boxes when you start your computer. One of these dialog boxes will say Welcome to Windows and ask for a user name and password. Then you will be asked for a user name, password, and host name for the secondary network. The order in which these dialog boxes appear and, in fact, which dialog boxes appear, depend on how your Windows 95 is configured.

Remember, however, that if a user bypasses the network log-in by pressing **Escape** or **Cancel**, they won't be able to access network resources but will have access to the local machine.

We show you in Chapter 9 how to change the basic Windows 95 configuration to set up the same password for Windows and a networking client, and how to improve Windows security.

After the first time, you will see a network log-in dialog box whenever you start your computer. Simply enter the user name and password you established when you first set up Windows and your system will start normally.

NOTE If you receive an error message while starting a networked Windows 95 machine, refer to the troubleshooting hints in Chapter 10.

LAUNCHING (RUNNING) APPLICATIONS

In many respects, a networked computer works just like a standalone machine. For most of us, the main difference in the two is the number and type of disk drives and printers available to an individual computer. When you set up a network and properly share resources, the machine in your home office will have its local drives—usually floppies A: and B: and a hard disk C:—plus the drives you have shared from other machines.

Suppose you have a second machine in a study, that it is networked, and that it also has two floppies, a hard drive, and a CD-ROM drive. If you share the hard drive and the CD-ROM with the network (we show you how to do that in Chapter 3), then you can access them from the machine in your office.

N O T E Normally you won't share floppy drives with the network because (1) they are slow, (2) they store relatively small amounts of information, and (3) the data on them depends on the floppy disk that is inserted in the drive. You can share a floppy with the network if you want to, and you might want to if, for example, you have a notebook machine that has no floppy drive and you want to copy information off a floppy disk onto the hard drive on your notebook.

In this case, the machine in your office would have its local drives—A:. B:, and C:—as well as two more drives from the networked machine in the study. In this case the D: drive on your office machine would point to the hard drive on the machine in the study, while the E: drive on your office machine would point to the CD-ROM drive on the study machine. This configuration is shown in the drawing in Figure 4.1.

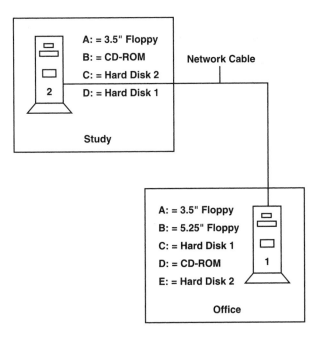

FIGURE 4.1 Drawing of two networked machines sharing drives.

Now, because of the network, your office machine has a second hard drive and a CD-ROM player it didn't have before. Make sense? Beginning to see the value of the networked connection?

How do you run programs on the machine in the office? That depends on where they are stored. If the programs you want to run are on your office hard drive, then nothing changes. You will access them and run them just as if that computer were not part of a network.

Whether you can run on the office machine an application that is installed on the machine in the study depends on the application and how it is installed. In the Windows environment a program (application) has many components, some of which are installed in the Windows or Windows\System directory. If you attempt to run a single-user program installed on a remote hard drive, you'll probably see an error message to the effect that Windows can't find a required program component.

How do you fix this problem? Again, the answer depends on the program you're trying to access. If this is a single-user application—one that is designed for one person and one computer—you'll just need to install the program on each machine where you want to run it.

NOTE   Computer software is protected by copyrights. You can't use someone else's software. In fact, most contemporary licenses restrict you from running one copy of a program on more than one machine at a time. Consult your license for details.

If you have software designed for a network, on the other hand, then you will install just the remote or networked components on the machine that does not have the primary installation. The Microsoft Office suite is an example of software of this type. The documentation with your software will tell you whether it is designed for a network and how to make the networked installation.

If you have to install software on all machines in the network, what's the advantage of running applications over the network?

There is less of a storage requirement for one thing. Whereas a full application such as a comprehensive word processor or spreadsheet may require 15, 20, or even 25 megabytes for a complete installation, you may be able to install the second, networked, version of it in only 5 megabytes or less.

Lower cost is another reason. It usually is less expensive to purchase a multi-user license than to install separate single-user versions.

And, when you install software designed for a network, you have the right to run the same software on more than one machine at a time.

There are disadvantages, of course. Network traffic is increased since some or all of the instructions for the application must be transferred across the network to your desktop before it can be run. With increased network traffic comes slower program and network performance.

When you click on the **Start** button on the Windows 95 task bar, you should see the names of programs you have previously installed. To run a program, follow these steps:

1. Click on **Start** on the task bar to display the Start menu.
2. Select **Programs** from the Start Menu to display available programs.
3. Choose the program you want to run from the popup list.

For programs you run regularly, you may want to set up a shortcut on your desktop. Follow these steps:

1. Double-click on the **My Computer** icon on your desktop to display your computer's resources. Figure 4.2 shows a typical My Computer dialog box from a networked computer.

FIGURE 4.2 My Computer dialog box example.

2. Double-click on the icon that represents the drive letter where the application you want to run is stored. Windows will display a graphical directory of this drive, like the one shown in Figure 4.3.

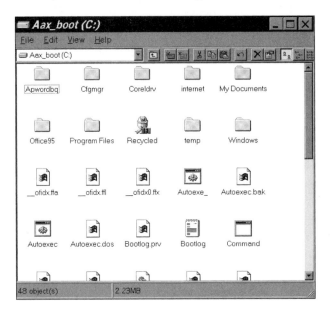

FIGURE 4.3 Drive directory.

3. Double-click on the folder that contains the program for which you want to create a shortcut. You will see a list of files and, perhaps, additional directories.

4. Keep choosing folders until the file you want to use is displayed in the list.

5. *Right-drag* the file name out of the directory dialog box and onto the desktop (that is, move the mouse over the file name, depress and hold the right mouse button, and drag the file name onto the desktop). Figure 4.4 shows the popup menu Windows displays.

Figure 4.4 Right-drag popup menu.

6. Choose **Create Shortcut(s) Here** from this menu. Windows places an icon to represent the chosen program on your desktop with any other icons that may be there.

You can tell if an icon is a shortcut by noting whether it includes a short curved arrow. The arrow indicates a shortcut. An icon without the arrow means that the icon points to a file actually stored in the desktop folder.

N O T E

Now to run the program, simply double-click on the **Shortcut** icon you just created on the desktop.

LOADING AND SAVING FILES

When you install a computer on a Windows 95 network, you generally share some or all of the resources it contains, such as a disk drive. Once a disk drive is shared (see Chapter 3 for information on how to do this), you can access it from other machines on the network. In fact, this is the real strength of a small, Windows 95 network. As you learned from the last section, running applications over the network isn't desirable, or may not even be possible. But storing data files in a central location where other users on the network can access them *is* desirable.

Sharing data files across the network has the following advantages:

❍ Reduced storage requirements when compared to storing individual copies of shared files on individual computers.

❍ Less redundant storage of files. This makes it easier to maintain files, making sure you always are working with the latest version.

❍ Easier data sharing. In an environment where two or more users need access to the same information, a central file accessed from multiple PCs is faster, easier, and less likely to access the wrong version of a file.

Accessing information on a networked drive is as simple as accessing it on a local drive. Remember that when you install Windows 95 networking and connect to a shared drive, your computer automatically assigns a drive letter to each remote drive.

To access data on a shared drive, use the built-in file management features of your application and specify the proper drive letter. For example in Microsoft Word, when you use **File Open** to access a file and choose **My Computer** from the list of options, you will see the dialog box in Figure 4.5.

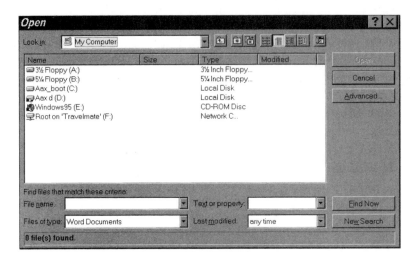

FIGURE 4.5 Microsoft Word File Manager dialog box.

As you can see, the F: drive on this machine is a network drive. You can see the Network designation in the Type column of this display.

If you double-click on a networked drive in a dialog box such as this, you'll see a display of folders and files available on that drive. Simply select the file you want to load and click on **OK**. The file will be loaded into the application as if it were stored on a local drive, and you can use it in much the same way.

However, remember these general considerations when using files across a network:

○ Access will be slower than from a local drive. The speed difference could be slight, or, depending on network traffic and the type of hardware you are using, significant.

○ You can't disable the network, reboot, or turn off the machine where the file is stored, or disconnect the network cable while the file is open. If you do, you may damage the file, losing data.

○ If the network is down you can't access files stored on a remote drive.

Designing Directories for Networking

We've said that at the basic level, using disk drives over a network is similar to using them on your local machine. There are a few considerations in designing shared directory structures that can make network life a little easier for users.

We suggested earlier that when you share a networked drive you use a share name that is descriptive enough to help remote users understand easily what computer and what drive they are using. This is even more important in Windows 95 than it was in Windows for Workgroups because in Windows 95 you normally don't see the full path to a drive or directory. All you see is a folder with a name.

So, too, for directories. Be creative and descriptive as you name directories. It will help users find their way around your system. Also, think about the directories on each networked machine in terms of how it fits with the rest of the network

What does that mean? One advantage of a networked environment is the extra storage available to all machines. Windows 95 is peer-to-peer networking, remember, so once several machines are connected they all have the advantage of the storage and other resources on the connected machines. This does two things for you as a user and administrator of data: 1) more resources than you have on a single machine, and 2) you have redundant resources—disk storage, printers—for data backup and to ensure that something is working.

You provide expanded resources to an individual computer each time you hook another machine to the network. One machine standing alone has one or maybe two hard drives. When you connect the second machine, you now have two or four disk drives. Accessing expanded resources—primarily disk drives—is as easy as sharing the drive on one machine and mapping it on the other.

But actually using the resource will be easier if you can plan how each piece is designed. For example, consider planning for each drive a disk directory structure that is predictable, repeatable, and easy to understand. This involves segregating programs and data, and grouping programs and data by type or function.

Figure 4.6 shows a sample directory structure that should help you with the idea. If you put the same or a very similar structure on each drive, then finding a specific file or directory should be fairly easy.

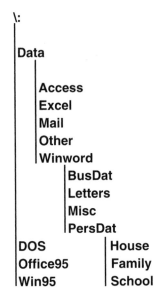

FIGURE 4.6 Sample networked directory structure.

Notice how in Figure 4.6 we have generally used short file names. You can use long names in Windows 95, and as you get more experience with how this functions, try it out. However, we find that new users to Windows 95 sometimes get carried away. The names become too long, difficult to enter, and difficult to display on file lists and directory dialog windows.

NOTE   One of the real strengths of Windows 95 is its support for long file names. No longer are you stuck with simple, eight-character file names. However, Windows for Workgroups and older Novell hosts won't support long names. If you are networking in a mixed environment, you'll need to stay with eight-character file names.

Of course the reality of a growing network is that you probably will start with machines that already have some directory structure in place. You will start with the structure you have, of course, but don't hesitate to make a change as you learn your way around networking. One of the biggest errors beginning network users make—and one of the easiest one to let snowball—is lack of control, a failure to direct the evolution of the network.

COMMUNICATING WITH OTHER USERS

Although the primary function of a network is to share storage, printers, and other resources, another useful feature is the ability to communicate with other users on the network by means of electronic mail or direct chat. We'll give you some hints on getting the most out of these features in the following sections.

Network E-Mail

Electronic mail is an interesting and useful facility that is available as soon as you network two or more computers. And, E-mail is one of the most popular and common facilities accessed by networked users. We are aware of at least two surveys that show that approximately 95 percent of Internet users say E-mail is their primary application. We work with many large and small companies that rely on internal networking as well as the Internet, which is just a huge, global network, to conduct their day-to-day business.

And we use E-mail on networked computers at home as a convenient way of keeping other family members up to date on schedules and plans. In a busy household where computer use is common, E-mail can serve as a flexible message board.

E-Mail Defined

E-mail is popular and useful. But what is it, really?

Basically, E-mail is the ability to send and receive messages electronically. On a local area network (LAN) you might use the built-in E-mail facility to inform coworkers or family members about your schedule, to remind others about upcoming events, to report on the progress of pending projects, to send documents for review and editing, and so on.

If your computer is part of a larger network, such as the Internet, then the same applications apply, plus virtually unlimited coverage. You can maintain regular contact with distant family members or business associates. Even with a global connection such as the Internet, E-mail is almost instantaneous and the cost is virtually nil, given the low cost for online time today and the quickness with which you can send and receive a message.

Whether the message is going to the other side of the room or around the world, the principle is the same. With the proper address you can send messages quickly and easily. The format of the specific address depends on the destination, but in general it consists of a user name, a machine name, and a network identification.

In addition to the network connection, you need software to manage your mail. Network E-mail software usually has the following functions:

○ An editor so you can compose messages.

○ A reader so you can view received mail.

○ A file manager to track and store mail.

○ An address manager to store frequently used E-mail addresses.

○ Facilities to send messages out on the network and to receive incoming mail to your desktop.

Microsoft Exchange

Later we'll show you how to send messages through the Internet and other services, but let's start with a relatively simple Windows 95 network. Included with Windows 95 is a software utility called the *Microsoft Exchange*, a multifaceted application that lets you exchange E-mail with a variety of networks and mail facilities. Once you learn how to use it inside a Windows 95 workgroup, you can use it to exchange mail with just about anybody anywhere.

Microsoft Exchange supports the following features:

○ Windows 95 Workgroup E-mail.

○ E-mail with a number of external network services, including the Internet.

○ Attaching files and other objects to E-mail messages.

○ Separating folders for E-mail organization.

○ A personal address book to store E-mail addresses.

○ Fonts, colors, and text alignment.

○ Fax transmission and reception through your computer.

To use the Microsoft Exchange Client for workgroup E-mail, you need to perform the following steps:

1. Install Microsoft Exchange if it wasn't installed during your Windows 95 setup.

2. Specify the E-mail system you want to use with Exchange. Remember, Exchange can work with a number of E-mail systems.

3. Setup an E-mail Post Office. This is a file system that resides on one of the computers in the workgroup to manage incoming and outgoing E-mail.

4. Configure Microsoft Exchange Client.

We'll show you how to complete each of these steps.

If Microsoft Exchange wasn't installed when you set up Windows 95, you'll need to install it before you can use workgroup E-mail facilities. Check out your desktop display. Is there an icon labeled Inbox? If so, you probably have Microsoft Exchange installed. If you don't see this icon, you probably need to install the Exchange client.

Even if you don't see the Inbox icon, make another check to see whether you have Exchange installed. Click on **Start** on the task bar and choose **Programs**. Is Microsoft Exchange listed? If not, proceed with the instructions in this section. If it is listed, skip to the next section.

To use Microsoft Exchange you need to have a post office installed somewhere on the network. If you are running a small network at home or in a small office, this probably hasn't yet been done. Set up the Post Office first. Then installing and configuring Exchange will be automatic and painless.

To set up a Post Office, follow these steps:

1. Click on **Start** on the Task Bar, select **Settings**, and choose **Control Panel**.

2. Locate the Microsoft Mail Postoffice icon in the Control Panel (see Figure 3.6) and double-click on it. The Workgroup Postoffice Admin wizard will launch.

NOTE If you don't see the Microsoft Mail Postoffice icon in the Control Panel, it means you either didn't install Microsoft Mail as part of your original installation, or you removed it some time after the installation. The only way to get the Postoffice Icon back is to re-install Microsoft Exchange. You can install Exchange over an existing installation at any time. You won't damage anything and you will restore the missing components. If you are sure you installed the Postoffice in the beginning, choose **re-install** from the install wizard. If you're not sure, choose **complete install** when you run Windows 95 setup. See page 82.

3. Click on the **Create A New Workgroup Postoffice** button on the opening screen of the wizard, and click on **Next** to continue. You will see the dialog box in Figure 4.7.

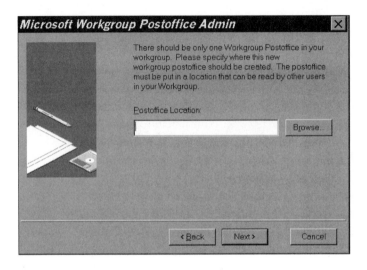

FIGURE 4.7 Choose Postoffice Location dialog box.

4. Type a path to the disk and directory where you want the Postoffice installed. You can click on **Browse** to use the Windows directory dialog box to find the right location for your Postoffice. The Postoffice wizard will create a directory within the last directory you specify on this screen.

5. Click on **Next** when the directory path to the Postoffice is correct. The wizard will display a dialog box to confirm your directory choice. Click **Next** to go on.

6. Fill out the information requested on the Administrator Account Details dialog box (see Figure 4.8). The wizard automatically inserts your user name and the default password **PASSWORD** on this dialog box. For an at-home network, erase the password and don't worry about it. For an office network, enter a unique password you can remember. You don't need to fill out this whole dialog box in a small installation. The mailbox and password are enough.

Enter Your Administrator Account Details
Name:
Mailbox:
tom
Password:
PASSWORD
Phone #1:
Phone #2:
Office:
Department:
Notes:
OK
Cancel

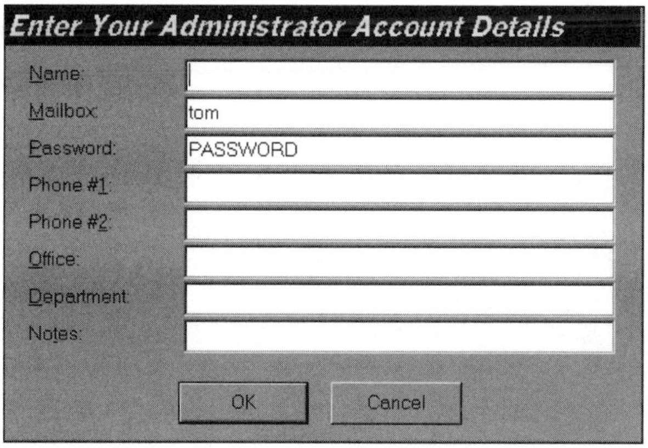

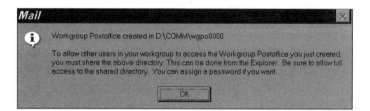

FIGURE 4.8 Administrator Account Details dialog box.

7. Click on **OK** to close the Account Details dialog box. You will see the instruction dialog box shown in Figure 4.9. Click on **OK** to close this dialog box.

Mail
Workgroup Postoffice created in D:\COMM\wgpo0000
To allow other users in your workgroup to access the Workgroup Postoffice you just created, you must share the above directory. This can be done from the Explorer. Be sure to allow full access to the shared directory. You can assign a password if you want.
OK

FIGURE 4.9 Final Postoffice Instruction dialog box.

8. Open the Explorer by clicking on **Start**, selecting **Programs**, and choosing **Explorer** from the displayed list.
9. Select the disk drive and directory just created for the Postoffice.
10. Use **File Properties** to display the **Properties** dialog box for the Postoffice directory.
11. Click on the **Sharing** tab on this dialog box (see Figure 4.10).

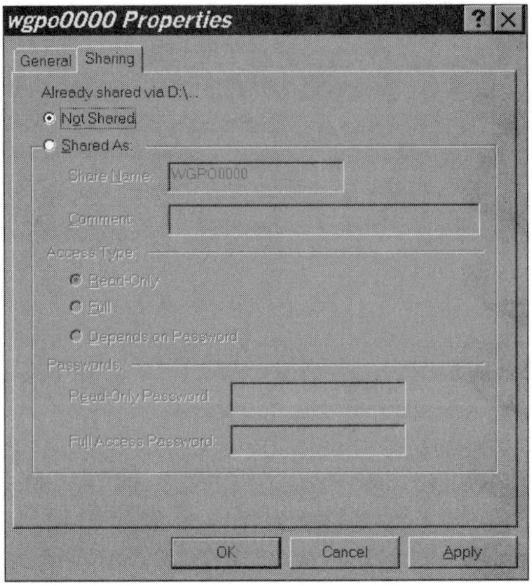

FIGURE 4.10 Sharing Tab of Postoffice Properties dialog box.

12. Click on the **Shared As** button to enable sharing features.

13. Either accept the default share name, or enter a share name of your own choice. We suggest you type **Postoffice** in this field.

14. Choose the **Access Type**. **Full** is the right choice for most networks.

15. Click on **OK** to start sharing and close this dialog box.

16. Close the Explorer.

Once you have a postoffice set up, you are ready to configure Microsoft Exchange. However, at this stage, there is only one user registered with the Postoffice to receive mail. That's you. If you want other users on the network to be able to receive mail, you need to take some additional steps:

1. Re-open the Microsoft Mail Postoffice Admin dialog box by clicking on the **Postoffice** icon in the Control Panel (Figure 3.2).

2. Choose **Administer an Existing Workgroup Postoffice** if this button is not already selected, and click on **Next**.

3. Specify the **Postoffice** directory if it is not shown by default and click on **Next**.

4. Enter your E-mail name and password on the next dialog screen, and click on **Next** to show the dialog box in Figure 4.11.

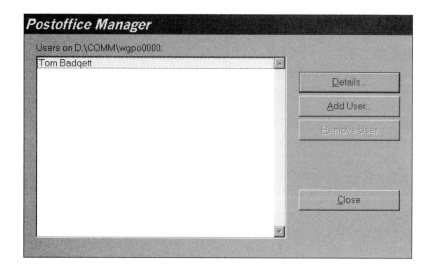

FIGURE 4.11 Postoffice Manager dialog box.

5. Click on **Add User** to display the Add User dialog box, shown in Figure 4.12. This is the same screen you used previously to set up your own mailbox as Postoffice Administrator.

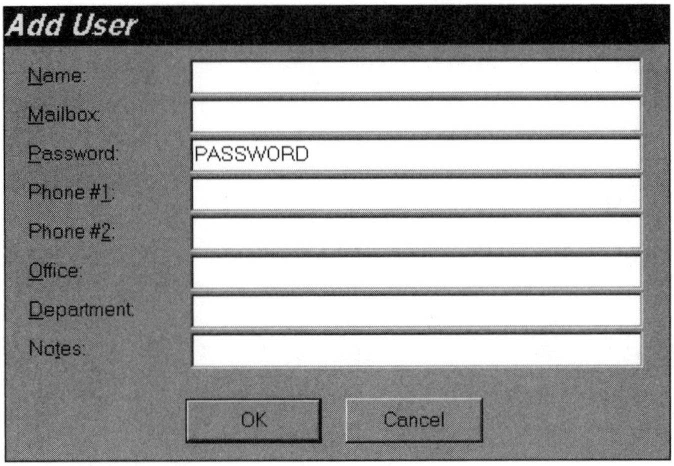

Add User

Name:

Mailbox:

Password: PASSWORD

Phone #1:

Phone #2:

Office:

Department:

Notes:

OK   Cancel

FIGURE 4.12 Add User to Postoffice dialog box.

6. Fill out the form with information for the new user. Be sure to remember the password you use. You can leave the password blank in small networks, especially at home, unless you receive business-related E-mail that you need to keep private.

7. Click on **OK** to enter the new user and return to the Postoffice Manager dialog box.

You can add more users at this time by clicking on **Add User** and filling out another form, or you can click on **Close** to close out the Wizard and return to the Control Panel display.

NOTE If you've found the facilities for installing a Workgroup Postoffice in Control Panel, then Microsoft Exchange is already installed. Double-click the **Inbox** icon on your desktop and answer the questions from the Wizard to configure Exchange. Skip to page 85.

To install Microsoft Exchange, follow these steps:

1. Click on **Start** on the Task Bar, select **Settings**, and choose **Control Panel**.

2. Double-click on **Add/Remove Programs** to display the tabbed **Add/Remove Program Properties** dialog box, shown in Figure 4.13.

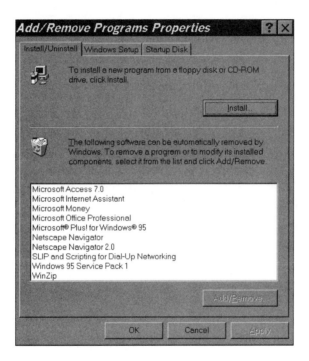

FIGURE 4.13 Add/Remove Program Properties dialog box.

3. Click on the **Windows Setup** tab to display the setup dialog box.

4. Click on **Microsoft Exchange** in the displayed list. Windows will show you how much storage is required for this addition and will also install some related components automatically (see Figure 4.14).

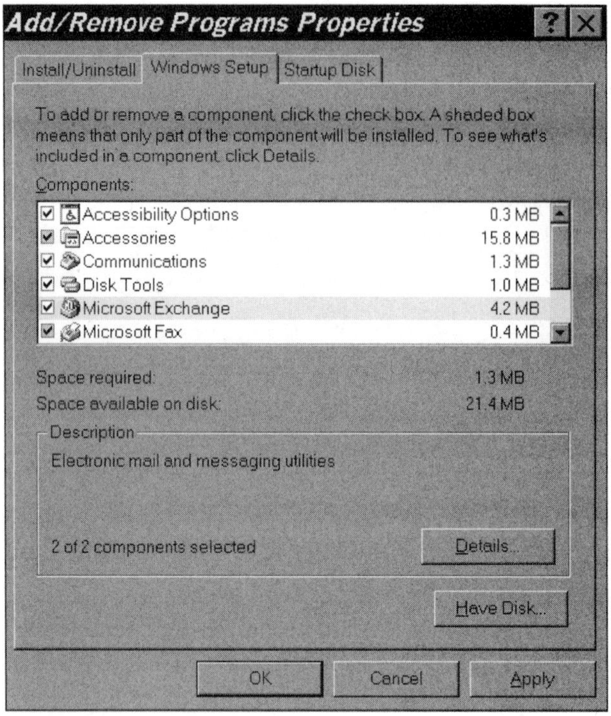

FIGURE 4.14 Windows Setup dialog box.

5. Click on **OK** to start the installation process. You will be asked to insert the Windows 95 CD-ROM disk or the installation floppies so that the installer can access the files required for Microsoft Exchange. After the necessary files are copied, Windows launches the Inbox Setup Wizard.

6. Click on **Next** on the first Wizard screen.

7. Accept the Windows defaults on the second Wizard screen, unless you do not wish to configure Internet mail at this time. Make sure that Microsoft Mail, at least, is selected on this screen and click on **Next**.

8. Accept the default Postoffice directory if it is the correct one on the next wizard screen. If the wizard chooses the wrong Postoffice directory, type the correct directory on this dialog box.

9. Choose your name from the list on the next dialog box. In a small network where you are also the network administrator, only your name is likely to appear on this dialog box.

10. Type the password to your mailbox on the next dialog box. This is the same password you created when you set up the Postoffice.

11. Click on **Next** to move to the next dialog box.

12. If you are configuring access to the Internet, choose the type of Internet access. For most of us, Modem (the default) is the proper answer.

13. Continue with the following dialog boxes to configure your Internet access (We'll give you more details on using Windows 95 with the Internet in Chapter 6).

14. Accept the default when the wizard asks for the name of your personal address book. You could change the path here, but it is easier to use the Windows default.

15. Click on **Next** on the Personal Folders dialog box to accept the defaults.

16. Choose whether or not you want Windows 95 to add the Inbox to your startup group. If you want Windows to launch the Inbox when you boot the computer, click on **Add Inbox**. If not, accept the default by clicking on **Next**.

17. Click on **Finish** to close the Exchange wizard.

Using Windows 95 E-Mail

Once you have a Postoffice established and you have installed and configured the Exchange client, you are ready to use the networked mail utility.

Sending Messages

To send an E-mail message across the Windows 95 network, using Microsoft Exchange:

1. Double-click on the **Inbox** icon on your desk to open the Microsoft Exchange Client, shown in Figure 4.15. The first time you use Exchange you will see messages welcoming you to the Exchange Client.

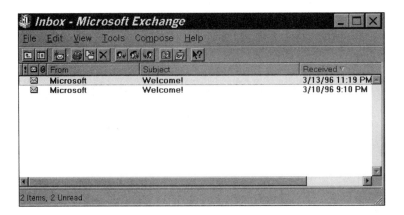

FIGURE 4.15 Microsoft Client opening screen.

NOTE

As the Postoffice administrator you probably will get right into the Exchange Client and the Postoffice. If you are a new remote user, then you may be asked for the path to the Postoffice and for your user name and password. If you didn't set up the Postoffice, then you may not know which directory holds the Postoffice; you may not even be sure what your user name and password are. Ask the person who set up the Postoffice for this information.

2. Click on **Compose** and choose **Message** to create a new E-mail message. You will see the dialog box shown in Figure 4.16.

3. Enter the name of the recipient for whom this E-mail message is intended in the **To:** field of this dialog box.

4. Enter a second E-mail address for another recipient in the Cc (carbon copy) field of this dialog box.

5. Type a subject on the **Subject** line of this dialog box.

6. Type the message in the message area.

NOTE

You can use the **Tab** key to move to the next field on this dialog box, or you can use the mouse to place the insertion point where you want it.

7. Click on **Tools** and choose **Deliver Now Using** to display delivery options. Choose **Microsoft Mail** from the popup menu. If the address is valid, the message will be sent to the addressee.

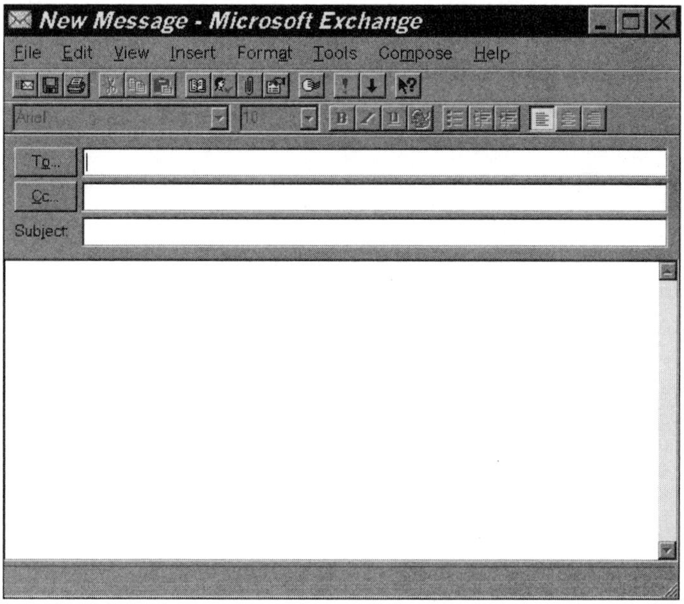

FIGURE 4.16 New Message dialog box.

> While you can type individual addresses each time you send a message, you also can build a personal address book of frequently used E-mail addresses. On a small local network this may or may not be useful to you. But as the network grows and as you start experimenting with dial-up networking and sending messages through online services or the Internet, the Address Book is more important. You can experiment with the Address Book by clicking on **Tools** and choosing **Address Book** from the pull-down menu. Refer to Chapter 6 for more information on configuring and using the Address Book.

Reading Messages

Reading a message transmitted over the Windows 95 network is equally easy. Just follow these steps:

1. Double-click on the **Inbox** icon to open Microsoft Exchange.

2. Double-click on the message displayed on the main Exchange screen that you want to read. A second dialog box will pop up with the chosen message displayed. You will also have a toolbar and a menu bar that let you reply to the sender, reply to everyone on the distribution list, forward the message to another user, and more.

3. Use the File menu to save a copy of this message to a disk file, to print the message, and to conduct other file operations.

4. Use **File Close** to close this dialog box and return to the list of incoming mail messages

Notice that the dialog box that lets you read a message includes a typical Windows menu and a toolbar beneath the menu (see Figure 4.17).

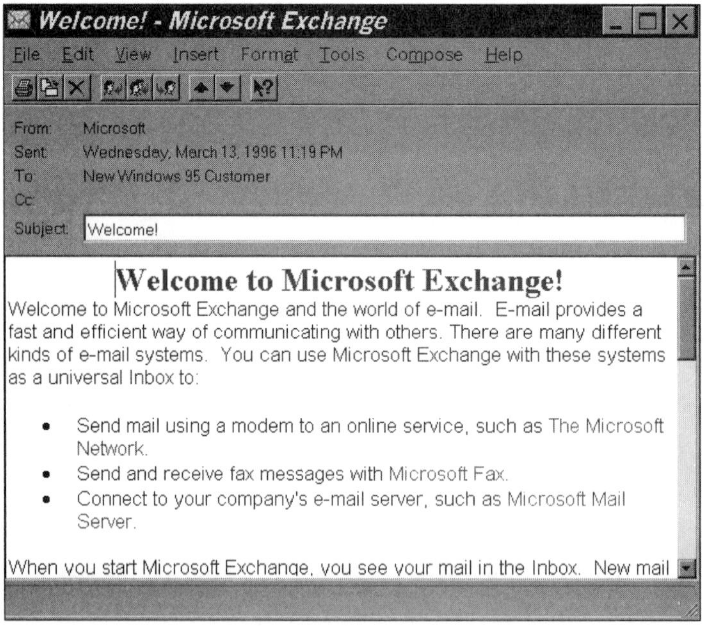

FIGURE 4.17 Exchange Read a Message dialog box.

The easiest way to manipulate the displayed message is to use the toolbar. Typical of Windows dialogs, this one includes tool tips, so if you point your mouse cursor to one of the images on the toolbar and pause for a second or so, a one- or two-word description of this button will appear.

For example, you can print the displayed message to the current printer by clicking on the first icon (it looks like a printer). Other icons let you respond to the sender, respond to everyone on the address list, forward the message, and so on. These functions are also available from the menu bar. And, you can respond to or forward messages and the like from the inbox (message list) display as well as with the text of the message displayed on the screen.

Use the View menu to customize the way the Exchange dialog box appears by adding the format toolbar display, for example. This is an intuitive utility that you should find really easy to use. For more help in learning your way around message handling with Microsoft exchange, click on **Help** to see a list of topics like the one in Figure 4.18.

FIGURE 4.18 Microsoft Exchange Help dialog box.

Network Chat (WinChat)

Electronic Mail is a store and forward system. That means the messages you create on your desktop may reside there temporarily until you are ready to send them to the host or post office. Once they have been transferred to the first move up the line, the messages are stored there until the recipient picks them up or they are sent on to the next host in the sequence to the final destination. Store and forward.

There may be times on a network, however, when you'd like to talk with another user in real time, keyboard to keyboard. That's where the Windows 95 Networking WinChat utility comes in.

NOTE If you upgraded a Windows for Workgroups installation that was using WinChat, then WinChat should already be installed. If yours is a fresh Windows 95 install, or you were not using WinChat in Windows for Workgroups, then you'll need to install WinChat to use it.

If WinChat is not already installed, you can install it by following these steps:

1. Open the Control Panel (Figure 3.2) and choose the **Add/Remove Programs** icon.
2. Click on the **Windows Setup** tab of this dialog box.
3. Click the **Have Disk** button at the bottom of this dialog box to display the **Install from Disk** dialog box, shown in Figure 4.19.

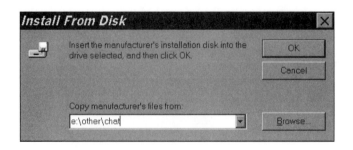

FIGURE 4.19 Install From Disk dialog box.

4. Type the drive letter that represents your CD-ROM drive (D: for most users), and then the path **\other\chat** (you will type **d:\other\chat** if your CD player is on the D: drive).

NOTE If your version of Windows 95 was supplied on floppy disks instead of CD-ROM, you don't have the WinChat program. You can get it from Microsoft as part of CD-ROM extensions that you can download free over the Internet. Point your World Wide Browser to **http://www.microsoft.com/windows/soft-ware.htm** and choose **Windows 95 CD-ROM Extras.** Click on **Other Utilities** and choose **Windows Chat Utility** to download.

5. Click on **OK** to begin the installation.

6. Click the check box beside Chat on the Have Disk dialog box (see Figure 4.20).

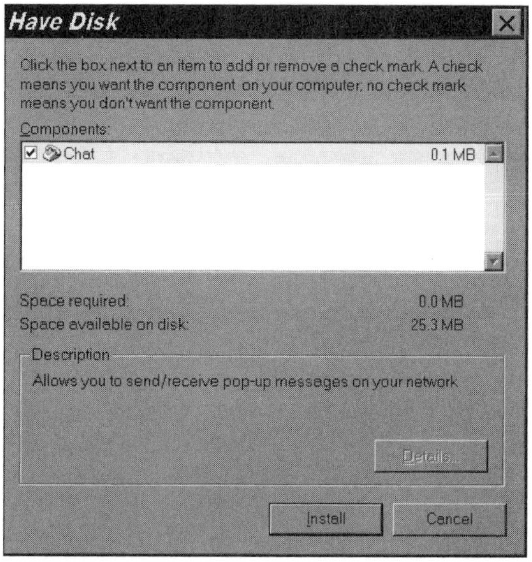

FIGURE 4.20 Have Disk dialog box, with Chat checked.

7. Click on the **Install** button.

8. After the installation is complete, click on **OK** to close the Windows Setup dialog box.

9. Close the Control Panel.

The **winchat.exe** program is now installed in your Windows 95 directory. For most users this is the **c:\windows** directory. You can run the Chat utility from the Run dialog box by clicking on the **Start** button on the task bar and choosing **Run**. In the **Open** field on this dialog, type **c:\windows\winchat** and click **OK**.

It will be easier to use this utility, however, if you create a shortcut to WinChat. You can do this from the Run dialog box by using the following steps:

1. Click on **Browse** instead of entering a path and filename.
2. From the popup directory dialog box, choose the **Windows** directory.
3. Use the horizontal **Scroll bar** to move the file list display to the right.
4. Right-drag the **Winchat** filename to the desktop.
5. Choose **Create Shortcut** from the popup menu.
6. Click on **Cancel** to close the Directory dialog box.
7. Click on **Cancel** to close the Run dialog box.

To open WinChat, double-click the shortcut you just created to display the WinChat application main dialog, shown in Figure 4.21.

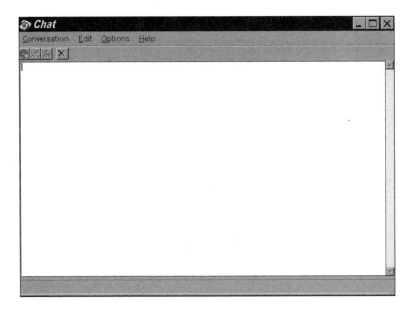

FIGURE 4.21 WinChat main dialog box.

Windows treats the WinChat program like a telephone utility. So to chat with someone at another workstation you make a "call." To do so, use the following steps:

1. Click on **Conversation** and choose **Dial** from the menu (you can also use the first icon on the toolbar). You will see the Select Computer dialog box, shown in Figure 4.22.

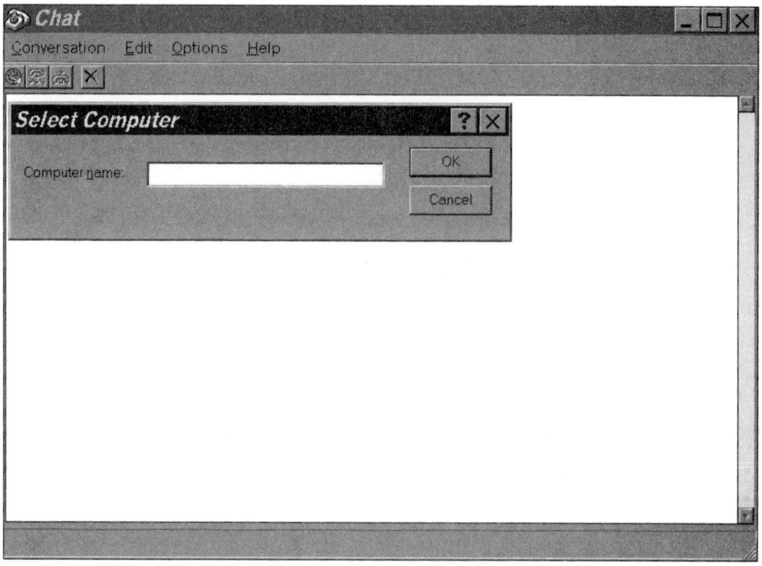

FIGURE 4.22 Winchat Select Computer dialog box.

2. Type the name of the computer you want to dial and click **OK**. If the computer you are using has a sound card installed, you will hear the sound of an outgoing ring, like the one you hear when you dial a telephone. If you don't have a sound card, your standard PC speaker will click or beep once for each outgoing ring.

N O T E

To chat with another user using WinChat, dial the name of the computer at which they work. You may or may not be able to dial a user name. If you enter a computer name that doesn't exist on the network, nothing happens. You won't see an error message; you simply won't be able to contact the person you want.

When the computer you dialed answers, the Chat window will split horizontally and you will see what the person is saying to you in the bottom window. You can answer their message by typing in the top window. This is a full duplex link, which means you can both talk at the same time. In fact, the messages you type appear in real time, character by character. If you edit a line, the edit appears on the destination screen at the same time you edit it on your screen. Chat is like having a copy of part of your computer screen in a popup window on a remote computer.

If you are working at a computer that receives an incoming call from WinChat, you will hear a ringing telephone, if your computer has a sound card installed. If you don't have a sound card, your speaker will click or beep with each ring.

NOTE The sounds you hear when you dial a number or receive a call depend on settings in the Sound utility of your Windows 95 control panel. The default sounds are standard telephone outgoing and incoming rings. The incoming ring sounds like an old-fashioned telephone bell. You can change what sounds you hear with WinChat by choosing **Sounds** from the main Control Panel dialog box and then selecting **Chat dialing ring** or **Chat incoming ring**. The name of the sound file used with each of these events appears in the **Name:** field in the Sound group on this dialog. Type a new sound file name or browse for the name and you can have any sound you want to notify you of an incoming call or to tell you that your computer is dialing another user. You could use cartoon sounds from a download or a sound effects CD, for example, or your could record a spoken message through your sound card. Windows 95 sound support is flexible and fun.

To answer an incoming call, use the following steps:

1. Move your mouse pointer to the bottom of the screen to pop up the task bar if it isn't already visible.

2. Click on the **Chat** button on the task bar. Windows 95 launches Chat automatically when a call comes in, but keeps it minimized on the task

bar until you open it up. When you open Chat, you will see a split screen and the phone sound will stop (see Figure 4.23).

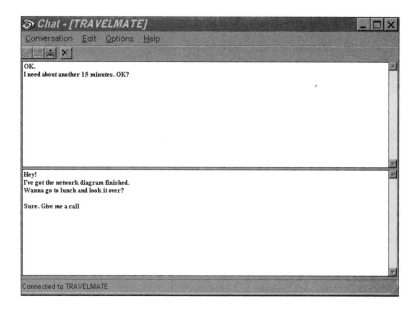

FIGURE 4.23 Chat split screen with messages.

At the bottom of the dialog box will be the name of the calling computer (not the name of the calling person, remember!). You can start typing immediately to the person on the other end of the link.

If Chat is already running and open when a call comes in, you'll need to use **Conversation Answer** or click on the **Answer** icon on the toolbar (the second from the left—the icon with the telephone off the hook) to pick up the call.

You can change a few things about the way WinChat operates with the Options menu. Click on **Options** to pull down the menu shown in Figure 4.24.

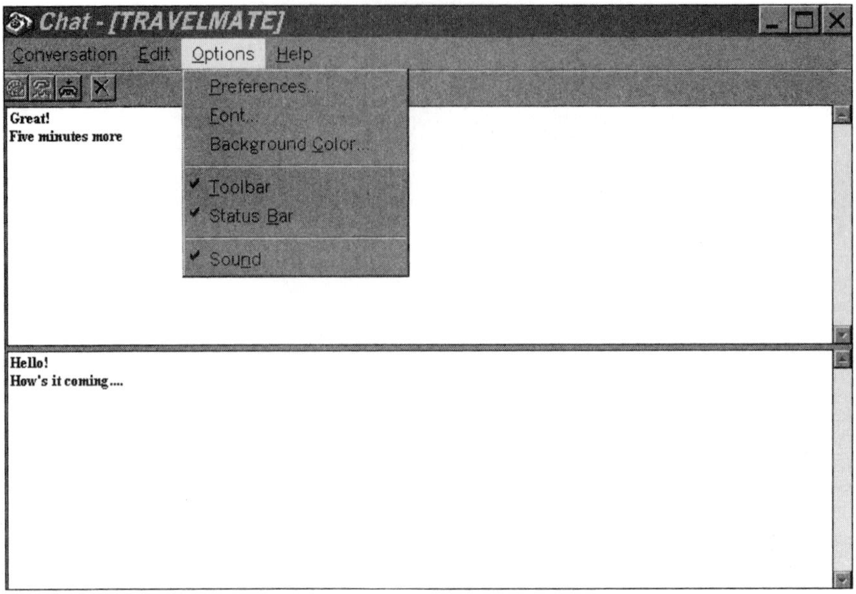

FIGURE 4.24 WinChat Options menu.

Turn off the toolbar (under the menu), the status bar (at the bottom of the dialog) or sound by clicking on the entry you want to change. The check mark beside any feature you turn off will disappear.

You can control the background color and the font you use by choosing these items from the Preferences dialog box. You'll see a standard Windows color chart for background color or a split, font dialog similar to the one in Microsoft Word or Excel if you choose to change the default font.

To change other operational parameters, use the following steps:

1. Choose **Preferences**... from the Options menu (Figure 4.24). You will see the dialog box shown in Figure 4.25.

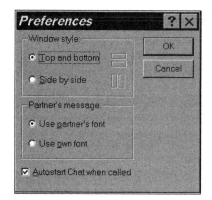

FIGURE 4.25 WinChat Preferences dialog box.

2. Change any of these features by clicking the appropriate radio button to enable or disable an item. Click on **OK** to effect the changes and return to the WinChat dialog box.

Network Messaging with WinPopup

In addition to interactive chat or talk, your Windows 95 network supports a messaging facility that lets you send short, popup messages to specific computers on the network. Unlike the WinChat utility, WinPopup is a one-way facility. But you can use it to send a message to an individual computer or to broadcast messages to an entire workgroup. You can even use WinPopup to display messages from your printer when it has finished a print job.

And, of course, the person receiving your popup message can respond to you through WinPopup as well, so that it becomes two-way in the same way that electronic mail is two-way. The difference is that with E-mail the messages are stored so that you can read them again or file them for future reference. With WinPopup, when you shut down the utility or reboot your computer, any messages you have received are gone.

Suppose you want to tell a coworker that your sales meeting has been delayed because the client will be late. Rather than interrupting with WinChat, or even a telephone call, you can send a quick popup message that will show up on the computer screen. Or, what if you need to reboot one of the computers in the network and you want to make sure no one is using files from it? Send a broadcast message telling everyone on the network that the machine will be rebooted in five minutes. Then you can send another broadcast one minute before rebooting the machine as a final alert.

To use WinPopup, each machine that you want to receive messages must be running the program. To make sure that popup messaging is available to everyone on the network, install **WinPopup.exe** in everyone's Startup folder.

To install **WinPopup.exe** follow these steps:

1. Click on the **Start** button on the task bar and choose **Programs** to display a list of available programs.

2. Choose **Windows Explorer** from the list.

3. Double-click on the folder that represents your Windows 95 directory. In most cases this will be **Windows**, though it might be **Win95** or something else if you installed Windows 95 in a separate directory while running an earlier version of Windows.

4. Click on any file name in the Contents of Windows side of the dialog and press the **W** key to move down in the directory list.

5. Use the **vertical scroll** bar on the right of this window to locate the **winpopup.exe** file and click once on the file name to select it. You can also use the **down arrow** key on the keyboard to scroll down in the display and select the file name. Your display should look like the one in Figure 4.26.

6. Use **File Copy** to make a copy of the file.

7. Press the **S** key to move back up in the directory display.

8. Double-click on the **Start Menu** folder to open it.

9. Double-click on the **Programs** folder to open it.

10. Use **Edit Paste** to place a copy of the application in the Start Up program directory.

11. Repeat this process for each computer you want to use the WinPopup utility.

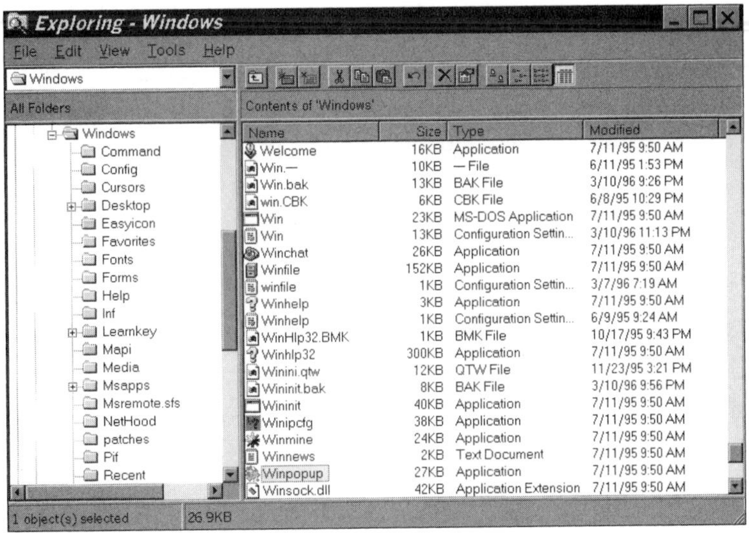

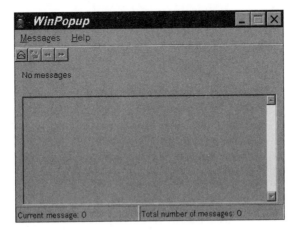

FIGURE 4.26 Windows 95 directory listing.

Now, whenever you start this computer, the WinPopup utility will load auto-matically and be available for use by anyone on the network. You can reboot the computer now to launch the program, or you can simply double-click on **WinPopup** in the current directory display to run it. When the program runs you will see a dialog box like the one in Figure 4.27.

FIGURE 4.27 WinPopup main dialog box screen.

Next you may want to configure WinPopup to behave the way you want it to. Use the following steps:

1. Run the program by rebooting your computer, by double-clicking on the program name in Windows Explorer, or by using **Start Run** to specify c:\windows\winpopup.

NOTE If you started WinPopup by booting your computer, it may be running minimized. Check the task bar to see if it is there. If so, click on the name to open the main dialog box.

2. Click on **Messages** and choose **Options...** to display the Options dialog box shown in Figure 4.28.

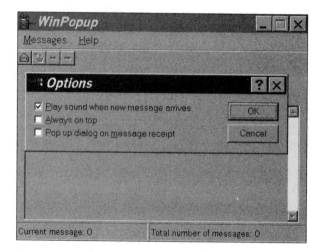

FIGURE 4.28 WinPopup Options dialog box.

3. Click on the options you want to enable or change.

By default WinPopup will play a sound when a computer receives a message. You can disable this if you wish. You also can tell WinPopup to always remain on top of whatever other programs or dialogs are displayed, and you can have the program open a message window automatically when a message is received. Otherwise, you will hear a sound when you receive a new message, but you will have to open WinPopup from the task bar to read it.

Figure 4.29 shows a WinPopup dialog box with a new message.

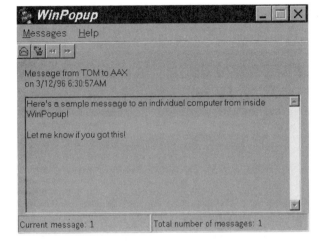

FIGURE 4.29 WinPopup dialog box with new message.

Each computer can receive multiple messages from WinPopup. If you have more than one message on your desktop, the right arrow on the toolbar will light to indicate that you can move to the next message. If there are additional messages prior to the current message, the back arrow also will be lit. Move among messages by clicking on the forward or back arrow.

The first time you view a new message, you also will see information about the source, date, and time of the message. If this information is dimly lit, you have already viewed this message. The status bar at the bottom of the dialog box shows you what message you are viewing and how many messages there are.

To send a message with WinPopup, use the following steps:

1. Open the main program dialog box if it is not already displayed. Use the task bar if the program is running or click on **Start** and choose **Run** if you want to start the program.

2. Click on **Message** and choose **Send** to display the Send dialog box shown in Figure 4.30. If a message from another user is displayed, WinPopup assumes that you want to respond to that user, so the name will be filled in automatically.

FIGURE 4.30 WinPopup Send dialog box.

N O T E Unlike WinChat, WinPopup can send messages to a computer, to a user, or to the whole workgroup. If User or computer is selected, you can type either a user name or the name of a computer on the network. If you want to broadcast a message to the entire Workgroup, then enter the name of the target workgroup in the **To:** field of this dialog box.

3. Select whether you want to send the message to a user or computer, or broadcast the message to everyone in a workgroup.

4. Type the name of the user, the computer, or the workgroup you want to receive the message.

5. Press **Tab** or click in the Message area of the dialog and type your message.

6. Click on **OK** to send it. After a few seconds a dialog box will pop up to show you that the message was successfully sent, or to report errors if the message was undeliverable because the destination machine was turned off or misnamed.

N O T E Although WinPopup includes an automatic feature to notify you when a print job sent to a network printer is finished, as this book is written it does not function in a Windows 95–only network. Microsoft technical people say they are working on the problem. If it were functioning as intended, all you would need to do to receive these messages would be: just make sure that WinPopup is running on the computer that has the printer you want to use, and run WinPopup on your own computer.

WHAT'S NEXT?

With the information in this chapter you have a good background for designing and building your own Windows 95 network, and in beginning to use the resources you build. In the next chapter, we'll start discussing some parts of Windows 95 networking in more detail, beginning with network printing in Chapter 5.

CHAPTER FIVE

Network Printing

Printing over a network is one of the really useful benefits of connecting computers. Although quality printers are cheaper than ever, most of us still don't want to purchase a high-quality printer for every computer. With Windows 95 networking, you don't have to. When you attach a printer to one of the PCs in a Windows 95 network, you can print to it from any other PC on the network. The transfer time may be slightly slower than if the printer were attached directly to your PC, but only slightly. Otherwise you'll never know the difference. And, if you own more than one printer—a laser printer for day-to-day work and a color printer for special projects, for example—then you can access them all from any PC on the net. Besides, by placing a printer away from your day-to-day work area, you'll notice a lower noise level and a reduction in indoor air pollution, an increasingly common problem with laser printers and copiers moving into every corner of the office.

ATTACHING A NETWORK PRINTER

For most of us, a network printer will be attached to a parallel port on one computer that is part of the network. In a small network, this is the way to go. Hooking up a parallel port printer is quick and easy, and configuring a PC-attached printer is also easy.

In larger networks and where speed of printing is very important, you may want to install a printer directly on the network, either with an internal network interface or with an external interface.

In Chapter 3, we showed you how to connect a printer to a PC and how to set up a printer with a direct network connection. The hardware part of setting up a networked printer is very simple. A cable from the printer to a PC or a print server box is about all you need to install a printer on a Windows 95 network. Of course you must turn on file and printer sharing from inside the Network dialog box of the Control Panel, and you will have to install some driver software to permit Windows 95 and your applications to use the printer's features.

The documentation that comes with any dedicated network print server hardware should show you how to hook up the hardware and what additional software, if any, you need to install to support it.

There are a few considerations in setting up the software part of a networked printer installation. We'll show you in the next section how to handle that process, and then we'll show you how to use a networked printer.

CONFIGURING A NETWORK PRINTER

You probably configured a printer attached directly to one of the PCs on your network when you installed Windows 95. Here, we'll assume you did not install a printer at that time . If you did install one, here's how to rework it and perhaps add some enhancements.

Specifying Printer Model

It may seem that you should be able to hook up a printer and just start sending documents to it. In the real world, however, things are never as simple as they should be. That's because each printer supports slightly different features, and each does its job in a slightly different way. That means you have to use special software (called *driver software*) to support each particular printer.

The good news with Windows 95 is that the operating system contains all the software you are likely to need for most popular printers. And, if the printer is relatively new, chances are the printer can "talk" to Windows and report its brand and model number, and Windows can set up everything properly. This *Plug and Play* capability is one of the new and exciting features of the Windows 95 environment.

In addition, if you installed Windows 95 as an upgrade to a previous version of Windows and you are using the same printer or printers, then the drivers you need may have been kept from the previous installation. If the Windows 95 versions of hardware drivers are more current than the existing ones, on the other hand, you were likely prompted to allow Windows to replace them.

If your printer is a Plug and Play model, when you bootup Windows after hooking up the hardware, if the printer is turned on, Windows should report that it found a new printer and ask if you want to configure it. The installation process is handled by a printer wizard and is simple and straightforward.

If your printer and Windows can't work things out on their own, you can help by launching the **Add Printer Wizard** and answering some questions. You start the **Add Printer Wizard** from the main Printers dialog window.

NOTE You must complete this procedure for each PC with which you want to use this particular printer. Even though you install the printer and configure it on the PC to which it is physically attached, you must install software and configure the printer for each computer that will use it. The process described here is for the PC that is directly attached to the printer. Later we will show you how to configure a remote printer across the network.

You can open the Printers dialog window in three ways:

❍ Click **Start** on the Task Bar, point to **Settings**, and choose **Printers**.

❍ Double-click the **My Computer** icon to open the My Computer dialog box, then double-click the **Printers Folder**.

❍ From Control Panel, double-click the **Printers** icon.

Whichever method you choose, you should see the Printers dialog box, shown in Figure 5.1.

FIGURE 5.1 Printers dialog box.

Notice that in this example other printers are already installed. Also visible in this dialog window is an icon that represents the **Add Printer Wizard**. Double-click on this icon to launch the wizard and display the dialog window shown in Figure 5.2.

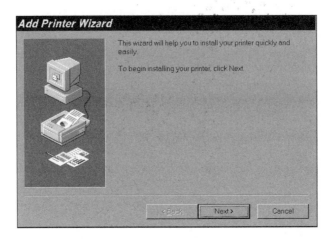

Figure 5.2 Opening dialog window of Add Printer Wizard.

Proceed with the Add Printer process as follows:

1. Click on **Local Printer** to select that option if it is not already selected, and click **Next**. The Printer Selection dialog window shown in Figure 5.3 should appear.

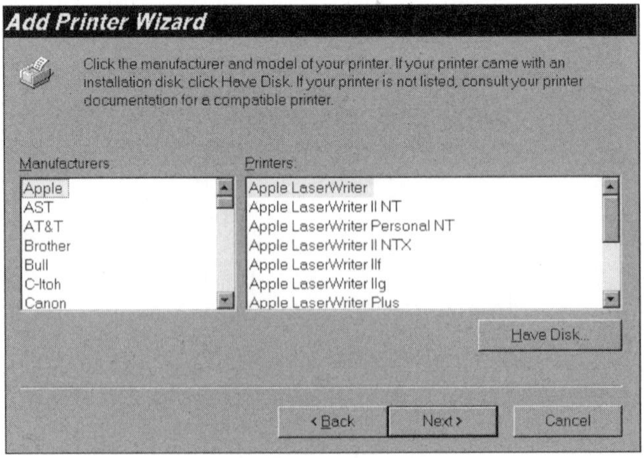

FIGURE 5.3 Printer Selection dialog window.

2. Use the scroll bars in the Manufacturers: window of this dialog window to choose the maker of your printer. A list of models for which Windows 95 includes drivers is shown in the Printers: window of this dialog window.

3. Use the scroll bars in the Printers: window to choose the particular model you are installing, and click **Next**.

N O T E

Don't install a driver for a model that doesn't exactly match the printer you have. A Model 12A is probably not the same as a Model 12. In this case, select a printer that is close, then click **Have Disk** to install the driver that came with your printer.

4. Choose the port to which the printer is attached from the next dialog window in the wizard. For most of us, this is the default, **LPT1**:. If you are using a serial printer, choose **COM1:** or **COM2:** from the display.

5. Click **Next** to display the Printer Name: dialog window.

6. Accept the Windows default name or enter a unique name of your own for the printer you are installing. In most cases, the default name is best, because it is descriptive of the brand and model you have. But if you want to call your printer *Yellow Submarine*, go ahead.

7. If you want this to be the default printer for this computer, click **Yes** at the bottom of the dialog window.

8. Click **Next** to display the printer test page prompt. It is a good idea to send a test page to the printer at this point. You can bypass the test by clicking **No** before you click **Finish**.

9. Insert the floppy disk or CD-ROM for Windows 95 when the wizard asks for it.

The driver will be copied, an icon for the new printer will be placed in the Printers dialog window, and you will see a message indicating that a test page has been sent to the printer (if you chose this option). Check the printer to see if the page came out OK, and click **Yes** if it did. (It almost certainly did print OK.)

N O T E

If the page didn't print properly, click **No** and Windows will load a help dialog window to help you troubleshoot the problem. Answer the questions in the dialog window and you should be able to locate the problem.

Now you are ready to configure the printer.

Specifying Printer Settings

To configure your new printer, open the Printers dialog window and follow these steps:

1. Right-click the icon that represents the printer you want to configure.

2. Choose **Properties** from the popup menu to display the dialog window shown in Figure 5.4. This is a tabbed dialog window with seven choices, with the **General** tab on top.

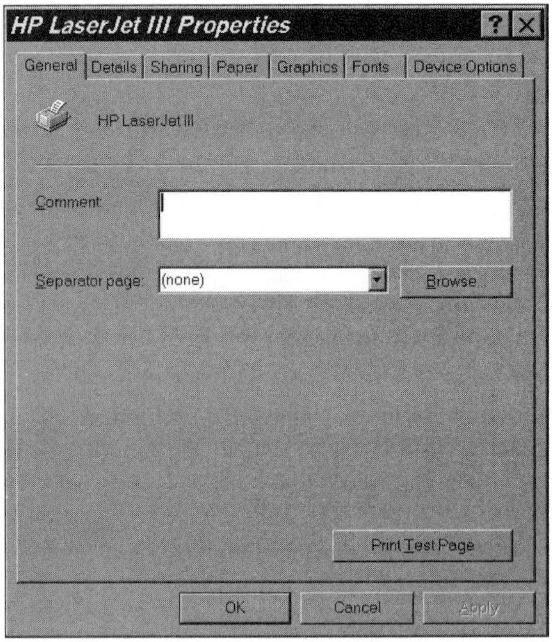

FIGURE 5.4 Printer Properties dialog window.

The Properties dialog window you see may not look exactly like the one in Figure 5.4 because different printers support different properties.

N O T E

3. Click on the tab whose properties you want to review or change and make any changes required. For example, you can specify a separator page on the General tab. A *separator page* is inserted at the beginning of each new print job to identify the sender. In a small network, separator pages just waste paper. As the network grows, however, they are useful to keep the pages of a job together so the right person can find them among the piles of paper that tend to accumulate around a shared printer.

4. Click on the **Sharing** tab and choose **Shared As**.

N O T E If your Properties dialog window doesn't show a Sharing tab, then printer sharing was not enabled when you installed the networking components. Open the Control Panel and choose **Network**. Click on **File and Printer sharing** and choose **Share printer**. Also, refer to Chapter 3 for information on configuring your Windows 95 network.

5. Enter a share name or accept the Windows default. The *share name* is used to identify this printer to other users on the network. When you see this share name from a remote PC you will also see the name of the PC to which it is attached, so you don't need to make that part of the share name. However, you should use a share name that uniquely identifies this printer to everyone on the network.

6. If you want to provide shared access to this printer only to those who have the proper password, enter a password in the Password field of this tab on the Properties dialog window.

7. You can also enter a comment to further identify this printer, if you wish.

Another tab you should view is the **Device Options** tab, if it appears with your particular printer. With a Hewlett-Packard printer, for example, this tab lets you specify how much memory the printer contains. **One megabyte** is the default, but if your printer has more, it will probably print graphics and large files faster and better if you enter the correct memory size on this dialog window. This and other dialog windows will let you set some operation parameters specific to your printer model and brand.

INSTALLING A REMOTE PRINTER

Once you have hooked up the hardware and installed the software on the computer that has the printer attached, you need to install software on all the PCs in the network that will use that printer. Remember that just having the physical connection is not enough. You have to tell Windows that you have a particular printer installed and where it is. In addition, Windows has to install the driver software so that it can take advantage of the features of your printer and allow applications such as word processors and spreadsheets to print to it.

You could follow essentially the same process for a remote printer as you used with a locally attached printer by running the **Add Printer Wizard**. However, there's another way to get the job done, and it demonstrates some of the integrated features of Windows 95.

A feature called *Point and Print* lets you simply locate the printer on the remote computer and tell Windows you want to use it on your local PC; Windows 95 does the rest. You can "point" to a remote printer by entering the path name on the Run dialog window available from the Start menu, but it is easier to use Network Neighborhood. Follow these steps:

1. Double-click on the **Network Neighborhood** icon on your desktop to display the Network Components list shown in Figure 5.5 (your list won't look exactly like this one, of course).

FIGURE 5.5 Network Neighborhood dialog window.

2. Double-click on the computer name that is set up as a print server. If you are not sure which one that is, double-click on each one in succession until you find one that displays the printer you want to use. You will see a list of shared resources available on that machine, similar to the list in Figure 5.6.

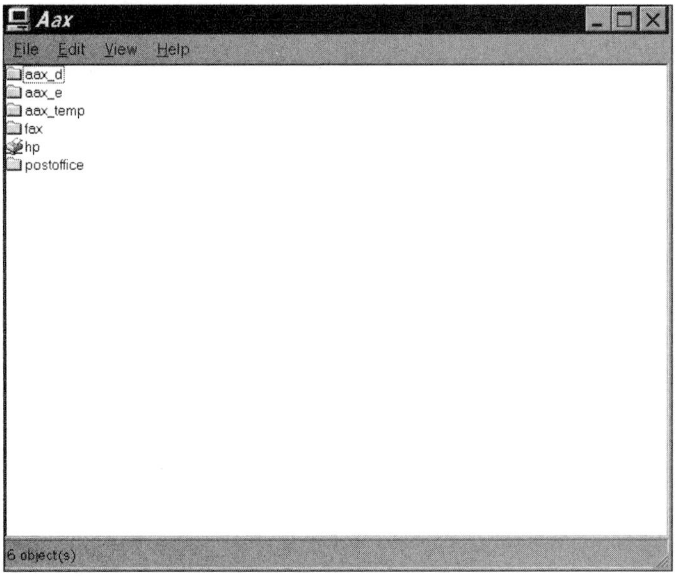

FIGURE 5.6 Shared Resources list on remote computer.

3. Double-click on the printer name that represents the printer you want to use from your remote PC. You will see the dialog window shown in Figure 5.7. Click the **Yes** button.

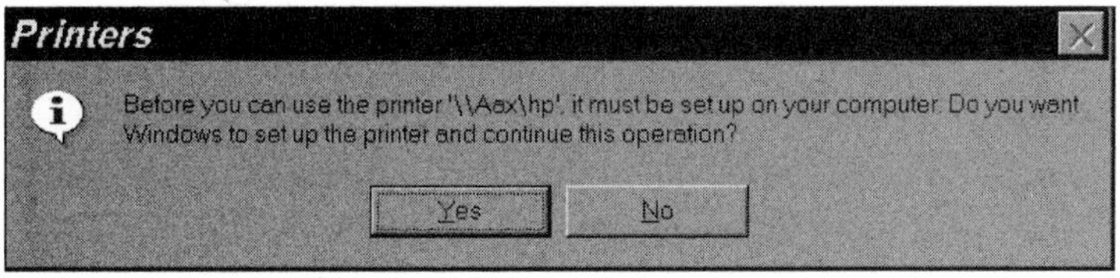

FIGURE 5.7 Printer Must Be Installed dialog window.

Windows launches the **Add Printer Wizard**, which analyzes the printer and the configuration of your local PC and then installs the required drivers and other information to allow you to use it from your local machine.

MULTIPLE VERSIONS OF SAME PRINTER

There may be times when you want to install more than one instance of the same printer. You will do this primarily when a printer supports multiple configurations—such as color and black and white, simplex (printing on one side of the paper) or duplex (printing on both sides of the paper) printing, and so on—and you want to be able to choose a configuration easily and quickly.

Printing to a File

You may also want to install a version of a printer that is set up to print to a file instead of to the printer itself. Do this from inside the Add Printer Wizard when you are asked for the printer port. Your choices will include **LPT1**, **COM1**, **COM2**, and perhaps some other choices, in addition to **File**. Choose **File** and give this printer definition a different name from the installation that prints directly to the printer.

Now when you print to this printer, the information goes to a file in the format of the specified printer. If this is a PostScript printer, for example, the resulting file contains PostScript commands. If it is a Hewlett-Packard printer set for PCL, then the file contains PCL commands.

To physically print a document that you have sent to a file, copy the file to the printer by using the DOS command: **copy /b <filename> lpt1**. The **/b** switch in this example tells the **copy** command to send the data to the printer in binary format, ensuring that the printer interprets the commands instead of trying to print them.

When you do this, you can also copy the file to a floppy disk. Then you can carry the disk to a computer that is connected to the printer you specified. This is a good way to create a printer file for a coworker who is not part of your network and doesn't have the same printer you do. You can also transmit this file over the Internet or other online service for printing at a remote location.

USING A NETWORK PRINTER

Like networked disk drives, when networked printers are properly installed, they become like local resources. As far as you and your applications are concerned, a networked printer is attached to your local PC and is using the standard printer port, LTP1. When you install new software or configure a printer for existing software, configure it as if the printer or printers you want to use are attached to your local machine. The networking components of Windows 95 then reroute any information sent to the printer on LPT1: to the proper location on the remote printer server.

It should be fairly easy to understand the benefits of network printer sharing. You have one printer but two, five, ten, even fifty users. Everyone on the network can use the printer, reducing hardware costs and space requirements.

NOTE You don't have to open an application, such as Microsoft Word, before printing a document. Open a dialog window that displays the files you want to print (such as by opening **My Computer** and choosing a drive and folder) and drag the icon that represents the file you want to print onto the icon that represents the printer you want to use in the Printer dialog window.

Also, inherent with a printer server is the concept of *job spooling*, the ability to send a print job out of the local computer much faster than a printer can accept it. Information that is waiting to print is stored at the print server in RAM and on disk. With disk storage of print jobs, many users can send data to a printer very quickly and free up local resources. Then the printer management software running on the PC to which the printer is attached sends the jobs, one by one, to the printer.

Anyone on the network can view the progress of printing—their own print jobs and any others in the queue—by opening a dialog box associated with the printer being used. Here's how:

1. Use **Settings** from the Start menu to access the Printers dialog window, shown in Figure 5.8.

NOTE

Several printer icons are shown in this sample. You can have multiple printers on a Windows 95 network, sending printouts to the appropriate printer, depending on the location of the printer, type of printer, and what data you are printing. The hand that is part of the HP LaserJet III printer indicates that this printer has been shared with the network from the local machine. The Apple LaserWriter, on the other hand, is obviously a remote printer because of the network cable that runs beneath it.

Printers
File Edit View Help
Add Printer
Apple LaserWriter II NTX
Fujitsu DL 1100 Color
Generic / Text Only
Microsoft Fax
HP LaserJet III
1 object(s) selected

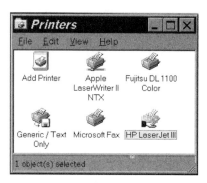

FIGURE 5.8 Printers dialog window.

2. Double-click on the icon that represents the printer you want to view. A printer dialog window named after the printer you selected is displayed (see Figure 5.9).

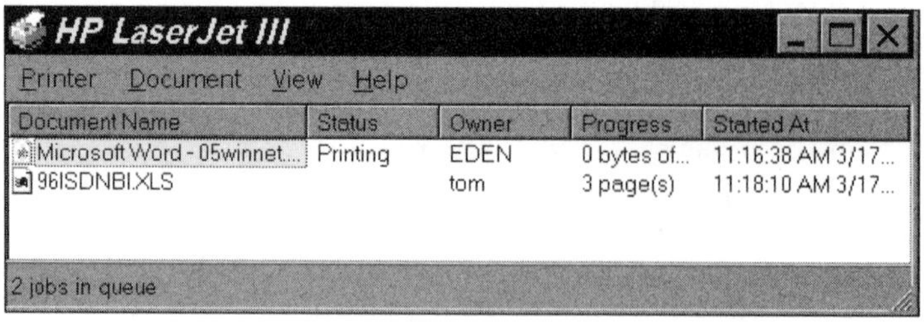

HP LaserJet III
Printer Document View Help
Document Name
Status
Owner
Progress
Started At
Microsoft Word - 05winnet...
Printing
EDEN
0 bytes of...
11:16:38 AM 3/17...
96ISDNBI.XLS
tom
3 page(s)
11:18:10 AM 3/17...
2 jobs in queue

FIGURE 5.9 HP LaserJet Printer dialog window.

3. Use the menu displayed with this dialog window to inspect and manipulate print jobs as desired.

As you can see from Figure 5.9, this dialog window shows all pending print jobs from anywhere in the network to this printer. (There may be other pending print jobs going to other printers; to view them you must open the printer dialog window associated with that printer.) You can see the name of the document, in some cases the name of the application that created it, the status, who is printing it (the Owner), how far along the job is (the Progress), and the date and time it was sent to the queue.

You may never see information about small files that are going to a printer with a reasonable buffer inside it unless the printer dialog window is displayed when you send the file to the printer. That's because the job comes into the queue and leaves very quickly.

However, with longer jobs and, especially, when there are multiple people using the same printer, you can use this dialog window to monitor progress of each job, pause a print job, or cancel a job. You can also view continuous progress reports as information is sent continuously to the printer.

NOTE You can only control print jobs you own unless you are the administrator with all rights to the network. If you try to pause or cancel a print job you don't own you will see an error message indicating you don't have permission to control that print job.

You can use the File menu to pause or cancel a print job, or you can right-click the name of the document you want to manipulate, to pop up a Pause/Cancel dialog window. If you click elsewhere in the line—on the Owner name, for example—you will see the rest of the File menu, allowing you to purge print jobs, view printer properties, set or remove the default printer setting, and pause printing. When you choose **Pause Printing** from this dialog window, all print jobs will be halted because you are controlling the printer. When you choose **Pause Printing** from the document popup, you will pause only the selected print job.

If you pause a print job, the status for that job changes from *Printing* to *Paused*. Jobs behind the top job will show a blank status because they haven't moved up the queue to where they can stream out to the printer. You may see a blank status on the top document if you have selected **Pause** for the printer. The document is ready to print, but it can't print because you have turned off printing at the printer level.

If you pop up the Document Control menu for a paused document, you will see a check mark beside the **Pause** entry. To resume printing this document, click **Pause** to deselect it and send the document on to the printer. The same technique works to pause or resume printing at the printer level.

Solving Common Network Printer Problems

Windows 95 is a strong network environment that is tolerant of user mistakes and hardware problems. However, there may be times when you experience difficulties getting your documents to print. In this section we'll offer suggested solutions to some common printer problems in Windows 95.

Problem: A Job Sent to a Printer Is in the Queue but Doesn't Print

Solution: Open the Printers dialog window and choose the printer to which you sent the print job in question. Look at the status for the first job in the queue. Is there an error message indicating the job can't print? Is the job paused? Correct these problems for the top job and the jobs behind this one can print.

Solution: Clear the print buffer by choosing **Purge Print Job** from the File menu of the Print dialog window specific to the printer you want to use. Turn the printer off and back on.

Solution: Make sure all cables are connected, and ensure that there is paper in the printer and that there is no problem with the printer ribbon or toner cartridge. Choose **Properties** from the File menu and click on the **Print Test Page** button on the **General** tab of the Properties dialog window.

Solution: Try printing to a file (see "Multiple Versions of Same Printer" earlier in this chapter for more information), then copy the file to the printer. If that works, there is a problem in the network definition or other aspects of the printer installation. Try re-installing the printer.

Solution: If possible, move to the PC to which the printer is physically attached. Open the application and try printing again. If this works, you have a network communication problem. Reshare the printer, then return to your PC and attach to this printer again.

Solution: Try disabling the print spooler. Here's how:

1. Right-click the **Printers** icon in the Printers dialog window.
2. Choose **Properties** from the popup menu.
3. Click on the **Details** tab, then click on **Spool Settings**.
4. Choose **Print Directly to Printer**.

If this works, you may have a damaged disk or you may be out of disk space. Run **Scandisk** to verify disk integrity. Make sure you have at least 2 megabytes of free hard disk space. In most cases, Scandisk can repair damaged areas of your hard drive. If Scandisk cannot repair a damaged disk, it is time to call for professional repair.

If you don't have at least 2 megabytes of free space, use Windows Explorer to study your disk to remove files you no longer need or can do without. You can copy files to another hard drive, a floppy disk, or a data cartridge, to free up space. You can also use an archiving utility such as PKZIP to compress files you want to keep but don't need to access regularly. Of course, files you know won't be needed should be deleted.

Problem: You are Using a Laptop Computer that is Sometimes Attached to a Network, but You are Not Online and You Want to Proceed with a Print Job

Solution: You can print to a disk file, then send the job to the printer when you reconnect to the network. Open the Printer dialog window (from Control Panel or by choosing **Printers** from the Settings menu under Start). Single-click the icon for the printer you want to use, then use **File Work Offline** to turn on offline printing.

If you choose a printer that is directly connected to your PC and is shared with the network, you won't see the **Work Offline** option in the File menu. You would have to unshare the printer to be able to take it offline.

NOTE

The Printer icon will dim in the Printers dialog window display. When you reconnect to the network, open the Printers dialog window and open the File menu. Click on **Work Offline** to deselect this option and return to live printing.

Problem: You Can Print to a Printer, but Graphics are Incomplete or Information is Garbled

Solution: This is probably an application problem. Make sure the printer definition in your application is compatible with the configuration on the target printer. Try changing the configuration in your application or re-install the application.

Solution: Try printing a small job—one or two pages. If this works, there is a spooling problem. Follow the earlier instructions for correcting spooling problems.

Solution: Restart Windows 95 and try again.

Solution: Make sure the font you are trying to use is properly installed. Open Control Panel and double-click on the **Fonts** icon. Is the font you are using listed? If not, install it by clicking on **File** and choosing **Install a New Font**. If it is there, double-click on the icon that represents the font you want to use. Does it display properly? Click on the **Print** button to print the font test sheet to the printer. If that works properly, there may be an application problem. Check font settings in the application and re-install the application if necessary.

Problem: Printing Seems Slower than Normal

Solution: This could be a spooling problem. Use Scandisk and defrag to eliminate fragmentation or disk problems. Make sure there is adequate disk space available.

Solution: Check system resources by opening Control Panel, double-clicking on the **System** icon, and then choosing the **Performance** tab. If less than 10 percent of resources are available, see what else is running by displaying the Task Bar. Close any applications you aren't using. Restart Windows 95 and try again.

Solution: Re-install the printer driver. Make sure you specify that you want to load the driver from disk when the Add Printer Wizard tells you that a driver for that printer exists.

Problem: The Computer Stalls While Printing; Information May or May Not Appear on the Printer

Solution: Re-install the printer driver.

Solution: Re-install the video driver. If you are using a high-end video card, such as a video accelerator, try installing a driver for standard VGA, disabling your high-end video features. If printing works normally, contact your video card manufacturer for an updated driver.

Solution: Make sure you have adequate free space on your hard drive. Caution: If you have more than one hard drive, check which drive is being used for temporary storage. You can force Windows to use a specific drive by choosing **Performance** from the System dialog window and clicking on **Virtual Memory**. Click on **Let me specify my own virtual memory settings** and enter the disk drive you want to use.

WHAT'S NEXT?

Basic printing over a Windows 95 network is essentially simple. Once you install the printer on the server and all workstations that will use it, you should be able to print from all applications as if the printer you are using is attached to your local machine. We've shown you how to set up a printer, how to use it, and the basics for tracing down problems.

In the next chapter, we'll take you beyond Windows 95 basics to user profiles, dial-up networking, faxing, and more.

CHAPTER SIX

Using Other Network Features and Devices

The nearly automatic networking capabilities built into Windows 95 opens a world of possibilities, and the process of wiring up machines and configuring the network is relatively easy. You can now share disk drives and printers. Now... what else can you do with your network?

That's what this chapter is all about, those "other" features intrinsic to the Windows 95 environment that may not be immediately obvious, or that might take a little more effort to configure and use. For example, we will show you how to establish user profiles for each person logging into the network so that their own preferred setup is turned on each time they use a machine. We'll discuss dial-up networking between Windows 95 machines and from your Windows 95 computer to the Internet. We'll show you how to use a fax server so that anyone on the network can send and receive faxes without a standalone fax machine, and we'll look at some other outstanding features.

USER PROFILES FOR CUSTOM WINDOWS AND NETWORKING

Networking computers causes some interesting and predictable changes in the way you look at your computers. Strange as it may seem at first, you quickly get accustomed to the concept of sharing information and printing to any printer on the network when you feel like it. Then something else usually happens: you want any machine on the network to look and act like your own personal machine whenever you log on. Many of us quickly dismiss that idea as soon as we think of it. Not a reasonable expectation, you know.

That was before Windows 95. In this environment, you can set up user profiles so that when you log into the network from any machine, everything looks and feels familiar, just like your primary computer. Depending on how much you want to do, there may be some differences among the machines, but these differences may be slight or nil.

We'll show you in this section how to set up user profiles. But first, let's look at what you can expect from this Windows 95 feature, and what you can't do.

With the User Profile tools provided, you have control over the following components of your system:

○ *The Control Panel and Preferences dialog box.* These let you specify your own settings for the user interface, including the shortcut icons on the desktop, placement of these icons, what appears on the Start menu, the desktop background (or *theme*), and other related items.

○ *Network settings.* These let you specify what connections are *persistent* (they are there every time you log in), what printers and printer ports to use, as well as information about recently used resources, such as which documents you have opened.

○ *Application settings.* These include some applications that install with Windows 95 such as menu and toolbar configurations, fonts, colors, and so on.

In addition to these general possibilities, there are some additional configuration options and some restrictions.

○ You can establish user profiles for individual machines so that different users have their own settings when they log onto that computer. If they use another computer on the network, however, the profiles don't appear.

○ With some restrictions, you can set up user profiles to work across the network. With this profile configuration you can support "roaming" users who log onto different machines across the network but who still want their personal settings to be active.

○ You can let each user establish their own preferences, or you can set up networkwide user profiles for individuals or for groups of users.

And you can make profiles optional or mandatory.

The main restriction to establishing networkwide user profiles is the installation location of your Windows 95 files. For successful user profile configurations you need to have Windows installed in the same subdirectory on all machines. For example, if you have used **c:\windows** as the Windows directory on some machines and **c:\win95** for others, there will be problems in establishing profiles. This restriction also includes using the same disk drive. For example, you shouldn't install Windows on the C: drive on some machines and the D: drive on others. In addition, User Profiles are easier to establish and maintain, and you have some additional functionality, if you are using a Novell or Windows NT network. We are assuming for the purposes of this book, however, that you are using a Windows 95–only network, and the instructions that follow are for this type of network.

With these simple restrictions in mind, you are ready to design your user profiles. In general, here's what you do:

❍ *Enable* (turn on) user profiles.

❍ Specify what general features will be included in each user profile.

❍ Enable Roving Profiles, if you want users to be able to access their own profile from multiple computers on the network.

Finally, you will analyze how you use your computer and what features of your desktop are unique and important enough to warrant a custom profile. Then you can either allow each user to define individual profiles, or you can establish a standard user profile that will be used whenever anyone logs onto the network.

Turning On User Profiles and Setting General Features

Enabling user profiles is a simple dialog box interaction:

1. Open the Control Panel by choosing **Control Panel** from the Settings menu under Start.

2. Double-click on the **Passwords** icon (an image of a key) within Control Panel to display the Passwords Properties dialog box.

3. Click on the **User Profiles** tab.

4. Click on the **Users can customize their preferences and desktop settings** button. The display should look like the example shown in Figure 6.1.

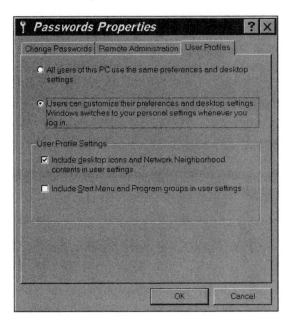

FIGURE 6.1 User Profiles tab of Passwords Properties dialog box.

5. Click on **Include Start Menu and Program groups in user settings** if you want to include these features in user profiles

6. Close the Password Properties dialog by clicking on the **X** in the upper right corner of the dialog box.

7. Use **Start Shut Down** to restart your computer and enable the changes.

NOTE   You can disable User Profiles for any PC by reversing the process. Open the Control Panel, double-click on **Passwords**, and uncheck the **Users can customize...** button on the **User Profiles** tab.

With User Profiles enabled, each user's settings for Network Neighborhood, desktop icons, and Start Menu programs (depending on what you enabled) will be available when they log into the network from the machine you just config-ured. Also, you must turn on User Profiles on each machine on which you want to use profile settings.

With all options enabled, users can specify what disk drive letter assignments they use, what remote resources they automatically attach to (disk drives, print-ers, and so on), what short cuts appear on their desktop, and what programs appear on the Start menu. Notice that you don't specifically program or set up individual profiles. Rather the settings that are current when each user logs off the network become the profile settings for the next session.

N O T E

With User Profiles enabled, when new applications are installed, only the user who was logged in during the installation will see the new application on the Start menu. Other users must create shortcuts to these applications and place them on their desktops or Programs menus to have automatic access to them.

Roving Profiles

If you are using a Novell, Windows NT, or other server-based network instead of or in addition to Windows 95, you can enable Roving Profiles. That means you can log on to any workstation in the network and still maintain your personal profile. In a Windows 95 peer-to-peer network, each user's profile is available only on a single machine. This is because the data file that stores individual settings resides on the local machine and is called up from the local machine during individual user log-in.

N O T E

Online documentation, and the Microsoft Windows 95 Resource Kit (in book form or on your CD with the Windows 95 system) describe at great length how to implement Roving Profiles in a peer-to-peer, Windows 95–only network.

It doesn't work!

We have spent hours talking to Microsoft's help desk and software engineering staff about this issue and the final ruling direct from Microsoft is that the documentation is mistaken. Perhaps it is an artifact left over from early designs that never got updated in the documentation; perhaps it is a misunderstanding among the technical writing staff that prepared the manuals. Whatever the reason, Roving Profiles cannot be implemented in a peer-to-peer environment in the initial release of Windows 95. A future update could solve this problem, of course, so check your Readme files and other documentation with your version of Windows 95.

If the profiles you are using aren't likely to change much, you can make profiles available to roving users in a Windows 95 Network by copying individual profiles to all workstations in the network. Profiles are stored in the \windows\profiles directory in subdirectories named for each user. User jordan, for example, has a profile on her personal machine in the directory \windows\profiles\jordan. There are several subdirectories stored under this directory, a separate subdirectory for each desktop component being tracked by the profile. There is a subdirectory for desktop settings (desktop), for example, one for Network Neighborhood (nethood) and others. Under each of these subdirectories are files that specify settings for these components.

In addition, there are two hidden files stored in each user's subdirectory: user.dat and user.da0. The user.dat file stores the main information about that user's profile; the user.da0 is a backup for this information. The files are stored as hidden system files, so if you do a directory in DOS or use Explorer to display the contents of a user directory, you won't see these files.

Suppose you want to copy the files from the user's workstation to other computers on the network. We are assuming for this example that all systems share the Windows directory with the network, either by sharing that directory specifically, or by making the entire hard drive that holds the Windows directory available to the network. If this is not the case, you can copy the user profile information to a floppy disk and then go to each workstation where you want it available and copy it from the floppy to the profiles directory. A typical profile requires between 80 and 100 files and from 300,000 to 500,000 bytes of storage. Use the following steps to copy user files to network computers:

Click **Start** and point to Programs.

Choose **MS DOS Prompt** from the pop up list of applications. The Windows directory—or the directory where your Windows programs are installed—should be the current directory.

Type **cd profiles** and press **Enter**.

Type **dir** and press **Enter**. This will show you what profile directories exist on this machine.

Type **cd dirname** (**dirname** is a directory named after one of the users on your network) and press **Enter** to make the first user profile directory that you want to copy become the current (or default) directory.

Type **attrib -a -h -s -r user.*** and press **Enter**. This will make the user.dat and user.da0 files visible and able to be copied.

Type **md driveletter:\windows\profiles\dirname** and press **Enter**. This will create a new directory on the remote machine represented by the drive letter designation. The drive letter will be d:, e:, f: or another alphabetic drive letter. It will be different for each machine you have mapped on the network. If the specified directory already exists—and it might if that user has logged onto the specified machine previously with user profiles enabled—then you will get an error message. That's OK. It simply means that the directory already is available to receive the files you will copy in the next step.

Type **xcopy *.* driveletter:\windows\profiles\dirname /s** and press **Enter**. This will copy all of the files in one user's directory to the remote machine. The previously hidden user.dat and user.da0 files will be copied along with anything contained in subdirectories beneath the specified directory.

Type **attrib +a +h +s +r user.*** to restore the hidden, system status of the user.dat and user.da0 files.

Repeat the copy process for each user whose profile you want to appear on a remote machine.

Remember that this is a workaround for the fact that peer-to-peer networking doesn't support Roving Profiles. It works, as long as users don't make changes to their profiles. If a change is made, the new profile settings are stored only on the machine where the user was logged in. Other machines in the network will retain the previous settings. Of course, you can update other machines in the network with the copy process described above. Just be very careful as you copy, being sure to copy the correct files to the correct location. Otherwise you will overwrite the new configuration with an older one.

DIAL-UP NETWORKING

We've examined several aspects of using your Windows 95 workstation over a Local Area Network so that you can share disk drives or printers. But the Windows 95 operating system also supports dial-up networking so that you can make a remote Windows 95 PC part of a LAN.

NOTE To get full functionality from Window 95's dial-up networking, including establishing a dial-up server, you must purchase and install the add-on Plus! package. The Plus! package includes a lot of software that adds significant functionality to Windows 95. This is software that should have been part of Windows 95, in our opinion, but at under $40, it is worth the price and we recommend that you purchase it.

You might want to implement dial-up networking for a number of reasons. For one thing, you might want to dial into a PC on your LAN from a laptop computer on the road. Or, you might want to dial up a UNIX host to access the Internet using the TCP/IP networking protocol. With Windows 95 you can have only one dial-up connection at a time, but for a small office or home installation, that should be adequate.

We'll show you how to use both of these aspects of dial-up networking in the following section.

Accessing Your Desktop on the Road

To set up your home or office Windows 95 network for remote dial-up access, you need a modem attached to one of the workstations on the network, a telephone line, and about 3 megabytes of free disk space to install the software.

Once you decide which computer will serve as the dial-up server (with the Plus! add-on installed), and you have a modem in place, you are ready to configure the system.

A dial-up networking setup in Windows 95 includes these basic components:

○ Dial-up software client(s)
○ Dial-up software server
○ Network protocol
○ Connection protocol

We show you in the next section how to set up the software required for Dial-Up clients and servers. The server software is part of the Microsoft Plus! add-on package that must be purchased separately.

A *network protocol* is simply the "rules" a network uses to communicate. The default protocols in Windows 95 are IPX/SPX-compatible (Novell Compatible) and Microsoft's NetBEUI. These protocols are installed automatically when you install dial-up networking.

A *connection protocol* is the method your client and server use to establish communications so they can then use the networking protocol. The default in Windows 95 is PPP, the acronym for Point to Point Protocol. This connection protocol is extremely common in dial-up networking, especially for Internet access (see the Internet Access section later in this chapter for more information on using your Windows 95 dial-up networking client to access the Internet). You will also use PPP to support dial-in clients to your Windows 95 LAN.

Configuring a Dial-Up Server

A *dial-up server* is the computer that is part of a local area network that will answer the incoming call from a client computer.

Before you can use the dial-up networking facilities built into Windows 95, you must install the basic software and protocols to support dial-up networking, and you must install a modem. For most users, dial-up networking was probably installed when you installed Windows 95.

You can check to see if it was installed on your system. Simply double-click on the **My Computer** icon to open the My Computer dialog window. If this dialog window contains a Dial-up Networking icon, then this facility has been installed; if not, you need to install it before you can proceed. Here's how to install it:

1. Open the Control Panel by choosing it from the popup Settings menu available on the Start menu.

2. Double-click on the **Add/Remove Programs** icon.

3. Click on the **Windows Setup Tab** to bring it to the front of the dialog box.

4. Click on the **Communications** entry in the Components window of this dialog box to select it.

5. Click on the **Details** button and make sure **Dial-up Networking** is selected in the Components window.

6. Click **OK** to close the Components dialog window.

7. Click **OK** again to close the **Add/Remove Programs** dialog window.

Installing a Modem

We learned (or relearned) about installing a modem with Windows 95 in Chapter 3. Let's review.

Windows 95 handles most of the work of installing a modem. If you are using a relatively new modem, you can simply plug it into a bus slot (for an internal modem) or connect it to a serial port (for an external modem) and reboot your computer. Windows 95 will tell you it detected a new piece of hardware and step you through the installation process.

If Windows 95 doesn't recognize your modem, you can manually start the install process, as follows:

1. Open the Control Panel and double-click on the **Modems** icon to display the Modems Properties dialog window.

2. Click the **Add** button. This launches an Install New Modem Wizard that will step you through the process of installing your modem. Notice that by default the Wizard is set up to automatically detect your modem.

3. Click on **Next** to accept the default of auto-detect and to move to the next Wizard screen.

If you have an older modem, or one that Windows does not recognize, you will be prompted to choose a modem from a list of available modems. Choose the manufacturer in the left window and the model number in the right window.

N O T E

4. Click **Next** and continue with the rest of the Wizard until your modem is installed.

Configuring the Server

Once basic dial-up networking is installed and available to the computer that will function as a dial-up client or server, and you have a modem installed, you are ready to complete the configuration.

You should have a modem installed and connected to your computer before beginning this configuration process. Part of the configuration will set the modem up for autoanswer so that an incoming call will be answered.

N O T E

Here's how to configure a server on your network to accept dial-in connections:

1. Double-click on **My Computer** to open the My Computer dialog box.

2. Double-click on **Dial-Up Networking** to open the Dial-Up Networking dialog box.

3. Click on **Connections** and choose **Dial-Up Server** from the menu to display the Dial-Up Server dialog box shown in Figure 6.2.

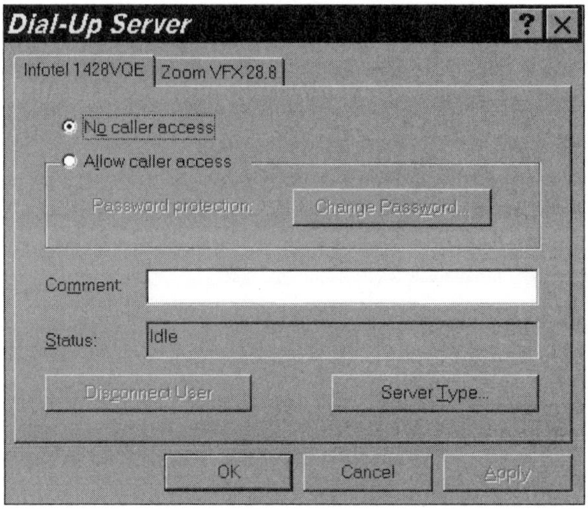

Figure 6.2 Dial-Up Server dialog box.

 If you have previously installed a modem, but haven't established a password for it, you may see a potentially confusing message that says you don't have a password for this modem. You will be told to click on Dial-Up Server from

N O T E the Connections menu to set a new password. Of course, this is what you just did to see this error message! Simply click on **OK** and the Dial-Up Server dialog box will be displayed.

4. Click on **Allow caller access**.

NOTE If you have configured more than one modem, then this dialog is a tabbed dialog, one tab for each modem. Be sure to click on the tab for the modem you will be using for the Dial-Up Server.

5. Click **Change Password** to display the Dial-Up Networking Password dialog box. You don't necessarily have to establish a password here, but if you don't, your network will be wide open to anyone who has the telephone number to your modem.

6. Enter a password for Dial-Up Networking and click **OK** to close this dialog box.

NOTE There are three fields on this dialog. The top field is for the old password. If you don't have a password established, leave this field blank. The middle field is for the new password, and the last field is for you to enter the new password again as a confirmation. If you enter the new password in the old password field, you will get an error.

7. Click the **Server Type** button to display the Server Types dialog box (see Figure 6.3). You should accept the defaults on this dialog box as you get started in Dial-Up Networking. View this dialog box simply to see what features are enabled. The default network protocol is PPP for Windows 95; this is what you will set up for the client (calling) computer as well.

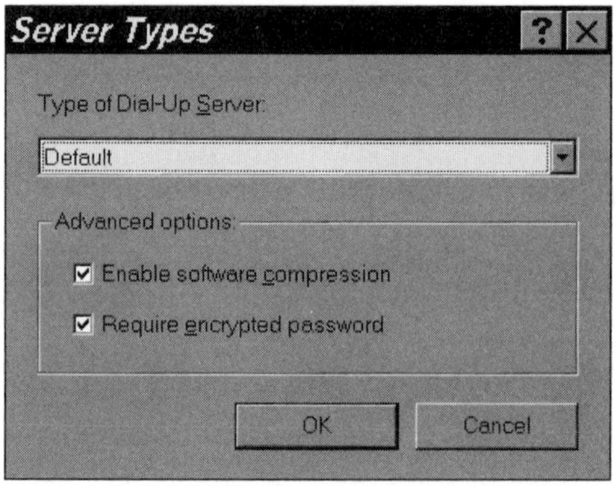

FIGURE 6.3 Server Types dialog box.

8. Click on **OK** to close the Server Types dialog box.

9. Click on **OK** again to close the Dial-Up Server dialog box.

You can disable Dial-Up Networking access at any time by opening this dialog box and clicking on **No caller access**.

N O T E

The computer is now ready to accept calls from a remote dial-in client computer running Dial-Up Networking. If the computer you just configured as a Dial-Up Server is part of a network, the remote machine will have access to the network. Alternatively, you may want to configure a standalone machine as a Dial-Up Server to give you access to that one machine while you are on the road.

After you turn on Dial-Up Network Server, your modem is set to auto answer, and the server software has control of the modem and your modem port. If you try to dial out using a 16-bit application you won't be able to access your modem. The solution: open Dial-Up Networking, click on **Connections**,

N O T E

choose **Dial-Up Server**, and click on **No caller access**. You'll have your modem back, but you won't have a dial-up server. Reverse the process when you are ready to set your computer up to answer incoming calls. You can use newer, 32-bit applications, such as those that came with Windows 95, to dial out of your computer with Dial-Up Server enabled.

Remember, too, that once you have a modem installed on a computer and you have configured it as a Dial-Up Server, the modem is set for auto answer. When the telephone line to which the modem is attached receives a call, the modem will answer, usually on the first ring. For this reason, it is a good idea to use a separate telephone line to support dial-up networking. At the very least, you should remember to turn off your modem or unplug it from the telephone line while you are at home or in the office and expect to use the telephone normally.

Configuring a Dial-Up Client

A *dial-up client* is the computer that will dial into the network. This is probably a laptop machine, or perhaps a desktop computer at home that dials into an office network. This remote client requires some of the same general setup as the server machine.

For example, you must enable Dial-Up Networking and you must have a modem physically installed and configured. See the previous section for details on performing both of these tasks.

With a modem installed and Dial-Up Networking enabled, you are ready to configure the dial-up client to make calls to the server. This involves establishing a Dial-Up Networking profile, and then configuring it. First, set up the new profile:

1. Double-click on **My Computer** to open the My Computer dialog box.

2. Double-click on **Dial-Up Networking** and choose **Make New Connection**. This launches a New Connection Wizard that will step you through the process of setting up the new profile.

3. Type a name for the profile. The default name is My Connection; you should use a name that describes the computer you will dialing: My Office, The House, AAX, and so on.

4. If the correct modem is not already displayed in the Select a Modem field of this dialog box, pull down a list of installed modems and choose the correct one.

If no modem has been installed, the Wizard will prompt you to install one and then lead you through the process.

N O T E

---

5. Click on **Next** to display the next Wizard screen.

6. Type the telephone number of the computer you want to dial, including the area code if it is different from the local one displayed by default.

7. Click on **Next** to display the final Wizard dialog, then click on **Finish**. The Wizard will close and an icon representing the new dial-up profile will appear in the Dial-Up Networking window.

Now you can enter some configuration information about this profile to make it function properly with the server you configured previously:

1. Right-click on the icon that you just created in Dial-Up Networking.

2. Choose **Properties** to display the configuration dialog box shown in Figure 6.4.

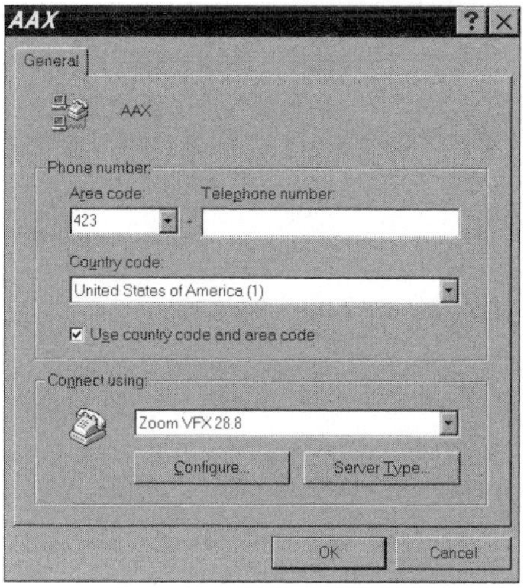

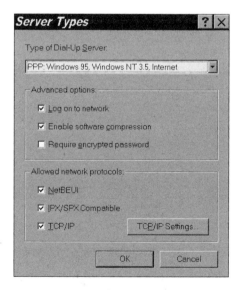

FIGURE 6.4 Dial-Up Networking Properties dialog box.

3. Type a telephone number for the Dial-Up Server you want to access. Be sure to include the area code if it is different from your calling location.

4. Click on the **Server Type** button to display the Server Types dialog box (see Figure 6.5).

FIGURE 6.5 Server Types dialog box.

5. Make sure that NetBEUI is the only protocol selected under Allowed Network Protocols. Uncheck other protocols that may be selected by clicking on them.

NOTE You may want to use TCP/IP protocol for Internet access or IPX/SPX if your computer is part of a network that uses Novell networking. We'll show you how to use dial-up networking to access the Internet later in this chapter.

6. Click on **OK** to close the Server Types dialog box.
7. Click on **OK** again to close the Properties dialog box.

With the server and the client configured, you are ready to dial that remote server. Use the following steps:

1. Double-click on the Dial-Up Networking icon that represents the server you want to call. You will see the dialog box shown in Figure 6.6. A default user name is shown.

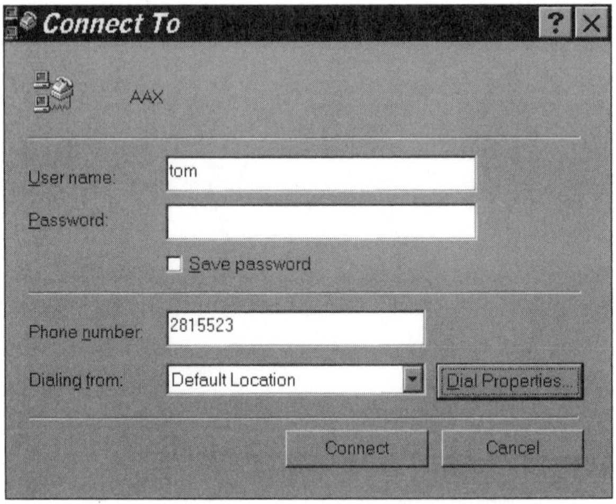

FIGURE 6.6 Connect To dialog box.

2. If you wish, type a different user name in the **User name** field of this dialog box.

3. Type a password in the **Password** field of this dialog box. In a closely controlled environment you might also wish to click on **Save password**. Next time you use this dialog box the password you entered will be retained and you won't have to enter it again.

4. Click **Connect** to dial the modem and log into the remote server.

If the log-in process proceeds OK, you will see a pop-up box that says you have connected to the remote server and will show you the speed of the connection and the total time you have been connected. At this point you are attached to the remote network and your client machine is a part of the remote network.

However, you won't see anything else on the screen. There will be no overt indication that you are part of a remote network. To use the remote facilities you must map a drive or access the remote machine in some way to use its shared resources.

One way to test your link is to double-click on **Network Neighborhood**, then double-click on **Entire Network**. You may be able to see the remote dial-up server and any other computers within its same network. Then again, you may not. Microsoft technical personnel say that for some reason (they don't know why, and we don't either), it can take 15 to 30 minutes for the software on your client to scan the dial-up connection and report accurately all the machines on the remote network. Then again, you may see these machines immediately. We have seen it go both ways.

You can also try the following steps:

1. Click on **Start** on the Task Bar.

2. Choose **Run** from the Start menu.

3. Type the server name on the Run line. Precede the server name with a double backslash: \\aax or \\iguana.

4. Click on **OK**. You will see a dialog box that shows all of the shared resources on that machine.

Another way to test the link is to map a new drive letter to the remote server. In any case, you'll want to do this the first time you establish this dial-up link. Thereafter the mapping will be in place and you should see it reappear whenever you establish another dial-up link. Here's how to map a drive to the remote, dial-up server:

1. Establish the dial-up network link as described above.

2. Right-click the **Network Neighborhood** icon and choose **Map Network Drive...** from the popup menu. The dialog box shown in Figure 6.7 will be displayed.

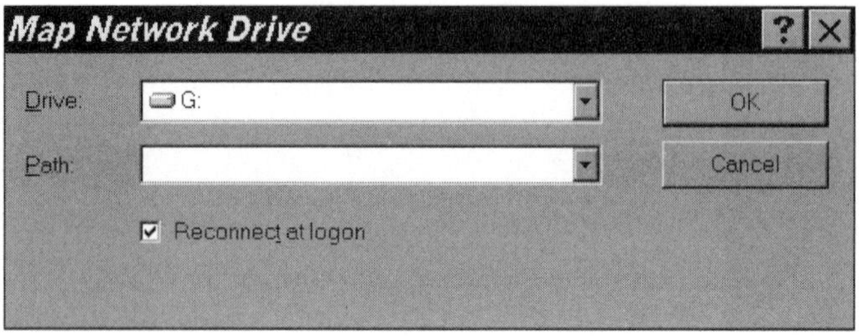

Map Network Drive ? X

Drive: G:

Path:

☑ Reconnect at logon

OK

Cancel

FIGURE 6.7 Map Network Drive dialog box.

3. Accept the suggested drive letter on the top line of this dialog and on the second line, type a path to a shared resource on the remote server.

NOTE

The path to a shared resource includes the name of the server and the share name of the resource you want to access. For example, if the name of the remote server is AAX and you have shared the C: drive on that machine as axx_root, you would enter the path as \\aax\aax_root. Another example: the server name is IGUANA and the disk drive you want to access is shared with the network as Reptile, then the path becomes \\iguana\reptile. You can use all lower case, all upper case, or a combination of upper and lower case in the path if you wish. Windows 95 doesn't care.

4. Leave **Reconnect at logon** checked and the next time you log on, Windows 95 will attempt to re-establish the drive letter link for you.

5. Click **OK** to establish the link.

Now you can access the remote shared resource by using the drive letter specified on the Map Network Drive dialog box. As long as you have dialed into and logged onto the remote server, that drive acts as if it were part of your local machine.

As indicated earlier, updates to the mapping and accessing information will be a little slower than over a local network, but the effect is awesome. Sitting at your desk at home, you double-click on **My Computer**, choose a drive, and the next dialog box shows you all the files and programs stored on your hard disk on the office computer. You can copy data files, sever the telephone link, edit the files or write reports, dial up again and copy the files back to your office desktop. The next morning when you arrive at work, the files you need are right there and you didn't have to remember (at home) to copy them to a floppy disk and carry them to the office.

The reverse works as well. Suppose you get to the office and discover that the latest proposal you were working on—the one that is due at 10:00 this morning—is tucked safely away on your hard disk at home. If you have set up your home machine as a dial-up server, you can call in from the office and copy the file quickly and easily.

Accessing the Internet

Accessing the Internet with Windows 95 Dial-Up Networking is very similar to dialing another Windows 95 machine with the Dial-Up Client software. The difference is in the networking protocol you use and—perhaps—some other configuration settings.

Microsoft has two "official" routes to the Internet: through Microsoft Network (MSN), and via the upcoming integration of Internet access in later versions of Windows 95. We can't go into the latter method because it doesn't officially exist as this book is written. As for MSN, use **Add/Remove Software** from the Control Panel to install the Internet browser and Internet access, if you haven't done so already. Be sure to study documentation included with your Microsoft Plus! Pak for more information on accessing the Internet with Windows 95.

N O T E
Each Internet Service Provider (ISP) requires slightly different log-on procedures. We will show you a common setup and procedure in this section, but to make Dial-Up Networking function with your computer and ISP configuration, you need to consult your ISP for details. If you access the Internet through America Online (AOL) or CompuServe, then you will be supplied special software to help make this process more automatic. In fact, many ISPs now offer Windows 95-compliant software for Internet access. Follow the instructions you are given.

Windows 95 Dial-Up Networking is responsible for dialing into your ISP and establishing a TCP/IP connection. Dial-Up Networking doesn't check your

E-mail, download files, or take you to the World Wide Web. Those things are done by other programs—such as Eudora, Winsock FTP, and Netscape—but those programs depend on Dial-Up Networking to make the connection to your service provider.

To get ready to use Dial-Up Networking to connect to the Internet you need to perform some of the same steps we described in the previous section. Specifically, do this:

❍ Make sure Dial-Up Networking has been installed on the machine you want to use.

❍ Add the TCP/IP protocol to your network configuration.

❍ Use **Make New Connection** to configure a new Dial-Up profile.

We showed you how to do some of this in the previous section, but we'll review some aspects here and show you the specifics you need to get Dial-Up Networking running with the Internet.

NOTE Some ISPs supply software as part of their service to new customers. When you open an account make sure the provider's software is Windows 95-compliant. Some popular Internet access software won't work with Windows 95. Other software—the Trumpet Winsock TCP/IP utility, for example—will work with Windows 95, but will force you to use 16-bit mode. That means that you can't use the 32-bit Netscape and other software specifically designed for Windows 95.

In addition, you will need some basic information from your service provider:

❍ Your user name. This is the name or personal identifier that you will use to log into the Internet host. You chose your name or were assigned a name by your ISP when you opened your Internet account. User names are usually lowercase with no spaces. Sample user names would be bob-smith and darkstar.

❍ Your password. This is a unique combination of characters that help identify you as the authorized user of a log-in account and to prevent other people from using your account. You were assigned or were allowed to choose a password when you signed up. Passwords are *case sensitive*: uppercase and lowercase letters are not interchangeable.

❍ Your Internet Protocol (IP) address. This is a unique number that identifies your computer to the rest of the network. If you are using static IP addressing you will always use the same number. Most ISPs, however, use dynamic (server-assigned) IP addressing, so you may not need this value, but you should ask your ISP about this. A typical IP address is 199.1.48.3.

❍ The access telephone number you need to call with your modem.

❍ A host name for your PC. In most cases you will use your user name. The host name should be all lowercase with no spaces.

❍ The ISP domain name. This is a network name for the company that provides your Internet access. For example, if you are accessing the Internet through U.S. Internet, your domain is usit.net. If you are using Netcom, the domain name is netcom.com.

❍ The Primary Domain Name Server (DNS) address assigned by your ISP. This is an IP address that identifies the computer your ISP uses to store other Internet address information—for example: 199.1.54.4.

Once you have this information, you are ready to configure your computer. You'll need to add the TCP/IP protocol to your network configuration. TCP/IP, the acronym for Transfer Control Protocol/Internet Protocol, is the networking protocol commonly used on the Internet and other UNIX-based networks. Remember that a network protocol is the underlying software that allows components of a network to communicate with each other. There are many protocols; TCP/IP is simply one common protocol.

Here's how to add TCP/IP to your Dial-Up Networking configuration:

1. Click the **Start** button.
2. Select **Settings**, then **Control Panel**.
3. Double-click the **Network** icon.
4. Select the **Configuration** tab.

5. Set **Windows Logon** as your Primary Network Logon.

6. If you see both Dial-Up Adapter and TCP/IP (or 'TCP/IP → Dial-Up Adapter), then your system already has TCP/IP installed. You can skip the rest of the steps in this section.

7. Click the **Add** button.

8. Double-click **Protocol**.

9. Select **Microsoft**.

10. Choose **TCP/IP** and click **OK**.

Now you have TCP/IP installed in addition to your local networking protocol. Your Network Configuration Tab window should show a Dial-Up Adapter (installed previously), NetBEUI attached to your Ethernet card, and TCP/IP attached to your Dial-Up Adapter. If this window shows that TCP/IP is also associated with your Ethernet adapter, click on this entry and then click **Remove**. Likewise, if NetBEUI is shown associated with the Dial-Up adapter, you should remove this entry. Your ISP probably won't appreciate your sending NetBEUI information over the TCP/IP link. It may not hurt anything, but then again it could cause problems.

If you are using for Internet access a machine that you also use to dial into a Windows 95 Server, then you will need to re-install NetBEUI before you can make that connection.

N O T E

With a Dial-Up adapter installed and the TCP/IP protocol available, you are ready to configure the TCP/IP part of the setup:

1. Open Control Panel (**Start** button → **Settings** → **Control Panel**).

2. Double-click the **Network** icon.

3. Click **TCP/IP**, then click the **Properties** button; this will give you a tabbed dialog with six sections, similar to the one in Figure 6.8. (Note: if you have more than one TCP-based network component, the one you want will be called "TCP/IP → Dial-Up Adapter").

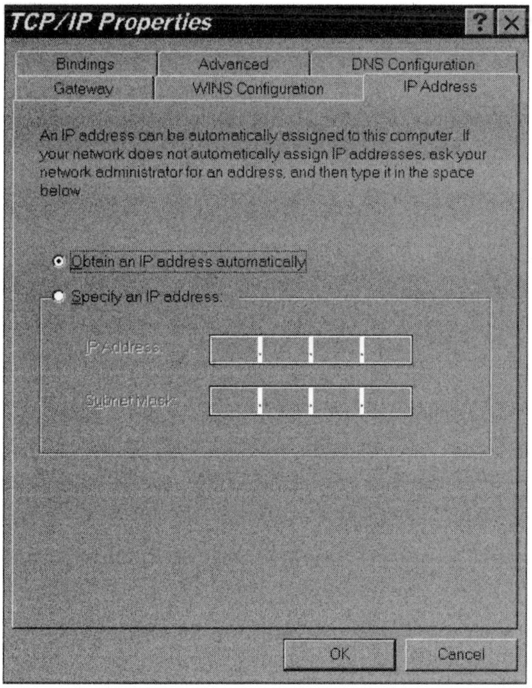

FIGURE 6.8 TCP/IP Properties dialog box.

4. Click the **IP address** tab and select **Obtain an IP address automatically**.

If your ISP requires a static IP address, select **Specify an IP address** and enter the number you were assigned. Press the **space bar** to move to the next field in this dialog box if the number in any field is less than three digits long.

NOTE

5. Click the **WINS Configuration** tab and select **Disable WINS Resolution**.

6. Click the **Gateway** tab. Enter **0.0.0.0** (or the static gateway address, if you were assigned one by your ISP) and click **Add** (use the **space bar** to move to the next field after you enter each number).

7. Click the **Bindings** tab. There should be no information on this screen.

8. Click the **Advanced** tab. There should be no information on this screen.

9. Click the **DNS Configuration** tab. Select **Enable DNS**.

10. Enter your assigned user name (such as bobsmith) in the Host box. Use all lowercase letters with no spaces.

11. Enter the Domain name you were assigned in the Domain box. Use all lowercase letters with no spaces.

12. Enter the assigned IP address for your Domain Name Server in the DNS Server Search Order box and click the **Add** button.

13. Enter your assigned domain in the Domain Suffix Search Order box. This should be the same value you entered in the Domain box earlier. Use all lowercase with no spaces, and click the **Add** button.

14. Click **OK**, then **OK** again in the Network dialog box. Windows 95 will offer to restart your system so that the changes will take effect. You should restart your computer before continuing.

At this point you have configured your Dial-Up networking for the proper protocol (TCP/IP) and you have entered basic information about the host to which you will attach to make the connection. Next, you must put a 'front end' on this information by creating a dial-up configuration for your Internet host. We showed you earlier how to set up a dial-up icon for your Windows 95 server. The process is similar. Remember that each ISP will require slightly different information in this section. We'll show you here how to configure the Dial-Up Connection for a typical Internet connection. You can get specifics from your service provider.

Here are the steps to setting up a Dial-Up icon for an Internet connection:

1. Double-click the **My Computer** icon, then double-click the **Dial-Up Networking** icon.

2. Double-click **Make New Connection**.

3. Enter a name for this new Dial-Up configuration. The name of your service provider, such as U.S. Internet, would be a good choice.

NOTE Your modem should be in the "Select a modem" area; if it isn't, now is a good time to set up your modem to work with Windows 95. Use the Add New Hardware Wizard in Control Panel to do this.

4. Click the **Configure** button.

5. In the General tab, select your modem speed. For 14.4 modems, use 19200; for 28.8 modems, use 38400.

DO NOT select Only connect at this speed. You can ignore the settings in the Connection tab.

NOTE

6. Click the **Options** tab.

7. Select **Bring up terminal window** after dialing and click **OK**.

Consult your service provider on using a terminal window. The terminal window is used to enter manual log-on information, such as choosing from a menu, typing your user name, and so on. Unless you have the Plus! package installed (see information later in this chapter), you will have to log into the Internet provider's network manually. For this reason, this terminal window probably will be required.

NOTE

8. Click the **Next** button.

9. Enter the access phone number you were given and click **Next**.

10. Click the **Finish** button.

Remember from the earlier description of Dial-Up Networking that you must now configure—set properties of—the new connection. Here's how to do that for the Internet connection:

1. Right-click the new icon and choose **Properties** from the popup menu. You should now see a dialog box named after your icon.

2. Click the **Server Type** button.

3. In the Type of Dial-Up Server choose **PPP: Windows 95**.

4. Make sure there is nothing checked in the Advanced group on this dialog box.

5. In the Allowed network protocols group, make sure that only TCP/IP is checked.

6. Click the **TCP/IP** settings button.

7. Select **Server assigned IP address**.

8. Select **Specify name server addresses**.

9. Enter the IP address of your assigned Primary DNS.

10. Select **Use IP header compression** and **Use default gateway on remote network**.

11. Click **OK** to close the TCP/IP Settings window.

12. Click **OK** again to close the Server Types window.

13. Click **OK** again to close the Properties window.

With the properties settings complete, you are ready to use Dial-Up networking to call your Internet Service Provider and log onto the Internet. The process from this point on is simple. Use the following steps:

1. Double-click **My Computer** to open the My Computer dialog box.

2. Double-click the icon you just created for your Internet connection. You should see the dialog box shown in Figure 6.9.

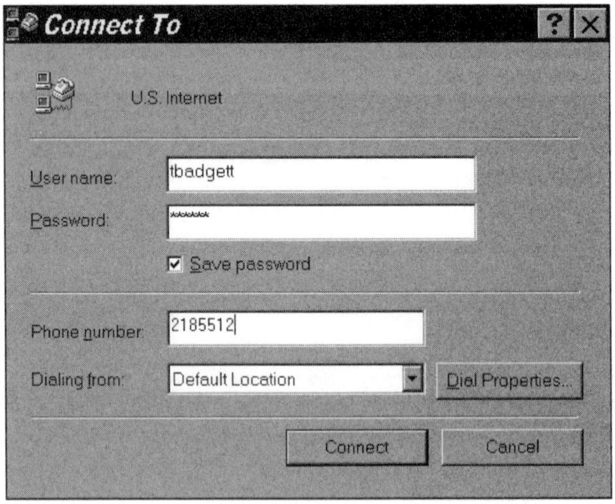

FIGURE 6.9 Connect To dialog box for Internet connection.

3. Enter your user name when the host asks for it.

4.   Enter your password when you are asked for it.

5.   Make any menu selections required in the terminal window.

6.   When all required entries are complete, you will see random characters ("garbage") appear at the bottom of the dialog. This is the host PPP trying to communicate with Windows 95. Press the **F7** function key or click on **Continue** to close the terminal window and complete the connection.

When the connection is complete, you will see a small box in the middle of your desktop showing that a connection has been made. You will see the connect speed and the name of the connection. At this point you have logged into the ISPs network. You computer is now a network member with the host machine and with anybody else who has logged into the host in the same way.

Nothing else will happen until you do something. Dial-Up Networking has done its job. It has dialed a remote host and established a TCP/IP-protocol network connection. Now you are ready to do something with the network. For example, you could run the Netscape program to browse the World Wide Web, or launch Eudora to check your E-mail, or run FTP to download some files, and so on. Many users assume that there is a problem with their connection at this point because nothing happens. Nothing is supposed to happen until you take the next step by running a program that makes use of the network connection you just established.

Using the Microsoft Plus! Scripting Tool

If you have installed the Plus! package, you can automate the log-on process for your local Windows 95 network or to an Internet host. Automatic log-ins are done with a simple script that watches your screen for certain characters, then sends the proper response to the host.

N O T E   You can learn more about the scripting tools included with Plus! from a readme file installed on your hard disk when you installed Plus! Use WordPad, Microsoft Word, or another text tool that can handle large files (Notepad won't work) to open the Script.doc file in the main Plus! directory. In addition, you might want to view the Internet.txt file located in the Microsoft Internet directory under the main Plus! directory on your hard disk. The Readme.txt file, also in the main Plus! directory, discusses these and other documentation files that will help you use the Plus! software.

In general, here are the steps to setting up a Plus! script for use with your Internet or Windows 95 Dial-Up Network connection:

❍ Write down the specific steps required during the log-in process. You must show every step of the log-in process and make sure that you have spelled all host prompts and your required responses correctly. Remember that most Internet hosts are case-sensitive, so if you use a capital letter to begin a prompt, but the host uses all lower case, your script won't work.

❍ Write a script, using the proper commands in the Plus! scripting tool, to watch for host prompts and to provide the correct responses. You can use the sample script provided in the Script.doc file as a starting point, or you can start from scratch. To write your script, you can use NotePad or any other editor that saves plain text files.

❍ Use the Dial-Up Scripting Tool utility in your Accessories program group to install the script so that Dial-Up Networking will know to use it to log into the host.

We show you in the following pages how to complete each of these three steps.

Write Down Steps

Most log-on sequences are relatively simple. All you need to do is complete the log-on process once or twice and write down everything the host asked and everything you answered. If the process is very complex you may be able to turn on a log file as part of your software, but in general a pencil and paper is the easiest way to document the average log-on process.

For example, most Internet hosts ask first for your user name. The key to writing a successful script is to make sure you spell the prompt exactly as it comes from the host. For example, some hosts ask for Username. Others ask for User Name? and so on. In a networking environment, especially a network that uses the UNIX operating system, preciseness is extremely important.

When you respond to the user name prompt, what do you type? Then what do you do at the end of the typing? For example, do you press Enter to send your user name to the host?

You might write down this part of the process in the following way:

Username:

jjones <carriage return>

Notice that we have underlined the information that came from the host. We have placed the carriage return (enter) key in angle brackets, indicating that this is a single keystroke.

Continue recording the interaction with the host in this way. Show exactly what the host asked and what you gave as a response. Then log-off, and, while referring to your notes, log in again to check your work. Once you are certain you have recorded the process accurately, you are ready to write the script.

Write a Script

Although the Microsoft Plus! scripting tool is relatively powerful, you will use only a small portion of this power. Especially if your script will be for your own use, you can keep it simple. As you learn more about scripting, or if you have some experience with computer programming, you can use the documentation that comes with Plus! to help you incorporate other features in your script. For example, you might want to include some error checking to provide feedback to the user in the event of a log-on failure.

For the purposes of this book, we will show you a simple script that works. We'll leave it up to you and your MIS department to design fail-safe scripts with lots of error checking and user feedback.

Suppose you have taken notes on a log-on process that looks like this:

Username:

jjones <carriage return>

Password:

abcdefg <carriage return>

Your Choice?

4 <carriage return>

This is the sequence required to establish a PPP connection with a host at U.S. Internet. For a PPP connection, this is actually a fairly complex login sequence. Now, let's see how to write a Plus! script to handle this log-on automatically. Again, refer to the documentation included with your Plus! package, especially the text files installed on your hard disk along with the software.

Here's a basic script to handle the log-on to this host:

```
;        SAMPLE Windows 95 Log-in Script

;
```

```
proc main

    waitfor "sername:"

    transmit $USERID + "^m"

    waitfor "sword:"

    transmit $PASSWORD + "^m"

    waitfor "oice ?"

    transmit "4^m"

endproc
```

If you understand the required log-in steps as previously described, then the inner workings of this script should be fairly straightforward. Typical of programming and script languages, this scripting tool requires that you define each process you want to execute. The declarative statement, proc main, defines the beginning of the main process (proc).

Any line that begins with a semicolon is a comment, a way of documenting the program. Statements that begin with a semicolon aren't processed by the program interpreter. Otherwise this script uses only two commands: waitfor and transmit. Enclose in quotes the text you want to capture with waitfor or that you want to send to the host with transmit. Notice that we have shortened some of the text the host sends to the client. This avoids the question of upper and lower case. If we look for sword: instead of Password:, there's no concern about whether the p in password is upper- or lowercase.

Notice, too, that the scripting language depends on the configuration of the dial-up networking component of Windows 95 to understand your user name and password. The variables, $PASSWORD and $USERID are filled in by the values you enter when you configure dial-up networking. This is a plus, since you don't have to rewrite the script if you change your password.

The final value that this script sends the host is the carriage return, represented, as it is in many scripting languages, by the caret m (^m). This is because the **Ctrl+m** keyboard combination sends the proper codes for carriage return on most terminals. The ^m symbol is used to represent **Ctrl+m**.

You should now be able to understand the workings of this script. It waits for the host to send the user name prompt and responds by transmitting the user name you have stored in your dial-up networking definition, followed by a carriage return. Then the script waits again until the host sends a request for the password. The password stored in the dial-up networking definition is sent, followed by a carriage return.

On this particular host, the next screen is a menu where the user can choose a *shell* (text-based) connection, a slip connection, or a PPP connection. The PPP choice is menu item number 4. Thus, in this script, when the menu sends `Your Choice ?`, the script transmits the number 4 followed by a carriage return to complete the logon.

Create this script in any text editor or word processor that can save plain text and store it in the c:\program files\accessories directory. Use any name you wish, but use the file extension of **.scp**, which indicates to Windows that this is a script file.

Install the Script

After you have installed the Microsoft Plus! package, some new programs appear in your Program menu when you click on Start on the task bar. Among the new offerings is the Dial-Up Scripting Tool that appears under accessories. You will use this utility to turn on the script you just prepared:

1. Click on **Start** and point to **Accessories** to display the Accessories menu.

2. Choose **Dial-Up Scripting Tool** from the Accessories list to display the dialog shown in Figure 6.10. You will see the hosts installed through Dial-Up Networking listed in the left window of this dialog box.

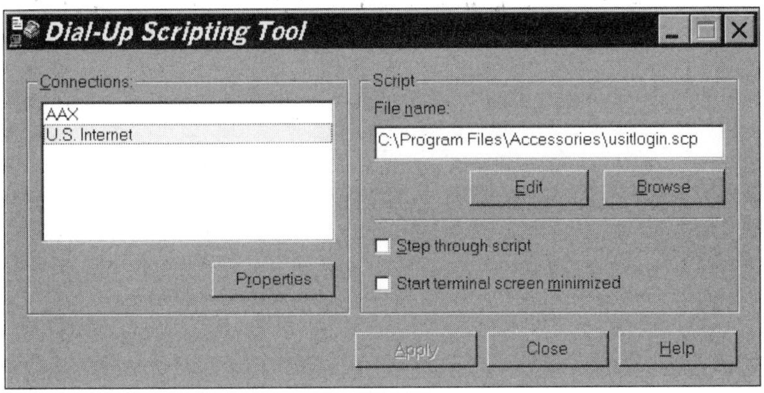

FIGURE 6.10 Dial-Up Scripting Tool dialog box.

3. Select the Dial-Up host to which you want to attach the script you just created.

4. Click in the **File name**: window and type the path to the script file. If you have installed the file in the \program files\accessories directory, then the path is the drive letter, plus this directory, then the name of the file (see Figure 6.10).

5. Click **Apply** to effect the connection between the Dial-Up host and the script.

6. Click on **Close** to close the dialog box.

Depending on how your Internet (or other Dial-Up) host is configured, you may need to make one change for the script to work properly. If you try the script and it doesn't work properly, first disable the **Bring Up Terminal Window After Dialing** that you specified when you configured the dial-up connection:

1. Double-click on **My Computer**.

2. Double-click on **Dial-Up Networking**.

3. Right-click on the icon that represents the host you want to change.

4. Choose **Properties** to display the General dialog box.

5. Click on **Configure**... to display the **Properties** dialog box.

6. Click on the **Options** tab.

7. Click on **Bring up terminal window** after dialing to disable this feature.

8. Click on **OK**.

9. Click on **OK** again to return to Dial-Up Networking and close this dialog box.

You can also reach the configuration dialog box from inside the Scripting Tool dialog. Select the host you want to configure and click on the **Properties** button.

N O T E

To use the script, all you need do is make a connection through the Dial-Up Networking dialog box. Double-click on the icon that represents the host to which you want to connect. The dial-up dialog box will be displayed. Type your password (unless you have previously selected Remember Password) and click on **Connect**. The script will do the rest.

NETWORKED FAXING

For several years, modem users have had access to digital faxing. Our experience has been that relatively few users actually use the fax capability built into their fax/data modem. With enhanced faxing features such as the ones built into Windows 95, however, perhaps this reluctance to using digital faxing will change.

So what can Windows 95 do for your digital faxing future? With the following basic features included (at no extra charge) with the Microsoft Exchange Client built into Windows 95, you can:

○ Create a mailing list of frequently-faxed individuals or companies.

○ Create fax groups so that you can send a broadcast fax to small or large groups by choosing a single entry in the mailing list.

○ Receive faxes from other Windows 95 workstations or any standard fax machine.

○ Send faxes to other Windows 95 workstations or to any standard fax machine.

○ Dial up and request a fax from a machine that supports fax polling.

And, you can do all of this over a Windows 95 network with only a single modem.

If you didn't install faxing when you installed Exchange or during the initial installation of Windows 95, you can do it at any time by using these steps:

1. Open Control Panel by clicking on **Start**, pointing to **Settings**, and choosing **Control Panel**.

2. Double-click on **Add/Remove Programs**.

3. Click the **Windows Setup** tab on this dialog box.

4. In the **Components** list box, click **Microsoft Fax**.

5. Follow instructions on the screen.

If you haven't previously installed Microsoft Exchange, the installation program will do that for you during the installation of fax features. These two utilities— faxing and exchange—work together.

Now you need to add some configuration information to the faxing utility. Use the following steps:

1. In Control Panel, double-click the **Mail and Fax** icon.

2. Click **Add**.

3. Click **Microsoft Fax** in the Add Services to Profile dialog box.

4. You will be asked if you want to type your name, fax number, and fax device modem. Click on **OK** to display the Microsoft Fax Properties dialog box shown in Figure 6.11.

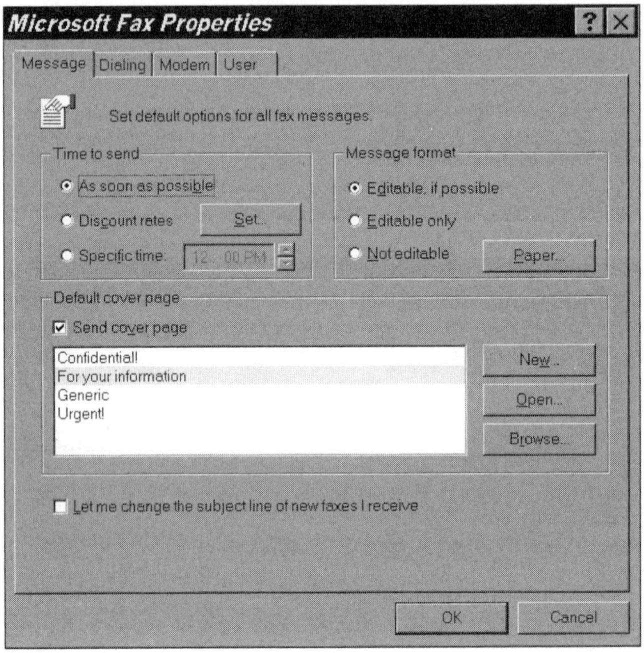

Figure 6.11 Microsoft Fax Properties dialog box.

5. Click each of the tabs on this dialog box in sequence and fill out the information on each one.

6. Click **OK** to close this dialog box.

In the following sections, we will show you how to configure the Exchange software and to use it for networked faxing.

Configuring Exchange for Faxing

We showed you in Chapter 4 how to install and configure Microsoft Exchange for electronic mail. The faxing facility is also part of the Exchange program. You can create a mailing list for future faxing, by following these steps:

1. Choose **Address Book** from the Tools menu in Microsoft Exchange (see Figure 4.17).

2. From the Address Book dialog box, select the **File** menu and choose **New Entry** to display the dialog box shown in Figure 6.12.

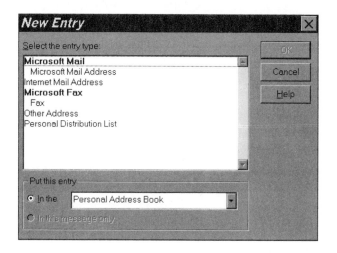

Figure 6.12 New Entry dialog box from Exchange.

3. Under the Microsoft Fax title in the Select the entry type window, double-click on **Fax**. You will see the dialog box shown in Figure 6.13.

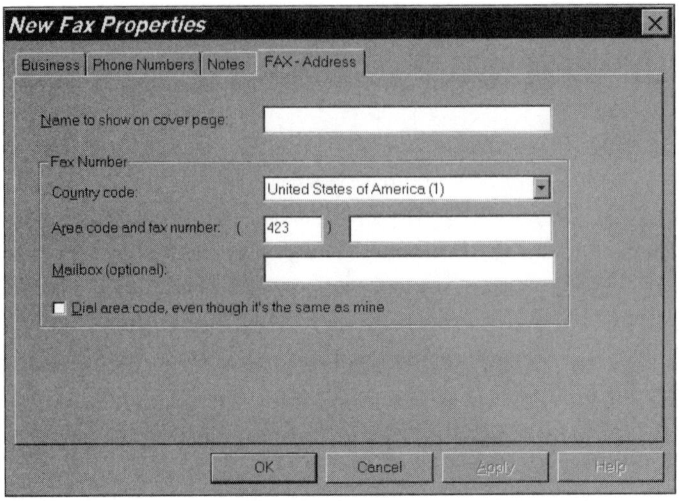

New Fax Properties   [X]

| Business | Phone Numbers | Notes | FAX - Address |

Name to show on cover page: [   ]

Fax Number
Country code: [United States of America (1) ▼]
Area code and fax number: ([423]) [   ]
Mailbox (optional):   [   ]
☐ Dial area code, even though it's the same as mine

              [OK]   [Cancel]   [Apply]   [Help]

Figure 6.13 New Fax Properties dialog box.

4. Fill out the **FAX-Address** fields on this dialog for a one-time fax or one that doesn't require additional information.

5. If you want to store more information about this fax recipient, click on **Business**, **Phone Numbers**, and **Notes** tabs to enter more details.

6. Click **OK** to close the dialog box.

You can create a mailing list for faxing as described in Chapter 4. You can also enter a fax recipient address "on the fly" when you create a new fax.

N O T E

Configuring a Network Fax Server

By configuring Microsoft Exchange you have set your system up for faxing. To send faxes over your Local Area Network, however, you need to conduct a few other steps:

1. On the computer that will serve as a fax server, open Microsoft Exchange by double-clicking on the **Inbox** icon on your desktop or by clicking on **Start**, pointing to **Programs**, and then choosing **Microsoft Exchange** from the list.

2. Click on **Tools** and point to **Fax Tools**.

3. Click on **Options** from the Fax Tools popup list.

4. Click the **Modem** tab.

5. Click on the modem you want to use for faxing.

6. Click the box beside **Let other people on the network use my modem to send faxes**. Accept the suggested path, or enter a drive and directory to use as the shared Fax folder.

7. Click the **Properties** button to display the Fax Modem Properties dialog box shown in Figure 6.14.

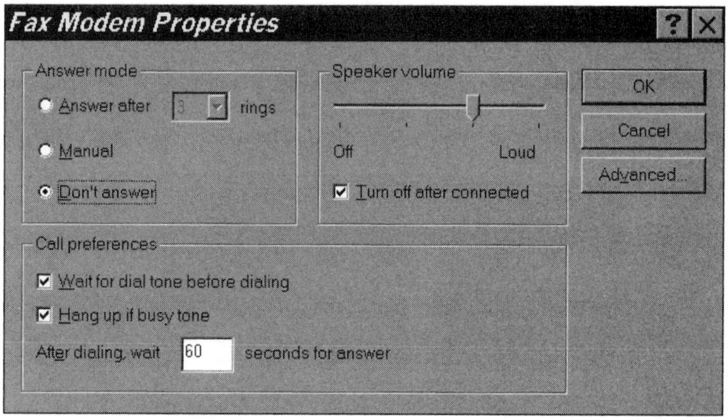

Figure 6.14 Fax Modem Properties dialog box.

8. If you want your modem to answer the phone and receive a fax, click on **Answer after** at the top of this dialog box and specify the number of rings.

9. Click on **OK** to close the Fax Modem Properties dialog box.

10. Click the **Properties** button on the Microsoft Fax Properties dialog box to change the share name for this fax server's modem, if you wish.

11. Click on **Set as Active Fax Modem** after selecting the modem you want to use for faxing. This selection may only be available if you have more than one modem installed.

12. Click on **OK** to close the dialog box and return to the Microsoft Exchange dialog box.

With the Server configured, you are ready to configure one or more client PCs to send faxes over the network through this server.

Configuring a Fax Client

Follow these steps to configure a client workstation to use the Server you configured earlier:

1. Open Microsoft Exchange by double-clicking on the **Inbox** icon on your desktop or by clicking on **Start**, pointing to Programs, and then choosing **Microsoft Exchange** from the list.

2. Click on **Tools** and point to **Fax Tools**.

3. Click on **Options** from the Fax Tools popup list.

4. Click the **Modem** tab.

5. Click on the **Add** button to display the dialog box shown in Figure 6.15.

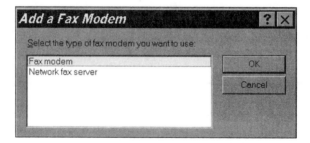

Figure 6.15 Add a Fax Modem dialog box.

6. Click **Microsoft Fax Server** and then click on **OK**. The Connect to Network Fax Server dialog box will be displayed.

7. Type the Network name of the fax server. This is the name you entered as the share name of the fax modem when you set up the server. Include the server name as part of this entry. If you didn't change the default name, your fax server is named NETFAX. If the server name is aax, enter **\\aax\netfax** in this field.

8. Click on **OK**.

9. Select the server entry you just specified in the Microsoft Fax Properties dialog box and click the **Set as Active Fax Device** button.

10. Click **OK** to return to the Exchange dialog box.

Faxing over a Network

To send a fax from a network fax client—or from the fax server—you have two options. You can create a fax message from within Microsoft Exchange, or you can print to a fax device from inside an application such as Microsoft Word.

Faxing from within Exchange

You can type a fax message from inside Exchange. Use the following steps:

1. Click **Compose** and choose **New Fax**. The Compose New Fax dialog box shown in Figure 6.16 will appear.

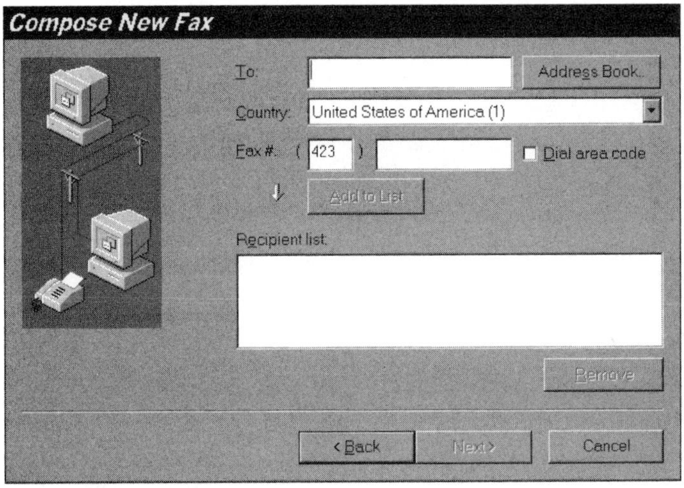

Figure 6.16 Compose New Fax dialog box.

2. Type the To: name in the **To:** field of this dialog box and enter the recipient fax number. Or, you can open the Address Book and choose a name or group to receive the fax.

3. Click **Next** and choose a cover page design from the next dialog box.

4. Click **Next**.

5. Type a Subject for this fax on the Subject line of this dialog box.

6. Type a cover page message for this fax in the Note: window of this dialog and click **Next**.

7. Click **Add File** if you want to attach a file to this fax. You can choose from a Microsoft Word file, an Excel spreadsheet, a text file, and so on. You can create a list of more than one file for this window if you wish.

8. Click on **Next**. The Exchange will tell you the fax is ready to send. Click **Finish** to send the fax.

The Exchange will attempt to dial the remote fax through the fax server. If the line is busy, it will redial several times to attempt to deliver the fax. If a problem occurs, a copy of the fax will appear in your Exchange InBox along with an explanation of what happened. You can send it again from the InBox by selecting it and clicking on **Re-Send**.

Faxing from an Application

You can access the Send Fax Wizard from within an application such as Microsoft Word. Here's how to do that:

1. Create the document you want to fax within an application that supports Microsoft Fax as a print device. This is almost any application you will run under Windows 95.

2. Click on **File** and choose **Print** to display the Print dialog box. Click on the **down arrow** to the right of the Name: field of this dialog box (See Figure 6.17).

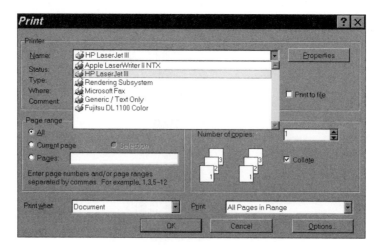

FIGURE 6.17 Pull-Down printer list on the Print dialog box.

3.   Choose Microsoft Fax from the list of printers.

Click on **OK** to start printing to the fax server. The application will launch the Fax Wizard where you can specify a recipient, create a cover page, and so on, as described in the previous section.

DIRECT CABLE CONNECT

So far we have described networking among computers with a standard network interface over coax or twisted pair cable. Windows 95 also supports connections between two computers using a serial or parallel cable. This permits a networklike connection between two machines. If one of those machines is also part of a conventional network, then the other computer has access to any shared network components that are not local to the machine to which it connects.

This is a handy setup when, for example, you have a laptop or notebook machine without a network interface and you want to download files from the network or use a networked printer.

To use direct cable connections you need to set up one computer as a host and another as a guest. To do this, you must create share directories or disk volumes on the host, and file and printer sharing must be enabled (refer to Chapter 3 for information on sharing resources).

In addition, you will need a special cable to connect the host and guest computers. If you are using a serial connection between two serial ports, you will need what is called a *null modem* cable. This is a serial cable with the transmit and receive wires crossed so that the transmitted data from one computer connects to the received data pin on the second machine. A computer dealer can supply a null modem cable for a serial direct connection.

A better choice, where available, is a parallel connection. Parallel connections send and receive data in parallel, eight bits at a time, whereas a serial connection sends information, well, serially, one bit behind the other. Therefore, a parallel cable will provide a faster connection. However, if you want to connect to a machine that has a parallel printer attached—perhaps to print something from a laptop computer—then you'll have to use a serial connection.

If you want to use a parallel connection, specify one of the following cable types at your computer dealer to make sure the connection will work:

❍ Standard or Basic 4-bit cable, including LapLink and InterLink cables available prior to 1992.

❍ Extended Capabilities Port (ECP) cable, if your computer has an ECP port. This type of connection is faster than a standard cable.

❍ Universal Cable Module (UCM) cable. This is the fastest possible connection and allows connecting computers with different types of parallel ports.

You can install direct cable connection by following these steps:

1. Open the Control Panel.
2. Double-click the **Add/Remove Programs** icon.
3. Click on **Windows Setup** tab in the Add/Remove Programs dialog box.
4. Click **Communications** in the Components list.
5. Click the **Details** button.
6. Click **Direct Cable Connection** in the Communications dialog box.
7. Click **OK**.

You must install Direct Cable Connection on each computer that you want to use in a direct cable link, and you must connect them with either a serial or parallel cable.

Now you are ready to run a Direct Cable Wizard to make the connection work:

1. Click on **Start** and point to **Programs**.
2. Select **Accessories** and choose **Direct Cable Connection** from the list. The Direct Connect Wizard will run and display the dialog box shown in Figure 6.18.

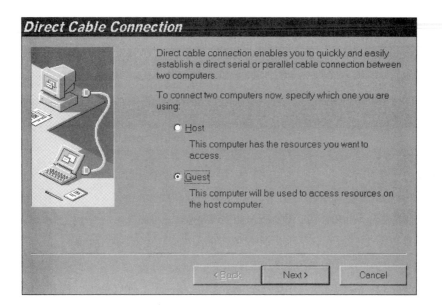

FIGURE 6.18 Direct Cable Connection Wizard opening screen.

3. Click on **Host** or **Guest** to tell the Wizard what role this computer will assume.

4. Click **Next** and choose the type of cable connection you are using from the next dialog box.

5. Click **Next** for the final Wizard dialog box and click **Finish** to start communications.

6. Run the same Wizard on the second computer and follow instructions.

WINDOWS 95 BRIEFCASE

The Windows 95 Briefcase is a useful if sometimes strange utility. We have found that most Windows 95 users either don't understand the Briefcase, or they just ignore it entirely. However, if you have multiple workplaces—say a desktop machine and a laptop—then the Briefcase is an excellent tool to help you keep the files you're working on synchronized. It also makes it easy to package multiple files from several applications into a file that you can copy to a floppy disk or to a laptop over a direct connection.

In addition, the Briefcase includes a reconciliation handler to help you merge changes to a file or files. Suppose, for example, you copy a file to the Briefcase and modify the file. In the meantime, someone using the network changes the source file that you copied to the Briefcase. Now that both files have been changed, which one is the correct version?

The Reconciliation Handler assumes that both versions are correct and merges both versions, keeping the changes made to both files.

To access these features you must first configure the Briefcase, and install it if it has not already been installed. If you chose Briefcase during a custom Windows 95 install, or if you specified a portable install, then the Windows 95 installer automatically installed the Briefcase and placed it on your desktop.

If you don't see the Desktop icon on your desktop, you can install it. Use the following steps:

1. Open the Control Panel.
2. Double-click on the **Add/Remove Programs** icon.
3. Click the **Windows Setup** tab.
4. Click **Accessories** in the Components list on the Setup dialog box.
5. Click on the **Details** button.
6. Click **Briefcase** in the Accessories dialog box and then click on **OK**.

To run the Briefcase utility, simply double-click on the **Desktop** icon. You will see the Briefcase Wizard dialog box shown in Figure 6.19 for instructions on using the Briefcase. Also on your screen will be a dialog box that shows the contents of the Briefcase. This dialog box resembles the Printer dialog box that shows pending print jobs.

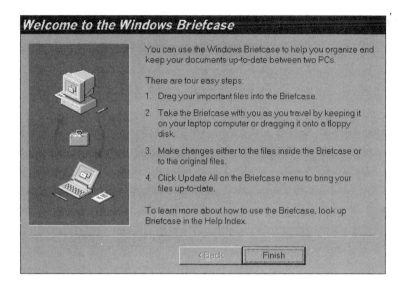

FIGURE 6.19 Briefcase Wizard opening dialog box.

To use the Briefcase utility:

1. Open **My Computer** and choose the disk drive that contains a file you want to copy to the briefcase.

2. Choose the directory and file you want to place in the Briefcase.

3. Drag the file onto the Briefcase. You will see the new file name and details appear in the Briefcase display (see Figure 6.20).

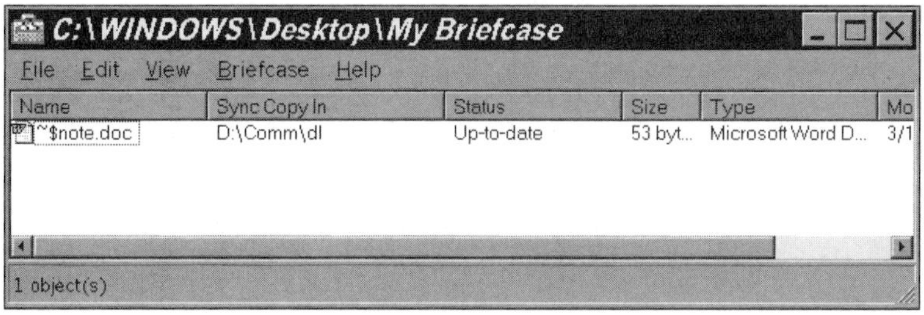

Figure 6.20 Briefcase file list.

You can drag files into the Briefcase by dropping them on the desktop Briefcase icon or into the open Briefcase dialog box that shows the file list.

NOTE

4. Copy the Briefcase by dragging it onto a floppy disk or an attached laptop or desktop disk drive.

5. Make any edits you want on the file or files contained in the Briefcase.

6. Copy the modified Briefcase back to its original location.

7. Double-click the **Briefcase** icon to open the Details dialog box.

8. Select the file or files you want to update.

9. Click on **File** and choose **Update**.

There is some useful information about using Briefcase in the Windows online help file. Click on **Help**, choose **Index**, and type **Briefcase** to get a list of topics.

NOTE

WHAT'S NEXT?

You now have enough information to go beyond simple resource sharing in a Peer-to-Peer Windows 95 network. You can use networked faxing, for example, dial-up networking to access a remote Windows 95 or Internet host, and the Briefcase to facilitate laptop computing in a networked environment.

In the next chapter, we will show you some real-world examples of these facilities. You will see in this chapter how to put to practical use the general information we have covered already in this book.

CHAPTER SEVEN

Ten Real-World Uses of a Windows 95 Network

We've covered a wide range of Windows 95 networking features in this book so far. You now have the basic data you need to set up a working Windows 95 network in a small office or at home.

In this chapter, we will turn the focus toward real-world uses of Windows 95–based networking. Instead of telling you how to wire this or configure that so you can do something useful, we'll start with something useful and show you how to make it work.

1. SHARING A HARD DISK

It seems as if there is never enough disk storage. The computers we see advertised today rarely have less than a gigabyte of disk space, and most users quickly find even that amount isn't enough. That's where Windows 95 networking can help. For example, you could establish one machine as the data server for word processing files, another machine for storing spreadsheets, another for database files, and so on.

To get this kind of functionality on your Windows 95 network, you need only to share one or more disk drives with the network:

1. Turn on file and printer sharing from the Networking dialog box (see Chapter 3 for details on this process; Figure 3.18 shows this dialog box).

2. Double-click on the **My Computer** icon to open a dialog box of disk resources.

3. Right-click on the icon that represents the drive you want to share and choose **Properties** from the pop-up menu.

4. Click on the **Sharing** tab on this dialog box.

5. Click on **Shared As** and type a name in the SHARED NAME field.

6. Click on **Read/Write Access** to enable full access to this drive.

7. Click on **OK** to effect the changes and close the Properties dialog box.

Now you have completed half of the process of exchanging data over the network. The other half of the process is to link to the shared drive from one or more other computers on the network:

1. Click on **Start** on the Task Bar and point to **Programs**.

2. Choose **Windows Explorer** from the list of available programs. You will see a display similar to the one in Figure 7.1.

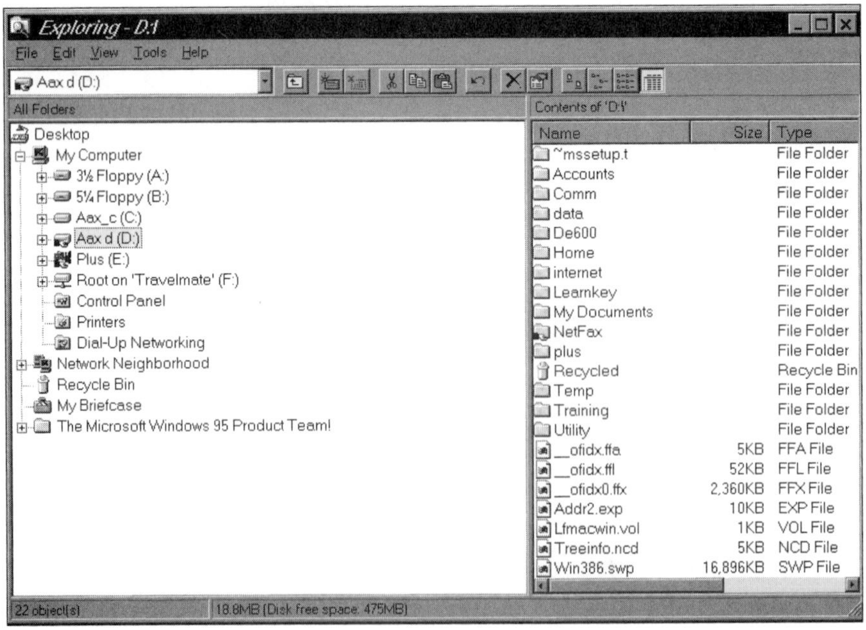

FIGURE 7.1 Windows Explorer main screen.

3. Click on **Tools** on the main Explorer menu and choose **Map Network Drive...** or click on the **Map Network Drive** icon on the toolbar to display the dialog box shown in Figure 7.2.

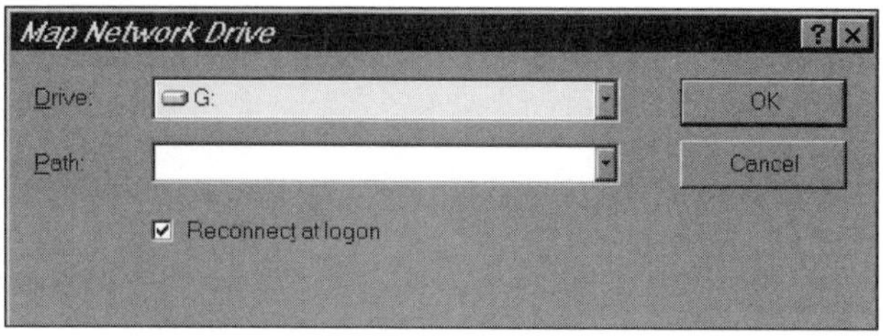

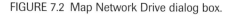

FIGURE 7.2 Map Network Drive dialog box.

4. Type the path to the resource you want to map, or pull down a list of available resources by clicking on the **down arrow** to the right of the PATH field on this dialog box.

Remember that the path to a shared network resource is entered as a double backslash, the name of the remote host computer, a backslash, and the name of the shared resource. For example, we use the share name **root** for the root directory of a hard drive. So the root directory of a laptop computer named **Traveler** on the network would be mapped as: \\traveler\root.

---

5. Click on **OK** to complete the process.

Repeat this process for as many shared network resources as you want to connect to your local machine.

2. SHARING A CD-ROM DRIVE

Aren't CD-ROMs wonderful? Software applications have grown to the point that you can hardly install anything with fewer than 25 floppy disks, but a CD-ROM can give you single-disk installation for nearly any application, plus interactive online documentation, tutorials, sample files, and more.

Unfortunately, even though most newer machines come equipped with a CD-ROM drive, anything more than a few years old won't have such a drive.

How can you install a new CD-ROM-based software package on a machine without a CD-ROM drive?

If you have another computer that does have a CD-ROM drive and both machines are running Windows 95, you can use the remote CD-ROM drive to install software on the local machine. Or you may want to access a CD-ROM-based database stored on another machine. You may want to do this even if the local machine you're using already has a CD-ROM drive installed. Why? That's the good news/bad news of the CD-ROM medium. The good news is that CD-ROM-based software or data lets you access a whole lot of information from a single drive. The bad news is that you have to change the disk to access something different.

Suppose you have a CD-ROM drive on your system and you leave an encyclopedia disk in the drive all the time because you want continuous access to the information it contains for an ongoing project. If you then decide you want to install new software or access a different type of data, you have to remove the encyclopedia disk and put in something else.

Now, suppose you have a Windows 95 network that contains two or more machines with CD-ROM players. If you share all of these drives with the network and then map remote drives from all networked machines, each machine on the network now has access to its own local CD-ROM player, plus any shared drive on the network. If you have a five-machine network and all machines have CD-ROM drives, then every computer on the network has access to five CD-ROM drives and five different, simultaneous kinds of data.

Do you see the value of sharing CD-ROM drives across the network? In addition, CD-ROM drives provide relatively slow access to information—fast enough for most of us, but slower than a local hard disk. However, when you share the drives over the network you'll hardly notice the access speed reduction the network imposes, because you're already used to slower access from the CD-ROM drive.

Ready to hook up a bunch of networked CD-ROM drives? Here's how:

1. Use the process described in Chapter 3 (Figure 3.20) to share the CD-ROM drive with the network.

2. Use the process described in the previous section to map the drive on the computer where you want to install software.

3. Click on **Start** on the Task Bar and click **Run**.

4. Type the path to the newly mapped CD-ROM drive and the name of the installation or setup file on the Run line of this dialog box. You can also choose **Settings** from the Start menu and double-click on **Control Panel** to display it, then choose **Add/Remove Software**.

5. Follow instructions for the software installation or upgrade, using the remote CD-ROM drive instead of a local drive as the source of your new software.

3. SUPPLEMENTAL OR ARCHIVE STORAGE

Among the most common questions about computers we receive from consulting clients, coworkers, casual acquaintances, friends, and family is this: "What should I do about that old, too-slow computer I've had for so long?"

Before the easy peer-to-peer networking brought about by products such as Windows 95, the answer to this question was pretty difficult. After all, a sufficiently old machine is all but worthless on today's used market. With a Windows 95 network, these machines may have a bit more life in them before you give them to charity.

We recommend placing older machines on a network for use as a data archive server, a place to mirror critical information from your main computer or disk drive. You shouldn't let this type of setup replace a regular backup strategy, but it surely can give you additional peace of mind by serving as a secondary or interim backup for current documents and files.

Older machines that may be too slow for comfortable use with today's sometimes ponderous software and that probably don't have enough disk space for both your applications and data can serve very well as a networked backup drive. Even if you have only four megabytes of RAM—nowhere close to enough memory to really use Windows 95—you can use this machine to store backup data, remotely, over the network.

Here's how to set it up:

1. If you haven't already installed Windows 95 on the archive machine, do so now. If you have installed Windows 95, make sure no applications except the operating system are running. You want to make available as much memory and CPU resources as possible for the archive tasks this machine will do.

2. Remove any unnecessary hardware and any associated drivers for it. Remove all shortcuts from the desktop. You want this machine as streamlined as possible.

3. Install the machine on the network. You can place the machine anywhere, but since you won't be using it as a workstation why not position the machine somewhere out of the way? We find that a corner, under a desk, or behind a desk are good places.

4. Share the hard drive on the archive machine with the rest of the network, making sure to provide full read/write access.

5. Remove the monitor and keyboard from the machine if you want to save room.

NOTE

If the archive machine is turned off or rebooted for any reason, you'll have to reconnect the monitor and keyboard to make sure it comes back up successfully and is configured to function as your network archive server.

4. SHARING A PRINTER OR MULTIPLE PRINTERS

One surprise you are likely to have as you work with computers is that they frequently don't have as many functioning ports for printers and modems and so forth as you thought they did. For example, there are four serial ports (COM1: through COM4:) logically configured for most machines, but in most cases only two physical ports exist, COM1: and COM2:. Moreover, COM1: is probably already used for your mouse, leaving only one available serial port.

The same deficiency arises when you want to connect more than one parallel printer. Two parallel ports (LPT1: and LPT2:) are typically configured for most computers, but most of the machines we see have only one physical parallel printer, LPT1:.

You can hook up a second printer on your one remaining serial port, but then don't try to install a modem—internal or external—because you've used your remaining port. Sure, you can install an internal modem and configure it for COM3: or COM4:, but you're likely to encounter software conflicts, especially if you try to run dial-up networking or a third-party TCP/IP driver.

With two or more machines running Windows 95, however, you can configure and use multiple printers—as many printers as you have computers. Here's how:

1. Go to the computer that is attached to the printer you want to use on a remote workstation.

2. Use the process described in Chapter 3 to share the printer with the rest of the network.

3. Go to the computer where you want to use this newly shared printer.

4. Click on **Start**, point to **Settings**, and choose **Printers** to display the Printers dialog box shown in Figure 7.3.

FIGURE 7.3 Printers dialog box.

5. Double-click on **Add New Printer** to display the Add Printer Wizard.

6. Click **Next** to move on to the next Wizard screen. Click on **Network printer** to specify a remote printer instead of a local printer.

7. Click on **Next** to display the next Wizard screen. Type the path to the printer you want to use, or click on **Browse** and choose the computer that is attached to the printer you want to use to display the dialog box shown in Figure 7.4.

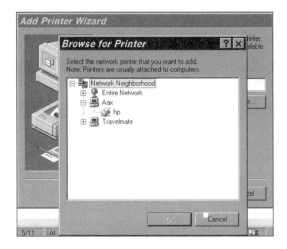

FIGURE 7.4 Browse for Printer dialog box.

8. Select the printer icon and name that represent the printer you want to use and click on **OK**. The Wizard places the proper path on the **xx** line of the Printer Wizard, as you can see in Figure 7.5. (You can type this path yourself if you know the host name and shared printer ID.)

FIGURE 7.5 Path to Printer in Printer Wizard.

9. If you have any DOS applications, click **Yes** beside the button that asks if you want to print from MS DOS programs. Leave the default **No** button checked unless you absolutely must print from DOS.

10. Click on **Next** to move to the next Wizard screen.

11. Click **Next** to accept the current driver, if one exists, or provide the driver software the Wizard requests.

N O T E

If you have previously installed this printer, you will be notified that a driver exists and you can keep it. If this is a new printer definition for this computer, you will be prompted to insert a diskette with the driver software in the **A:** drive of your machine (the drive letter depends on where you last installed software).

---

12. Click **Next** and follow the remaining Wizard instructions to complete the installation process. A new printer icon should appear in the Printers dialog box.

Now you can print to this new printer as long as the computer to which it is attached is turned on and online and the printer itself is powered up. Simply specify this printer as your default printer, either by pulling down the File menu in the Printers dialog box or by selecting this printer from inside the application print routine.

5. INTERNET ACCESS FOR MULTIPLE COMPUTERS

Once you hook up two or more computers using Windows 95 networking, you open up some interesting possibilities for online access. Suppose you have an Internet account and you'd like to be able to connect to it from any computer on your network without having a modem on each desktop.

Of course, if you are using a standard dial-up connection, you'll need to change the way you access the Internet. Check with your Internet Service Provider (ISP) about an Integrated Services Digital Network (ISDN) account. An ISDN connection provides high-speed access, fast enough to support real-time audio, video conferencing, and to provide simultaneous access for multiple network users.

N O T E

You can purchase third-party products that let you share a modem over a network, but Windows 95 doesn't include this functionality. A shared modem works for one-user-at-a-time access, but today's graphical interfaces for online services make a modem impractical for multiuser access.

NOTE   ISDN telephone lines are rising in popularity. Most ISPs provide ISDN access and you can get an ISDN telephone line from your local telephone company for very little more than a conventional line. Although this is a digital connection, you can order conventional telephone services for it, including call forwarding, call waiting, and the like. ISDN uses conventional telephone wiring and connects to the telephone company central office and to a destination location through a dialing interface similar to that of a standard telephone.

This digital link and a piece of hardware (similar to a modem) give you two functioning telephone lines that you can use for data and voice. The data component of this connection is generally 64K bits per second (bps) and can range up to 128K bps. With a 64K data link you can be online with your favorite Internet provider while you talk on the phone or receive a fax on the other half of the line.

Once you have established an ISDN link (or another type of high-speed access such as dedicated 56K bps, or even T1 for larger networks), you are ready to set up your end of the link for multi-user access. We assume at this point that you have already configured the Windows 95 network and that all machines on the network can communicate with each other.

As part of your ISDN configuration, you will need an ISDN bridge or router. Consult with your ISP about the particular hardware you need. Several ISDN connection hardware designs are available, but the easiest to use are the ones that attach directly to the network.

The bridge attaches to your local area network through one port and to your ISDN line through another port. The bridge should plug into your network hub through a standard 10BaseT cable as if it were just another workstation.

Remember that the Internet uses the TCP/IP protocol for its network communication, and that's what you'll set up to run over your LAN to communicate with the bridge and, ultimately, with the Internet host (see information in Chapter 6 about configuring TCP/IP for an Internet connection).

Your ISP will configure the bridge with its own Internet Protocol (IP) address so it becomes a member of the TCP/IP network just like one of your Windows 95 machines. In addition, the configuration of the bridge includes establishing what telephone numbers the unit will call when one of the computers on your network instructs it to connect to the Internet.

Once the hardware is configured and installed, all you have to do to access the Internet from any workstation on your Windows 95 network is to follow these steps:

1. Use the Networking dialog window from the Control Panel to enable TCP/IP networking protocol attached to your Ethernet controller for each machine on the network (see Chapter 6 for information on how to do this).

If you have the Microsoft Plus! package, you can install Internet facilities from your Plus! distribution disk.

NOTE

2. Install Internet software, such as Microsoft Internet Explorer (from your Plus! disk), Netscape (from your Internet Service Provider), Eudora for E-mail management, and so on. You should receive software and help in configuring your software from your service provider.

With TCP/IP enabled and Internet software installed and configured, you should be able to access the Internet directly from inside Netscape or other Internet applications. Simply launch one of your Internet software applications and it will request a connection to your ISP's host automatically. The bridge or router will dial the ISDN number and log you into the host, providing Internet access.

A configuration such as this makes your local computers act as if they are part of the network at your ISP. There will be a delay between the time you launch an application and when you see the Internet data appear, but the delay is only slight. It takes only a few seconds to complete the dial-up and log-in process across most ISDN circuits.

Notice, too, that this same technique works to provide high-speed network access to your office computers from home or another office. If you install an ISDN line at work and another at home or a second office site, then you can connect the two networks via ISDN bridges or routers just as you connect to the Internet.

At 64K bps or 128K bps your access won't be as fast as a direct Ethernet connection, but for most of what most of us do on a LAN (load a file, edit it, and save it back), the difference is hardly noticeable. In any setup such as this, make sure you have followed adequate security measures to prevent unauthorized access to your networked data.

6. Software Updates and Maintenance

If you are like many computer users, you can't stand out-of-date software. As soon as the latest version of something is available, you look for the lowest price and get it installed. Even more important to some users is keeping the current versions of the software they have updated. Many software companies continuously release software patches and updates to enhance their software and correct bugs that users have uncovered.

If you are using a single PC, then updating software isn't much of a problem. In a networked environment, however, it is more trouble to install software repeatedly on PC after PC. If the software is on floppy disk, then the process is slow and cumbersome. If it is on CD-ROM the installation is easier, but you must have a CD-ROM drive on each machine, or have access to a shared CD-ROM drive over the Network.

With a Windows 95 network, however, you can update or install software over the network itself, making the process fast and easy and removing the frustration of remembering where you left the latest set of update floppies.

N O T E   The process described here assumes you have purchased the required number of software licenses for your network. In most cases, you can install the same software to multiple machines as long as you have purchased and registered the proper number of copies. Some software is available as a network license, which means you have one physical copy of the software but it is approved for installation on a fixed number of machines simultaneously. Other software companies simply require that you buy one copy of the software for each machine on which it will be installed. Check your licensing agreement. One interpretation is that you can have multiple copies of a given package installed as long as only one person at a time is using it. If this is the case with your software, then you might have five users on the network, but only two copies of a particular piece of software because no more than two people at a time will be using it.

If the software you are installing is distributed on a CD-ROM, then use the techniques described earlier under sharing a CD-ROM drive with the network and installing software from it. You can insert different CD-ROM disks to install different software.

To set up a networked server for floppy-based software:

1. Create a subdirectory on a networked drive.

2. Share the directory with the network with read/write access (see Chapter 3 for details on how to do this).

3. Copy each diskette in the distribution set into the subdirectory. Make sure that any subdirectories on these diskettes get copied along with the files in the root. You can use the Explorer to drag and drop files and directories, or you can open an MS-DOS window and use `xcopy a:*.* c:<path> /s` to copy all the files and subdirectories to a server directory.

N O T E   You'll need to study individual software packages to find out whether the installation or setup routine included with them can find all the required files from a single directory. Some programs keep looking for the files they need in the specified directory and only ask for another disk when the required files aren't found. Other installation routines load the files thought to be from the first diskette, then request the next disk. For such programs you may need to create individual directories for the files on each disk. When required, we use *disk1*, *disk2*, and so on for these multiple directories.

To install the package on another workstation, use **Start Run** from the Task Bar, then enter the path across the network to the new directory you just created along with the setup or installation program required to set up the new software. The package should install across the network, without having to swap floppy disks, as if the source were your local floppy drive.

7. BACKING UP MULTIPLE DISKS

In our experience, one of the most neglected—yet crucial—procedures in computer networking is data backup. Unfortunately, the majority of individual computer users rarely back up hard disk data. And worse, users of small networks—those without a formal network or MIS manager—follow suit. The good news is that systems are very reliable today and the chance of losing more than a few files at a time is relatively small.

On the other hand, backup technology is relatively inexpensive and, especially in a networked environment, easy to use. What excuse do you have for losing a file that required many hours to produce?

Full documentation on backing up networked data is beyond the scope of this book, but in general, here's what you need to do to ensure against loss of data:

Make a Plan

This step is most often neglected. Whether you plan to back up information every day or once a week, whether you use floppy disks, a tape drive, or a redundant hard disk, making a plan and working it is sometimes the hardest part of a backup strategy, but it also is one of the most important parts.

Start planning by deciding how often and when you will back up information. Then make a chart to help you record the backups you've made. Also, label the backup media by day. Once you have a workable plan, if you label your disks or tape *Day1, Day2, Day3*, and so on, you'll know which is the most recent backup. Another mistake we have seen in managing data is restoring the wrong data when information was lost. If you are really serious about data backups, plan to keep one copy of your backup data in a safe place off site and rotate the off-site media with the local media daily, if possible.

If the network you are managing is at an office, for example, you might carry a tape or diskette home each night and return the previous day's backup to the office. If you are on a weekly schedule, you will always have five or seven tapes that hold backup information, each a little older than the next. And, you'll always have some backup information at the office and some at home. The chances of losing primary data off a network and simultaneously damaging the backup media at two locations are practically nil.

Choose Appropriate Hardware

Tape backup, floppy disks, zip drive or other removable storage, redundant hard disk—all of these hardware platforms can serve as a backup tool. Which one you use depends on the volume of data you need to back up, the type of data you are managing, your budget, and your own experience and expertise.

In a relatively low-volume environment, a workable backup strategy involves placing the most current files on a floppy disk at the end of a day or the end of a session. This technique works when the files you manage will fit on a floppy. Most word processing files and spreadsheet data usually will fit; database and presentation files frequently won't.

Also, in a networked environment where multiple users are creating data and changing it daily, this type of floppy backup strategy probably won't be successful because it depends on each individual remembering to back up their personal data. A better strategy for multiple users is to set up a central backup location and to copy information over the network.

Test Your System

We have had experience with several commercial network systems—systems that depend on accurate data, delivered on deadline, to run a business. Backups in this situation are important, and these companies began an aggressive backup procedure from the beginning. However, many of these companies with which we have experience have been surprised to discover, when backup data was required to restore lost information, that something was wrong with the software or hardware in the backup system. We learned from these experiences to test a backup implementation before it is actually needed.

The problem is that most backup schemes involve storing the data in something besides the native data format. For example, backup software compresses the information so that the archived information takes up less space than the original and will frequently store it in a combined file format. If the restore software can't read the stored information, you can't get it back. Of course, testing a backup system can be a little difficult when the live data you want to protect can be put at jeopardy if the backup goes awry. One way to conduct a safe test is to make a standard file copy to another hard disk on the network of the directory or directories you will restore. Then try restoring the information from your backup medium to the original location. If something goes wrong, you can always do a standard copy from the remote drive back to the original location, and nothing is lost.

Those are the basic concepts. How do you set up your Windows 95 network to help you back up everything on it to a central location? It is easy, and you probably have already done most of the work:

1. Decide which workstation will function as the backup server.

2. Make sure this machine can "see" all the other machines on the network and that the disk drives you want to back up have been shared with the network.

3. Install any additional hardware, such as a tape drive, that you need on the backup server. This may involve removing the cover to your computer and inserting a controller circuit board. You'll probably also have to install some custom software.

4. Run the backup software and back up key directories from all the drives on the network.

Depending on the backup device and software you are using, you may be able to write a simple script (program) to automate much or all of the backup process. Use a script if possible because this ensures that you will back up everything you need to and makes the process easier.

NOTE If you have the Microsoft Plus! utility, the included System Agent can help you schedule automatic backups and other tasks. If you installed Plus! with default settings, then the required System Agent components are installed and they run when you start Windows. By default, the Agent is set up to scan and defragment your hard disk after hours if you leave your computer turned on.

You can use the Agent for other automated tasks as well:

1. Open **System Agent** by double-clicking on the icon at the bottom right of the Task Bar, or by using the Start menu. Click on **Start**, choose **Run**, and enter the path to your Plus! directory, then the program name **sysagent.exe** (you can use **Browse** to help you locate this directory and file). You will see the dialog box shown in Figure 7.6.

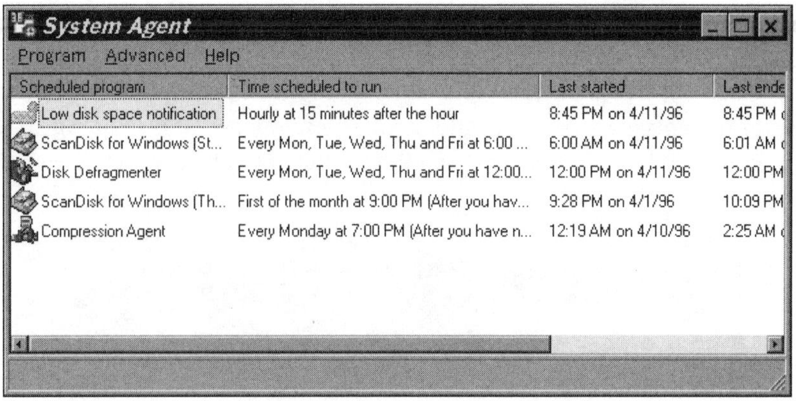

FIGURE 7.6 System Agent opening screen.

2. Click on **Program** and choose **Schedule a New Program** to display the dialog box shown in Figure 7.7.

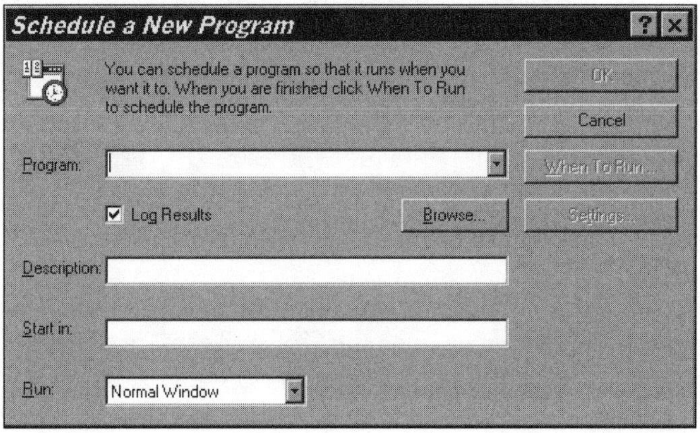

FIGURE 7.7 Schedule a New Program dialog box in System Agent.

3. Enter the name of the program you want to schedule in the **PROGRAM** field of this dialog box. Include a full path to the program and add any desired program switches such as names of files to load or configuration commands.

4. Type a description of the program, if you wish, in the **DESCRIPTION** field of this dialog box.

5. Click on **Settings** to display the dialog box in Figure 7.8 if the program you want to run is System Agent–aware. This dialog box lets you specify program parameters without having to enter them on the **PROGRAM** field.

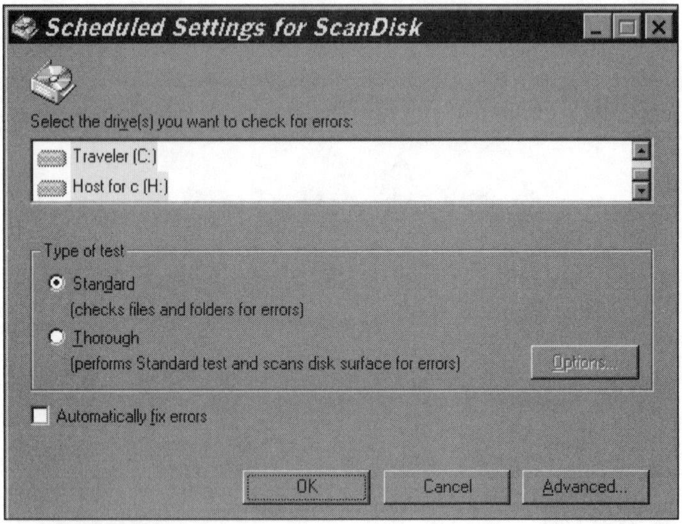

FIGURE 7.8 System Agent Settings dialog box.

6. Then click the **When to Run...** button to display the dialog box in Figure 7.9 and to specify when the System Agent should run the specified program. There are three control groups on this dialog box. The first lets you specify which days the program should run, the second sets the time, and the third lets you tell the agent what to do if you start using your computer while the specified program is running.

7. Click on **Advanced**, if you wish, to set some additional parameters that have to do with how the specified choices run under different conditions. Click on **OK** to return to the Change Schedule dialog box.

8. Click on **OK** to close the Change Schedule dialog box and effect the changes you've made.

9. Use **Program**, **Exit** to close the System Agent.

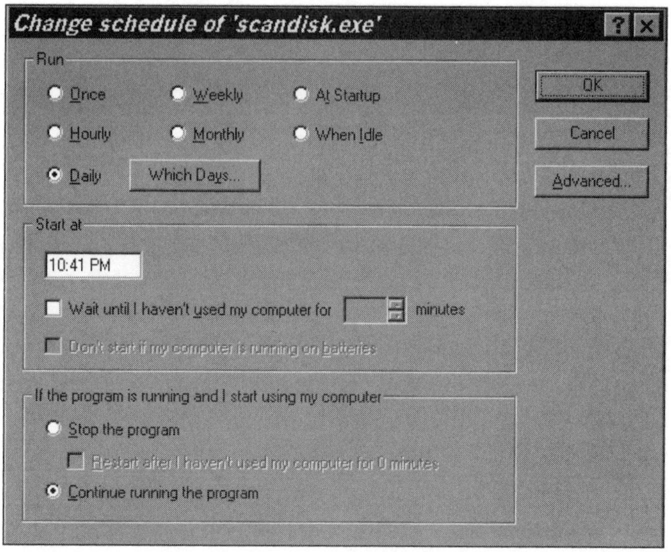

FIGURE 7.9 System Agent Change Schedule dialog box.

8. DIAL-UP NETWORKING

Suppose you have a small network at your office and one or more computers at home where you also conduct some of your work. We find (invariably, it seems), having moved a project from the office to the house for a little last-minute, late-night work, that we end up back at the office the next day without the file that contains the latest information. Dial-Up networking from the office to the house handles this problem nicely.

After setting up dial-up networking at home so the computer will answer the phone as a server and configuring a dial-up networking client at the office, we can log into the home computer over the phone and access all the shared drives and directories on the home network. In this configuration, all the shared resources on the home network appear on the office desktop as if they were local or attached as part of the office local area network.

NOTE In a small office, or one where you can establish a separate telephone line and phone number for your desktop computer, you can turn around this configuration to dial up and log into your office computer from home. Check with your office MIS staff to make sure you comply with any existing security requirements before you try any of these setups.

We showed you in Chapter 6 how to set up dial-up networking servers and clients. Review that material for the step-by-step process of establishing the basic dial-up link. As you establish a dial-up networking link from your home to your office, or the other way around, keep these ideas in mind:

○ Windows 95 Dial-Up Networking requires that you run the same network protocol on the server and client machines. If you are running native Windows 95 at the office and at home, then your default network protocol will be NetBEUI. If you are running a Novell network at either end of the link, then you will need the Novell drivers at both ends or you'll need to use the intrinsic IPX/SPX drivers from Windows 95.

○ NetBEUI and IPX/SPX protocols are installed automatically when you set up Dial-Up Networking. However, if you are running a secure Novell network at your office, you may not want to allow NetBEUI at the office. As network protocols go, NetBEUI is not very secure. Even if you haven't specifically shared resources in a NetBEUI network, under some conditions savvy users can access components of the network. You will need to use the Networking dialog window to disable NetBEUI on the dial-up adapter. Right-click the **Network Neighborhood** icon and choose **Properties** to display this dialog box.

○ If your office uses a digital telephone system you probably can't plug a modem directly into a telephone wall jack. You'll need to ask the vendor of the telephone system to break out a separate line for use by your computer.

○ Use adequate password protection to control access to the dial-up server. If you are new to the dial-up networking world, you are likely to be surprised to learn how vulnerable your dial-up server and the network to which it is attached are to unauthorized access. Hackers use ingenious (or diabolical, depending on your view) software to randomly dial numbers looking for modems, and then to guess passwords by cycling through dictionaries of 50,000 or 100,000 words. Chances are that if your password is a common name, a date, a street address, a noun, and so on, then it can be guessed within a few minutes. You don't want to jeopardize the security of your data in exchange for the convenience of picking up a forgotten file at home or at work.

❍ For added security you can consider disabling dial-up networking when you don't plan to use it. Of course, when you do this, you run the risk of having it unavailable when you do need it. After all, it is just as easy to forget to enable dial-up networking as it is to forget to copy a needed file to a floppy disk and put it in your briefcase.

N O T E   In addition to dial-up networking, Windows 95 includes a terminal emulation and dialer program you can use to connect to online services or other computers that aren't running Windows 95. The HyperTerminal application lets you configure different shortcuts for each service you want to use:

1. Click **Start** on the Task Bar. Point to **Programs** and then to **Accessories**.

2. Click on **HyperTerminal** to display the HyperTerminal program group (see Figure 7.10). Note that this program group changes as you create new HyperTerminal definitions. Your version may not look just like Figure 7.10.

FIGURE 7.10 HyperTerminal program group.

3. Right-drag the **HyperTerminal.exe** icon onto the desktop and choose **Create Shortcut**. This will place on your desktop a shortcut icon representing the HyperTerminal application. Now you can create as many HyperTerminal dial-up definitions as you want.

4. Double-click the **HyperTerminal** shortcut to display the dialog box shown in Figure 7.11.

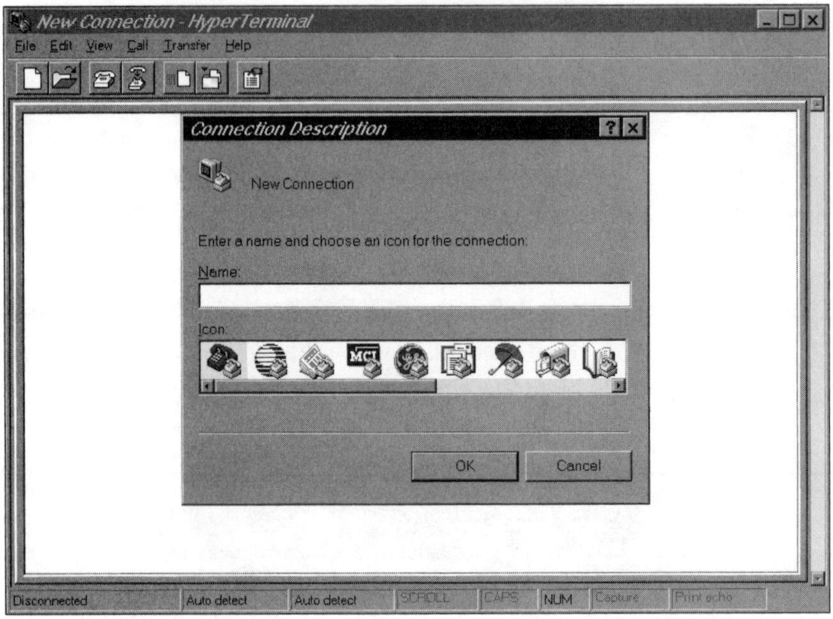

FIGURE 7.11 HyperTerminal Definition dialog box.

5. Type a name for the new dial-up definition in the **Name** field of this dialog box.

6. Choose an icon to represent this dial-up definition from the available icons in this dialog box.

7. Click on **OK** to display the Phone Number dialog box shown in Figure 7.12.

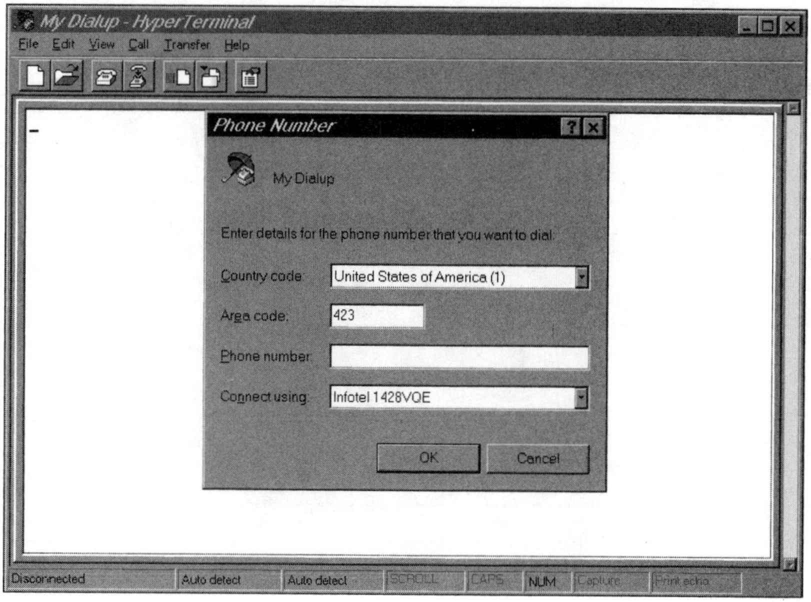

FIGURE 7.12 HyperTerminal Phone Number dialog box.

8. Type a telephone number in the **Phone number** field of this dialog box.

9. Change the area code, country, and modem, if you wish.

10. Click on **OK** to close the Phone Number dialog box.

11. From the Connect dialog box, click on **Dialing Properties** to display the Dial-Up Properties dialog box, shown in Figure 7.13.

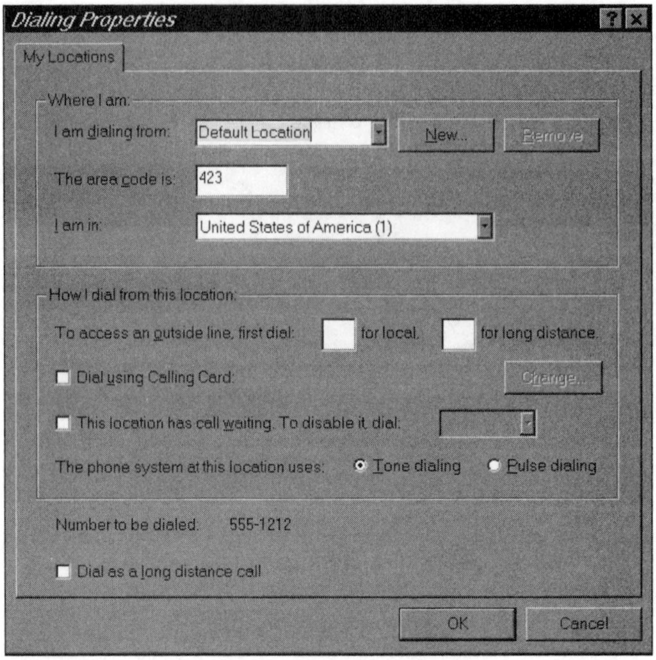

FIGURE 7.13 HyperTerminal Dial-Up Properties dialog box.

12. Make any changes required about the way this dial-up connection will work. You can turn off call waiting, for example, or specify a credit card connection.

13. Click on **OK** to close the Properties dialog box.

14. You can click on **Dial** to connect to the specified remote computer. For additional configuration information, click on **Cancel**, then choose **Properties** from the File menu to display the dialog box in Figure 7.14, which lets you change the phone number, modem, and other property values.

15. Click on **Configure** to display the properties of the specific modem you have specified on this dialog box. This will let you set the number of data bits, stop bits, and other communications parameters.

16. Close all dialog boxes, including the HyperTerminal dialog box. The shortcut icon for this new communications parameter will appear on

your desktop. Launch this dial-up connection by double-clicking on its shortcut icon.

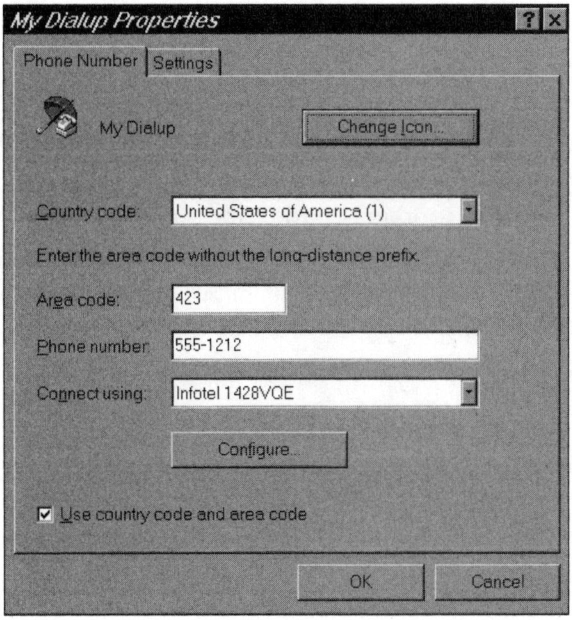

FIGURE 7.14 HyperTerminal Properties dialog box.

9. USING REMOTE MAIL

One of the desirable features of a networked operating environment is the ability to manage E-mail messages originating from or addressed to individuals on the network. Windows 95 and the Exchange client help you do this. Together they let you establish a post office that will accept outgoing E-mail messages from anyone on the network and accept incoming messages from outside the network and distribute the data as necessary. Suppose you are using Windows 95 networking and the built-in mail system at the office, but you'd like to be able to pick up your mail while traveling or from home. You can do that by following the procedures we outline in the following sections.

In general, here are the steps required to set up your Windows 95 network to manage mail messages for everyone on the network:

1. Install Microsoft Exchange, if it is not installed, and configure a network post office (see Chapter 4 for details on how to do this).

2. Install dial-up networking on the server (see Chapter 6).

3. Configure the server on which the post office resides for remote access (see Chapter 6).

4. Install dial-up networking on the remote client or clients.

5. Define a dial-up networking connection to the remote post office you want to reach. Do this on each client machine that will dial into the post office (see below).

6. Configure the remote client or clients for remote mail access (see below).

7. Specify a scheduled session time, if desired (see below).

Once you have conducted this basic setup procedure, you can send and receive mail to members of your network, whether your workstation is connected directly to the network via Ethernet or you dial into the network with a remote laptop or home machine.

In the following sections, we provide additional details on completing some of these steps, and on how to use the E-mail connection once you have successfully completed the configuration steps.

Define a Dial-Up Networking Connection

For each client machine that will dial into the LAN post office, you must define a dial-up networking connection. Do this using the Dial-Up Networking Wizard accessible from the My Computer group:

1. Double-click on the **Dial-Up Networking** icon to display the Dial-Up Networking dialog box.

NOTE

If you don't see the **Dial-Up Networking** icon in the My Computer group, you haven't installed it or it was installed and then deleted. Use the Add/Remove Software Wizard in the Control Panel to install dial-up networking before you try to complete these steps. You will need access to your Windows 95 distribution software—floppy disks or CD-ROM—to install dial-up networking.

2. Double-click on **Make New Connection** to launch the New Connection Wizard.

3. Type a name for the new dial-up connection. Use a descriptive name that will make it easy to remember what this configuration does.

4. If the modem you will use is not properly identified, choose a modem from the pull-down list on this dialog box.

5. Click on **Next** to move to the next Wizard screen.

6. Type a telephone number for the remote host you want to access on the next screen and click on **Next** to complete the Wizard. A new icon, with the name you just gave your new dial-up connection, should appear in the Dial-Up Networking group.

Once the new connection is created, you are ready to configure it. Right-click the new icon and choose **Properties** from the pop-up menu. Now use the procedure described in Chapter 6 to enable only the NetBEUI protocol. You should be ready to dial into the remote post office.

Configuring Clients for Remote Mail

Configuring a post office on a local area network is only half of the process required to let you manage remote mail. You also have to configure any client machines that will access the post office over a dial-up link. Here's how to do that:

1. Click **Start** on the Task Bar and point to **Settings**.

2. Click on **Control Panel** to open the Control Panel.

3. Double-click the **Mail and Fax** icon to open the dialog box shown in Figure 7.15.

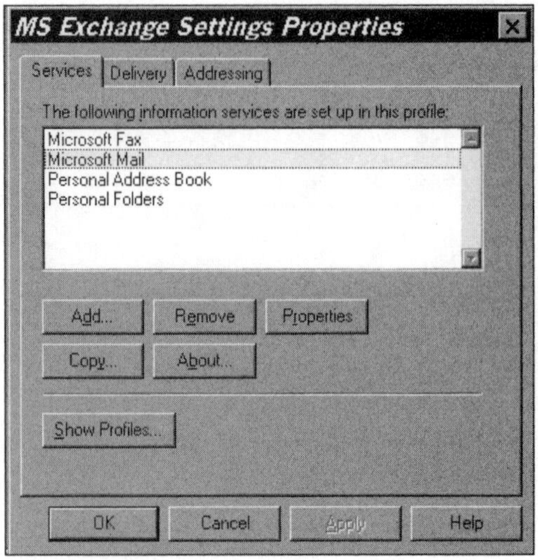

FIGURE 7.15 Mail and Fax dialog box.

4. Click **Microsoft Mail** to select it and click **Properties** to display the
    Properties dialog box shown in Figure 7.16.

FIGURE 7.16 Mail and Fax Properties dialog box.

5. Click the **Dial-Up Networking** tab to bring it to the front of the display, as shown in Figure 7.17.

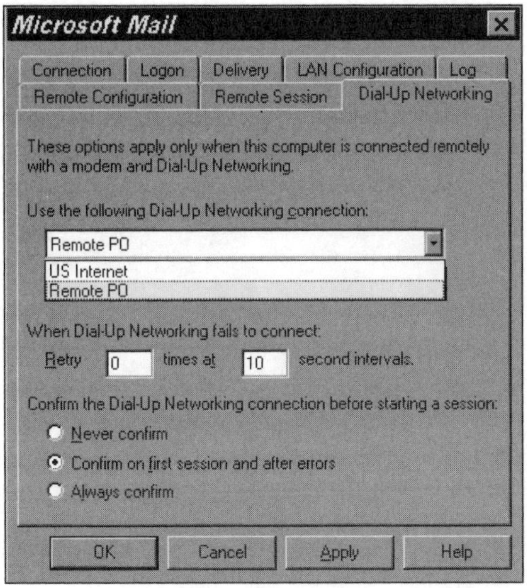

FIGURE 7.17 Dial-Up Networking tab from Mail and Fax Properties dialog box.

> If you don't see the Dial-Up Networking tab, then you haven't installed it or it was deleted. Reinstall Dial-Up Networking before continuing.

NOTE

6. Choose the new dial-up configuration you just created by pulling down a list in the USE THE FOLLOWING DIAL-UP NETWORKING CONNECTION field and selecting it as the default.

7. Click on the **Connection** tab on this dialog box to bring it to the front of the display (see Figure 7.18).

8. Click on the **Remote using a modem** and the Dial-Up Networking buttons.

9. Click the **Remote Configuration** tab to bring it to the front of the display (see Figure 7.19).

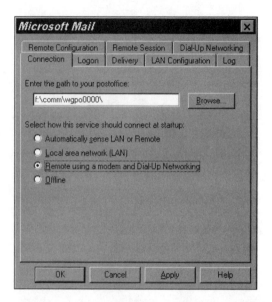

FIGURE 7.18 Connection tab of the Mail Properties dialog box.

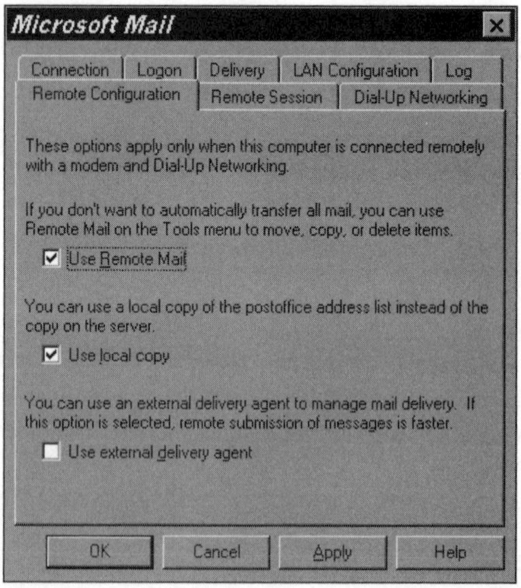

FIGURE 7.19 Remote Configuration tab of the Mail Properties dialog box.

10. You can accept the default settings on this dialog box, which require that you tell the system to download your mail after you are connected to the remote post office. If you uncheck the **Use Remote Mail** option, your mail will be automatically downloaded when you connect to the remote post office.

11. Click on the **Remote Session** tab to bring it to the front of the display (see Figure 7.20).

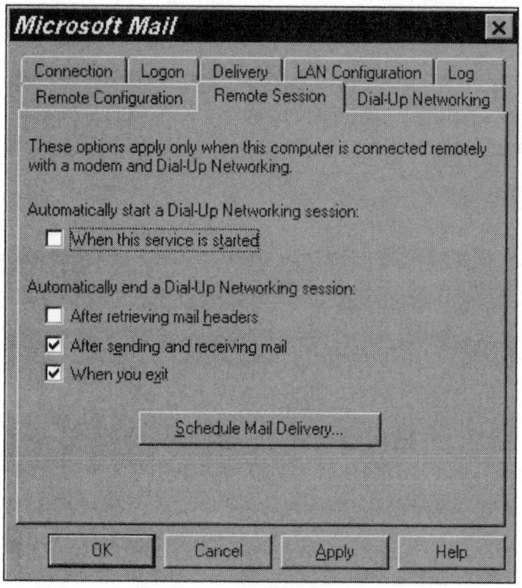

FIGURE 7.20 Remote Session tab of the Mail Properties dialog box.

12. Choose the configuration you want from this tab. You can specify when a dial-up mail session begins and ends. You can accept the default until you use the system a few times to determine what you want to do.

Defining a Scheduled Session

You can check your mail by dialing up the remote post office service through the Dial-Up Networking group. You also can schedule a remote mail session by specifying a time and connection method and storing it in the Exchange profile. Up to 16 sessions can be scheduled, including sessions by date and time, at prescribed intervals (check mail every three hours) or at specific times on specific days of the week.

To define a scheduled session, take the following steps:

1. Display the Mail Properties dialog box as described in the previous section.

2. Click on the **Remote Session** tab to bring it to the front of the display (see Figure 7.20).

3. Click the **Schedule Mail Delivery** button to display the Remote Scheduled Sessions dialog box.

4. Click on the **Add** button to display the dialog box shown in Figure 7.21.

FIGURE 7.21 Add Scheduled Session dialog box.

5. Choose the dial-up networking session you want to use.

6. Specify the time for a scheduled session.

If you specify **every**, then you must also specify an interval (every 2 hours, every 10 minutes). If you specify **Weekly**, then you will choose a day and a time. The intervals change with the specification you choose.

N O T E

7. Click on **OK** to close this dialog box.

Use the remote mail configuration you just created by selecting it in the Dial-Up Networking group from My Computer.

N O T E

Don't forget that Windows 95 also supports network faxing (see Chapter 6). You can fax across the network to a fax server machine set up somewhere else on the net. You can establish broadcast lists, and you can tell the program when to send your faxes so that, for example, you could write a fax message, specify a distribution list for it, and send the faxes late at night when rates are lower and telephone and fax facilities are less likely to be busy.

10. Data Sharing in a Workgroup Environment

One of the main objects of setting up a Windows 95 network in the first place is to share data among networked machines. As you start to do this, keep in mind how your information is distributed across the network, how you can be sure of using the correct version of a given file, and how to back up the data.

Although Windows 95 is a peer-to-peer network, we encourage you to think about it and use it as if it were a server network. When you do this, you set up a central machine as a shared data repository, a place to store all the data files you use across the network. When any files that are—or are likely to be—shared with other users are placed in a central location, it is easy to find the files you want, it is easier to back up the data, and it is less likely that someone will edit and/or distribute the wrong version of a file.

Also, it is a good idea to design the directory structure of this server to make it easier for users to determine what versions of files they are using. You might establish a central **data** directory, for example, and under that create sub-directories for each type of information: **Microsoft Word**, **Excel**, **Access**, **Mail**, **Graphics**, and so on.

Beneath each of the general categories, you might create directories for **Originals**, **Edits**, **Distribution**, or whatever grouping fits your usage patterns.

Where multiple users are sharing information and perhaps editing files prior to distributing them, it is a good idea to learn the habit of placing the file name, path, and date and time of last edit in the footer of each shared file. This is especially important for word processing and spreadsheet files that are likely to contain subtle changes that might be difficult or impossible to spot when you need the file in a hurry.

And, in addition to your regular backup procedure, which may place your files on an extra hard drive or tape system, practice extra-safe computing by copying the current versions of the files you need for current projects to your hard disk as well. Just remember to access the file for updates or printing from the networked server and to back up the current version to your hard disk. This will protect you from the frustrating situation of needing a file—say, to print a proposal for a new client—only to find that the network is down or the server machine isn't working properly.

WHAT'S NEXT?

The rest of this book will help you delve a little deeper into the concept of Windows 95 networking. In the next chapter we will expand the network design topic and discuss further network security topics.

CHAPTER EIGHT

Windows 95 Networking Reference

This chapter is designed to take you slightly beyond the basics of Windows 95 networking. If you want to know a little more about setting up servers on a peer-to-peer network, when you want to consider a more secure network or to learn something about network management, this chapter is a good place to start.

PEER NETWORKING DESIGN

Today's networking environment is an interesting mix. We hear more and more about the importance of networking and computer-to-computer communication, yet most information about computer networking deals with conventional server-based networking. As we told you in Chapters 2 and 3, Windows 95 is a peer-to-peer network where computers are connected as equals or near equals.

Why is so much emphasis placed on server-based networking?

Server-based networking is the design of high-end networking. It provides the best security and is the easiest network style to manage. Besides, millions of workstations using commercial server-based products such as Novell already are in place at all levels of corporate America.

A server-based network may connect multiple workstations in a variety of physical formats, but when it comes to sharing data, all workstations on the network store and share information only on one or more machines dedicated to file sharing. Likewise, shared network printers are attached to the server machine. The server-based design is particularly appropriate for larger networks because as the number of users and computers rises on a network, the management of software versions, backing up data, and so on becomes more difficult.

However, simpler, peer-to-peer designs made possible by Windows 95 and similar products bring networking down to the level where very small businesses and even at-home users can receive a lot of value from hooking computers together. A peer-to-peer design, as the name suggests, makes all machines on the network essentially equal. You can share resources on any machine with any other machine. In a relatively small network, this fact provides desired flexibility and expands the amount of disk storage and other resources each user can access. For example, you can achieve high levels of disk storage without having to invest in a single machine with lots of disk storage. The design is more appropriate for relatively small networks because you can manage distributed, shared data more easily if the number of individual machines is relatively small.

However, because of the flexibility of Windows 95, you can enjoy the advantages of easy-to-use peer-to-peer networking for some tasks while you maintain a strong, secure, server-based network for most of your business activities. Also, you can manipulate the standalone Windows 95 network design to make it more like a server-based network. For example, you may put your accounting data on a central server, but place sales department documents such as proposals and technical data on departmental machines to be shared freely among local users.

Peer Servers

What is a network server? We discussed this concept briefly in Chapters 2 and 3. Remember that a server is a computer dedicated to some specific task, such as managing a printer or acting as a data server.

Printer Servers

When you attach a printer to a PC, then share that printer with the rest of the network, the computer is functioning as a print server. All of the print traffic over the network flows through that computer on its way to the printer. That means disk, CPU, and memory resources on that computer will be partially allocated to managing printer data from other workstations on the network.

In a small network, the level of extra work a computer must do to support a shared printer probably isn't significant. In a large network, where many people will be using the print server simultaneously, you may need to consider what machine you assign to this duty, which printer you place on which machine, and so on. We have found in Windows 95 networks with ten people or so, for example, that when the computer that is handing print jobs also is used as a workstation, that machine is considerably slower than it would be without the added chore of print management. The user on the print server computer frequently has to wait for files to load or even for the mouse to move when managing graphics. At the same time, printing is relatively slow for others on the network.

In this situation, you will have better response from the print server if it is dedicated to printing and is not shared as a workstation on the network. The good news is you don't have to assign your fastest, most capable machine to this duty. In fact, if the machine is being used only to manage the printer queue you can press one of the least capable machines into service. Here is an opportunity to make good use of one of your older, slower machines with a relatively small disk drive, while you move a newer, more capable machine onto someone's desk. Figure 8.1 is a conceptual diagram of a small Windows 95 network with a single machine set up as a printer server.

Workstations

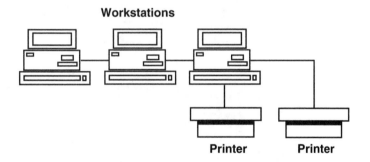

Printer   **Printer**

FIGURE 8.1 Windows 95 network with printer server.

If you want to make multiple printers available for network use, you can put two or more printers on such a dedicated server. You could attach your primary networked printer to the print server's parallel port, then hook up a less used, perhaps slower, printer to one of the server's serial ports. Need more printers? You could add a second parallel port. Adding that second port may simply require configuring an existing port on your I/O (Input/Output) card or on your motherboard; see your computer's documentation for assistance. Or you may have to add an expansion card to install additional serial ports. Modern machines with special cards can handle eight or more serial ports instead of the standard two or four. And because Windows 95 can distribute server machines across the network, you can attach additional printers to other workstations. As you do this, remember what the earlier warning about the limitations of sharing a workstation with a printer server.

You can adjust how the print server manages your print jobs by adjusting operation of the print spooler, as shown here:

1. Open the **Printers** group from the **Settings** option on the **Start** menu.

2. Right-click on the icon that represents the printer you want to configure.

3. Choose **Properties** to display the Properties dialog box.

4. Click on the **Details** tab to open the display shown in Figure 8.2.

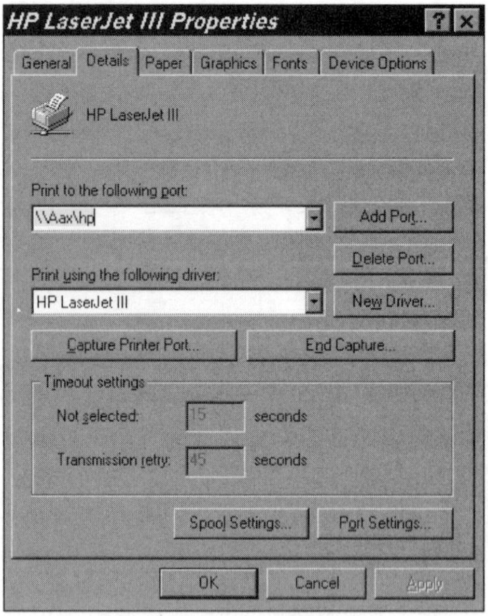

FIGURE 8.2 Details tab from Printer Properties dialog box.

5. Click on the **Spool Settings…** button to display the Spool Settings dialog box shown in Figure 8.3.

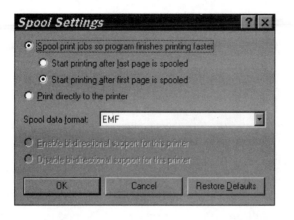

FIGURE 8.3 Spool Settings dialog box.

6. Click on **Spool print jobs**....

7. Click on **Start printing after last page is spooled** to speed up printing from networked workstations. This setting requires more storage than the default, but it is the best choice when multiple users are sharing one computer for printing.

8. Click on **OK** to effect the changes and close this dialog box.

Data Servers

You may also want to establish a data server as part of your Windows 95 network design. The concept is similar to setting up a printer server. You want to dedicate one or more workstations to the task of storing all shared information for everyone on the network. Remember that under Windows 95 you could share all the hard disks across the network so that every user could access their own local disk as well as every other disk on the network.

In a small network, this may be a desirable arrangement. With more than a few users, however, it will be easier to manage data, ensure adequate backups, and avoid data errors among users if you centralize storage of most information. Set up this configuration as you would a printer server. Share only the hard drive or drives on the machine designated as the data server. All other machines on the network will contain only local drives.

While you can use a conventional desktop configuration for the server— IDE hard drives, typical memory—you should consider upgrading this machine to make it a better performer and easier to expand as your network needs grow. For example, if you install a high-performance Small Computer System Interface (SCSI) controller in this machine, you can place up to seven hard disk drives, tape drives, or other devices on this machine without adding more hardware. Besides, all things being equal, a SCSI hard drive (if you use a fast controller) is a better performer than an IDE drive.

There are several versions of SCSI available for a machine capable of running Windows 95. You should check with your dealer or a knowledgeable LAN manager within your organization to determine which will provide the best cost/performance ratio in your situation. Newer SCSI designs—Wide SCSI, for example, and Fast SCSI—may provide better performance with fewer restrictions.

In addition, it will do little good to spend time and money on a high-speed SCSI controller if you are using a low-end, 16-bit network controller. The best I/O performance will be achieved with all high-end components, including a 32-bit, local-bus network interface.

Other data server considerations follow:

Make it a fast machine. Unlike a printer server where the computer spends most of its time waiting on the printer, a data server needs to be fast to manage the multiuser access requirements of network-shared disk drives. That means you should consider a Pentium or at least a high-end 80486-based machine (80–100 MHz CPU, for example).

Add extra memory. Windows 95 requires more memory than earlier operating systems to offer the same performance. We would consider 16 megabytes a minimum memory configuration for a Windows 95 workstation. If several users are accessing a machine, you'll probably achieve faster performance with even more memory. Doubling this minimum to 32 megabytes is a cost-effective way to ensure the maximum possible performance.

Add a dedicated hard drive. Windows 95 does a pretty good job of self-configuring to manage hard drives and memory—at least better than previous Windows versions. You must ensure that Windows has plenty of room on the main disk drive, where Windows 95 is installed, to create swap files and conduct other space management requirements. If you use a relatively large disk—say, 500 megabytes or so—and install on it only the Windows 95 software and other applications you need for this server, that should leave plenty of room for Windows 95 to work. The swap file will work best if it is on a drive that isn't too busy. It doesn't necessarily have to be on the same drive with Windows 95, but if it isn't, you'll have to set up a manual swap file. All in all, it is best to let Windows 95 dynamically manage the swap file on the same drive as the operating system itself. Next, install a second drive as large as you need for shared data. This will improve performance and make data management easier.

Optimize system performance. Windows 95 can configure individual machines to optimize performance for particular applications. For example, memory and disk usage are different when a machine is used in a portable environment as compared to a disk or printer server. To configure a machine as a server, follow these steps:

1. Click on **Start** on the Task Bar and point to **Settings**.

2. Click on **Control Panel** to open the Control Panel.

3. Double-click on the **System** icon to display the System dialog box.

4. Click the **Performance** tab on this dialog box to display the Performance dialog box, shown in Figure 8.4.

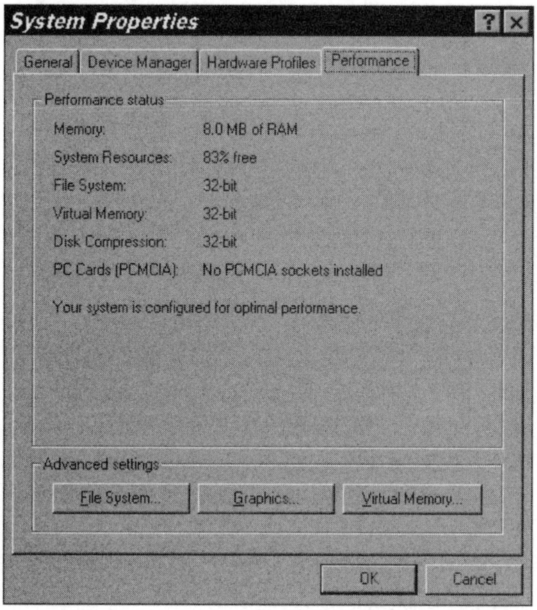

FIGURE 8.4 System dialog box from Control Panel.

5. Click on the **File System...** button to display the dialog box shown in Figure 8.5.

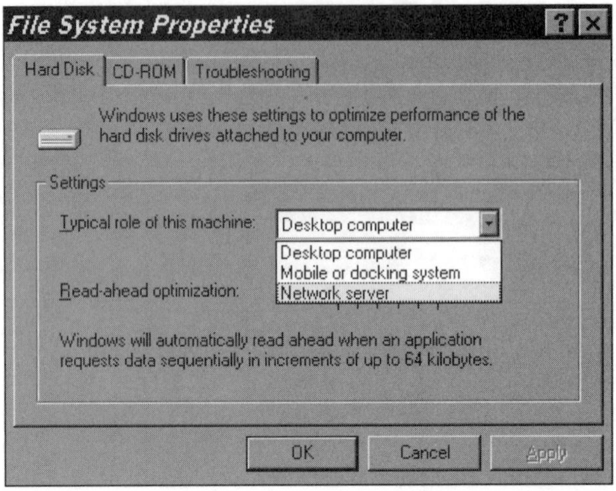

FIGURE 8.5 File System dialog box from the Performance tab.

6. In the list named **Typical role of this machine**, choose **Network Server**.

7. Click on **Apply** to make the configuration changes.

This change will tell Windows 95 to adjust certain settings in the system registry (the configuration file that controls how much of Windows 95 operates), including cache sizes, buffer operation, and so on.

If your data server contains a CD-ROM drive, you may also want to optimize the performance of this drive. These settings are similar to the hard drive settings but must be set separately, as follows:

1. From the File System dialog box on the Performance tab, click on **CD-ROM** to display the dialog box shown in Figure 8.6.

2. Make sure the proper type of CD-ROM drive is specified in the OPTIMIZE access pattern for field of this dialog box. Windows 95 probably chose the proper setting for this value, based on its scan of the CD-ROM drive during installation and the amount of RAM installed. Change the setting only if you are sure the values are wrong.

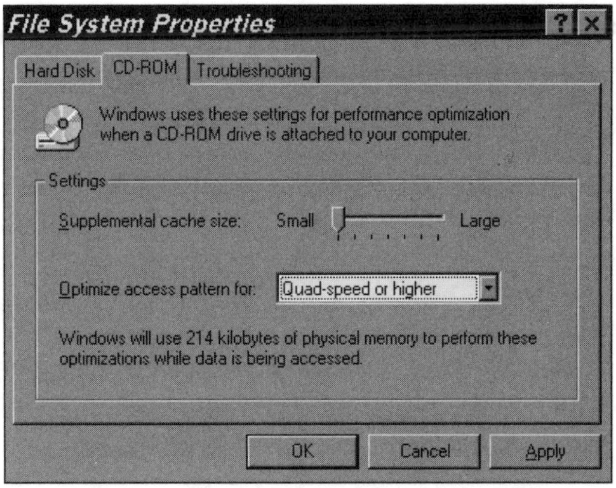

FIGURE 8.6 CD-ROM dialog box from Performance tab.

3. Drag the slider for the **Supplemental cache size** setting to increase cache size. The type of data you access from the CD-ROM drive affects the optimum setting. Experiment with different settings to achieve the best performance.

4. Click on **Apply** to effect the settings.

5. Shut down the computer and restart to make the change.

Upgrade the network interface. If the data server is using an older, 8-bit network interface, you can improve performance by upgrading to a 16-bit card; an existing 16-bit card could be upgraded to a local bus, 32-bit adapter. In general, newer network hardware provides better performance than older hardware.

USING MULTIPLE NETWORKING PROTOCOLS

The primary focus of this book is on using the networking facilities built into Windows 95. However, in a business environment particularly, you may want to run additional protocols. Probably the most common dual-network protocol combines Windows 95 with a Novell network. If you have even one Novell server configured on your network, then any of your Windows 95 workstations can access the server and use Novell protocols.

NOTE Check with your network administrator or LAN manager. Your company may want you to use a native Novell network driver instead of the intrinsic Windows 95 drivers. Your networking people can install and configure any additional required drivers for you.

Configuring Windows 95 to support another network in addition to the native Windows 95 protocol is easy. Take the following steps:

1. Right-click the **Network Neighborhood** icon on your desktop and choose **Properties** to display the Network Properties dialog box (see Figure 8.7).

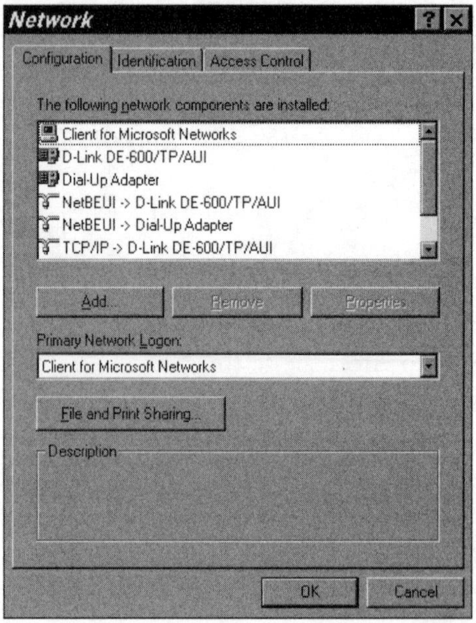

FIGURE 8.7 Network Properties dialog box.

2. Click on **Add...** to display the Select Network Component Type dialog box.

3. Double-click on **Protocol** to display the Protocol dialog box, shown in Figure 8.8.

4. Choose a company and product from the dialog box. Windows 95 will install the drivers for the selected protocol.

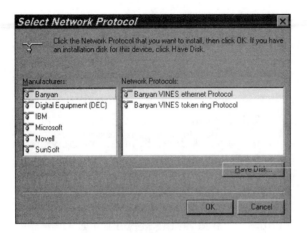

FIGURE 8.8 Network Protocol dialog box.

Click on **Have Disk** if you want to install a protocol not supported by Windows 95 or if you want to install a different version of the specified driver.

N O T E

5. If Windows 95 doesn't automatically install a client to support the new protocol, then double-click on **Client** in the Select Network Component Type dialog box and choose a company and product to install a client.

In some business situations you may find yourself in the reverse of this situation. Instead of adding another protocol to a Windows 95 network, you may want to add Windows 95 networking to an existing Novell or other network configuration. Why? To achieve peer-to-peer functionality, primarily.

We are familiar with one incident in which Windows 95 capability solved a serious problem for one company. It was a Novell network company with about 40 workstations heavily dependent on a server-based Novell network. During an effort to upgrade the server, something went wrong and the server disk was damaged. It required several days to get the system functioning again, during which time no one on the network could access server files or print anything because all printing was routed through one of several networked printers.

The short-term solution was to enable peer-to-peer networking on selected Windows 95 machines. This let users access archive versions of some files stored on individual workstation hard disks. Also, printers were moved from the

Novell network server to a couple of Windows 95 machines to enable shared printing. The network cable was already in place. All that was required to enable shared computing quickly were a few simple steps, as follows:

1. Enable Windows 95 networking using the procedure described in the previous section.

2. Share the disk drives and printers attached to select workstations.

3. Map the printers and disk drives from remote computers so that users can access these shared resources.

You don't need a network server disaster to appreciate the value of Windows 95 peer-to-peer networking. Suppose you have a functional, server-based network with heavy-duty printers shared on the network. Does it make sense for all the printing from all departments to go through the public printers? What about payroll checks and other financial reports? You could install a small, dedicated printer in the accounting department and share it among all the accounting machines using Windows 95 peer networking.

 Check with your systems people before implementing such a system. Depending on what else your network connects to, Windows 95 could compromise overall network security if proper precautions are not taken.

N O T E

NETWORK SECURITY

Windows 95 is actually several products in one. For many of us, it is a simple, functional way to connect two (or a few) computers to make computing life easier at home or in a small office. On the other hand, the Windows 95 system is strong enough to support serious networking for serious business if (1) you plan the network design carefully; (2) your network isn't online to the outside world through a corporate wide area network or the Internet; and (3) you use the security features it contains.

We examined network design earlier in this chapter and in sections of Chapters 2 and 3. We place the restriction on external connections because at least with the initial release of Windows 95, there are some flaws in the way device restrictions work. We feel that these flaws can probably be managed adequately in a closely held environment within a workgroup or even through a relatively large user population if all users are in one location under one management structure. However, if you open your Windows 95 network to a larger community—especially through an Internet connection—it may become difficult to ensure data and device security. Note also that even the kind of access restrictions frequently employed through network routers may not be able to overcome a serious hack attempt from outside.

N O T E   A full discussion of internetworking and using hardware routers is beyond the scope of this book. If you aren't familiar with these terms, don't worry. We aren't advocating extending Windows 95 networks anyway, and your network manager is familiar with these terms. We mention these suggested restrictions so that you will understand when your MIS staff limits the type and scope of peer networking connections supported by Windows 95.

At the same time, however, the security features intrinsic to Windows 95 are adequate to protect relatively sensitive files and to manage access to devices such as printers and CD-ROM drives on most networks at home and in small businesses. There is no such thing as guaranteed security in any computing endeavor, of course, and Windows 95 is no exception. But the techniques we describe in this section can help you control and manage access adequately in most cases.

Basic Windows 95 Security Features

Windows 95 in conjunction with a more robust network environment such as Windows NT or a Novell network offers some fairly powerful security controls. Windows 95 by itself is less powerful but capable of managing access and offering a degree of security, nevertheless. In addition, the intrinsic system policies features of Windows 95 give the network administrator even more control over how Windows operates and what users can do with it. (We examine system policies later in this chapter.)

Windows 95 offers these basic security controls:

○ Password log-in to the Windows 95 network, to other associated networks (such as NT or Novell), and to the Windows 95 operating system.

○ Shared-level security to let you control who can access a shared disk drive, printer, or other resource.

○ User-level security to control computer and other device access based on user or group rights.

○ Password caching to permit single-password log-in to Windows 95 and associated networks; caching can be disabled if you want to require that a user enter a password for each level of log-in.

Enabling Share-Level Security

With Windows 95 alone, you can establish passwords to control access to individual shared components on the network. Here's all you need to do to establish share-level security for a single computer:

1. Right-click the **Network Neighborhood** icon.

2. Choose **Properties** from the pop-up menu to display the Network dialog box.

3. Click the **File and Print Sharing** button to display the File and Print Sharing dialog box, shown in Figure 8.9.

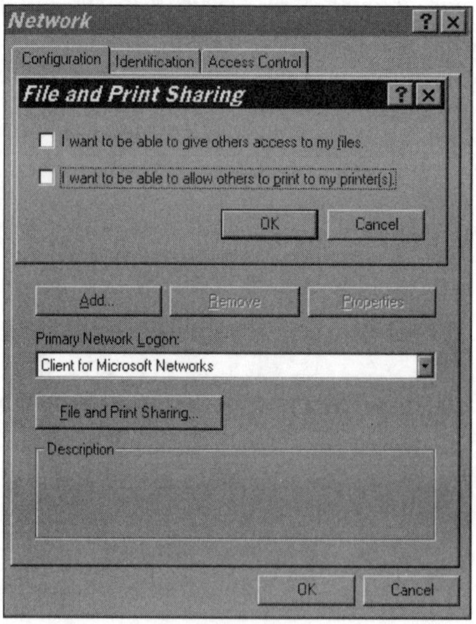

FIGURE 8.9 File and Print Sharing dialog box.

4. Click on the **File Sharing** and **Printer Sharing** boxes on this dialog box and click on **OK** to return to the Network dialog box.

5. Click on the **Access Control** tab of the Network dialog box to display the dialog box shown in Figure 8.10.

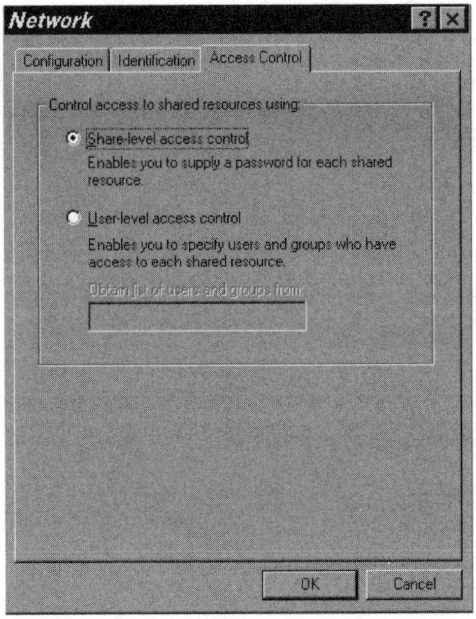

FIGURE 8.10 Access Control tab from Network dialog box.

6. Click on **Share-level access control** to enable share-level control (this option may already be selected).

7. Click on **OK** to close the Network dialog box. You will be prompted to restart Windows 95.

Once you have turned on share-level security, you can enable password protection for the shared devices on the network. You can share disk resources at the whole-disk level or at the directory level. Printers, of course, are shared one at a time, a whole printer at a time. You can turn on password protection when you share a network component, or you can reconfigure a device later, enabling password protection for a previously shared device.

To enable share-level security for a disk, directory, or printer, follow these steps:

1. Double-click the **My Computer** icon to open the My Computer group.

2. Right-click the icon that represents the disk you want to share or for which you want to turn on share-level security. The pop-up (context) menu shown in Figure 8.11 will be displayed.

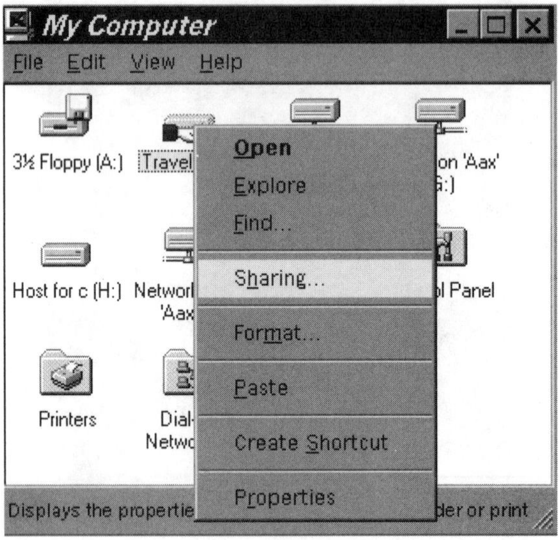

FIGURE 8.11 Disk Drive context menu.

NOTE
Double-click on the **Printer** icon to share a printer or turn on share-level security for a printer previously shared. Use Windows Explorer if you want to share a directory or turn on share-level security for a directory instead of an entire disk drive.

3. Click on **Sharing...** to display the dialog box shown in Figure 8.12. Click on the **Sharing** tab if it is not already on top of the display.

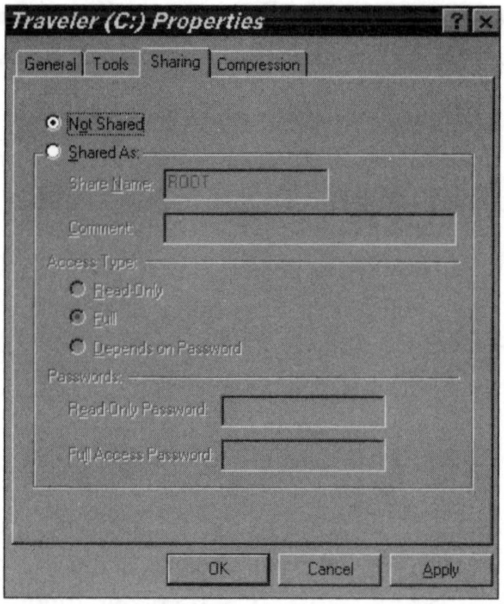

FIGURE 8.12 Sharing menu from Disk Drive context menu.

4. Click on **Shared As** and type the resource's share name.

> The actual name of the shared resource over the network will be the share name you type in this field, plus the name of the computer to which this device is attached. If the disk share name is *root*, for example, and the computer is *traveler*, then users on the network will access this disk by specifying \\traveler\root.
>
> **N O T E**
>
> As an added security measure you can share a resource with the network but hide it from the Network Neighborhood display. Simply add a dollar sign ($) to the end of the share name. In this example, you would enter root$ in the SHARE NAME field of this dialog box.

5. Click on **Read-Only** or **Full** to specify the level of access you want to grant to network users. The password field associated with the level of access you specify will be enabled.

6. Enter the password you want to use for the level of access you specified.

7. Click on **OK** to close this dialog box.

N O T E Click on the button beside **Depends on Password** to enable read-only and full access that is dependent on the password used. In this configuration, you can create groups of users who have read-only access and others with full access to the shared device. This feature approaches the user-level security available with more robust networks.

Now when you access this shared resource from anywhere on the network you will have to provide the proper password before you can use a password-protected resource. Remember, you can control access to any shared resource on the network, including disk drives, subdirectories, CD-ROM drives, and printers.

Setting User-Level Security

Although this book is primarily about using Windows 95 in a peer-to-peer network, we will introduce the concept of user-level security made available through a NetWare or Windows NT security server. If you are running a Windows NT or NetWare server, you can establish user-level security this easily:

1. Enable **File and Printer Sharing** from the Network dialog box.
2. Click the **Access Control** tab and choose **User-level access control**.
3. Type the name of the Windows NT domain, the name of the Windows NT workstation where the user accounts are stored, or the NetWare server name in the OBTAIN LIST OF USERS AND GROUPS FROM field of this dialog box.
4. Click on **OK** to close this dialog box and restart Windows when you are prompted to do so.

As with share-level security, user-level security requires that you share specific devices and specify which users or groups can access them. Do this from the Explorer or from the My Computer group as described previously, under "Share-Level Security." The display is different with user-level security enabled. You will be allowed to choose users and groups and, furthermore, to specify the level of access each user can have.

Consult separate documentation supplied with your NetWare or Windows NT software for additional information. In a moderately sized business environment, you probably also have access to a LAN manager or other technical support staff who can take you further into the issue of user-level security.

Setting Log-In Passwords

The first time you log into Windows 95 you will be asked to provide a user name and a password. If you have a network enabled, you will be asked to log into the network. If the user accepts the default on the Password dialog box, telling Windows to save the password (check the box labeled **Save this password** in your password list), this data is then stored for the next time you log in. This is another example of the semiautomatic nature of Windows 95. In many other systems, you must create a list of users and passwords from a default administrative account before anyone can log in and use the system. With Windows 95, new user names and the optional passwords are created on the fly as each new person logs into the system.

This is convenient, but it also demonstrates the relatively low level of security offered by the native, unaltered Windows 95. You can enhance the security by using System Policies (see the discussion of system policies later in this chapter). Remember, too, that there are actually two levels of password protection: Windows 95 itself and whatever network you are using. If Windows 95 is in a stand-alone environment, then the second password is to the Windows 95 network component. If, on the other hand, you are using Windows 95 with another network such as Windows NT or Novell NetWare, then the secondary log-in will be to this other network.

Whatever your network environment (Windows 95, Window NT, or NetWare), Windows 95 is configured to remember the password you use to log into Windows, to access a device protected by share-level security, or to log into the network—Windows 95 or something else. These passwords are stored in a password cache file, which the system checks when you log in. This cache arrangement assumes that if you provide the proper password for the Windows log-in, then you must be who you claim to be and the other passwords you have used to log into the network or to access shared devices are used automatically from the cache file.

Convenient as this may be, it is not very secure. Someone might steal or guess the password to your Windows system, which would be bad enough, but you wouldn't want them to be able to access your network or any other protected devices on the basis of that single password.

Again, in a small, relatively secure environment, minimum security often is best because when you make things too difficult, you slow down access and frustrate users. However, it is good practice to observe reasonable security in all environments.

Using Password List Editor

You could require users to use different passwords or disable password caching through the System Policy Editor. If you need to disable existing cached passwords, you can use the Password List Editor (**PWLEDIT.EXE**). This program is located in the **ADMIN\APPTOOLS** directory on your Windows 95 distribution CD. This utility is not supplied with the floppy diskette distribution of Windows 95. You can run this utility directly from the CD-ROM disk, or install it if you want to use it:

1. Open Control Panel by clicking on **Start** on the Task Bar, choosing **Settings**, and then double-clicking on the **Control Panel name** on the list.

2. Double-click on the **Add/Remove Programs** icon in Control Panel.

3. Click the **Windows Setup** tab.

4. Click the **Have Disk** button to display the dialog box shown in Figure 8.13.

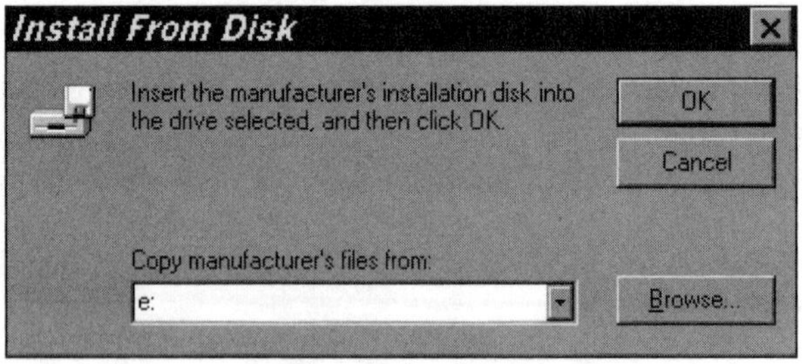

FIGURE 8.13 Have Disk dialog box.

5. Click **Browse** in the Install From Disk dialog box.

6. Choose the disk drive that points to your CD-ROM drive, and follow the path to **ADMIN\APPTOOLS\PWLEDIT\PWLEDIT.INF** on your distribution CD-ROM.

7. Click **OK**.

8. In the Have Disk dialog box, click **Password List Editor** and then click **Install**.

Once the utility is installed, you can access it from the **Start** menu:

1. Click on **Run**.

2. Type **pwledit** on the Run line of this dialog box.

3. Click on **OK** to launch the program and display the screen in Figure 8.14.

FIGURE 8.14 Opening screen of Password List Editor.

Notice that this editor really doesn't allow you to edit entries, and you can't even view the actual password information; the passwords themselves are encoded. However, you can remove a password entry by selecting it and then clicking on **Remove**. A password entry that is removed will force that user to enter a required password when logging in again or when accessing a protected device.

Separating Windows and Network Passwords

We showed you in Chapter 3 how to change an existing password. If you are in a dual networking environment with, say, a Novell or Windows NT server, then you may want to use different passwords for your Windows 95 log-in and the other network log-in. This can offer an extra degree of security. Here's how to make that happen:

1. Open the Control Panel.
2. Double-click the **Passwords** icon to display the dialog box shown in Figure 8.15.

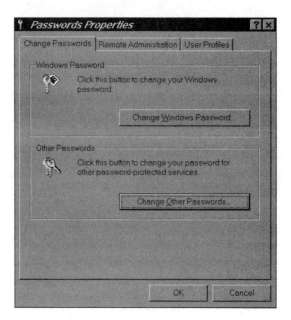

FIGURE 8.15 Password Properties dialog box.

3. Click **Change Windows Password**.

4. Type the old password in the first field of this dialog box.

5. Press **Tab** and type the new password.

6. Press **Tab** and type the new password again to confirm it.

7. Click on **OK** to return to the Password Properties dialog box.

8. Click on **Change Other Passwords** to display the dialog box shown in Figure 8.16.

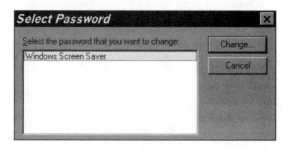

FIGURE 8.16 Change Other Passwords dialog box.

9. Click on **Change** to display a Change Password dialog box for these additional facilities.

10. Enter the existing and new passwords as before.

11. Click on **OK** to close the Change Password dialog box.

12. Click on **OK** again to close the Password Properties dialog box.

NOTE Windows 95 can't change the password for some network resources. If you click on **Change** with a network resource selected that Windows 95 can't change, you will see an error message that should tell you how to make the change.

Changing Network Resource Passwords

On the other hand, you may prefer convenience over security. Think carefully about the trade-offs. If you have separate passwords for your Windows 95 log-in and other network resources, you may want to edit the passwords so that they are the same. While not as secure as having separate passwords, combining the passwords can make online life easier for users. Here's how to do so:

1. Open the Control Panel.

2. Double-click on the **Passwords** icon.

3. Click on **Change Windows Password** to display the dialog box in Figure 8.17.

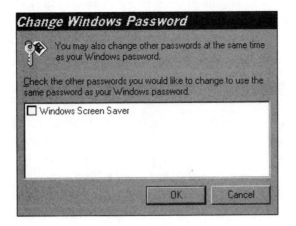

FIGURE 8.17 Change Windows Password with other resources.

4. Check other passwords you want to change to make them the same as your Windows 95 log-in password.

5. Click on **OK** to close the Extra Password dialog box.

6. Type the old password in the first field of the next dialog box.

7. Enter the new password and verify it in the final field of this dialog box.

8. Click on **OK**.

NETWORK MANAGEMENT CONSIDERATIONS

If you are accustomed to large, corporate network environments, you are aware that a sufficiently large network can take on a personality of its own. Connect enough computers and seat enough people at separate desktops, and you can build a data and hardware management nightmare. Whole industries have evolved around the concept of network management.

A relatively small Windows 95 network, on the other hand, doesn't require much management. Notice we said *much* management. All networks require *some* management. You need to spend some time with a stand-alone PC cleaning the disk of unwanted files, making sure critical information is backed up, installing software updates, and so on. You must do the same for each machine on a network, of course, but you also must be concerned with some connectivity issues: network loading, device sharing, software versions and licensing, intranet communications, security (see the previous sections of this chapter), and so on.

We can't provide a complete treatment of network management in this book (you don't need it, anyway), but we will in this section point out some of the issues and discuss what resources are intrinsic to Windows 95 so as to help you address them.

Resource Sharing

The key to successful resource sharing is a clear understanding of who is using the network, what resources the network contains, and what users are doing with the network. Resource-sharing strategies and hardware requirements are different for a two-machine at-home network for games and word processing and a ten-station network where most users are involved in graphics design.

In a small network, you probably will want to share nearly everything across the network. Remember that one of the useful features of networking machines in the first place is the ability to expand the resources at any given machine. If each computer on a two-computer network has a CD-ROM drive, for example, then by sharing both drives with the network and mapping the remote drives at each workstation, you have doubled the CD-ROM capacity for each machine. The same is true for hard disks. A machine with a 500 Kbyte hard drive on a network with another computer that has a 1.6 Gbyte drive has storage of more than 2 Gbytes available. If two computers have a printer apiece, then when you network them each computer has two printers.

You get the idea.

The same reasoning is true in a larger network, of course, but as the number of hard drives and other networked resources grows so does your job of managing the network. Again, the key to successful resource sharing is understanding what network users want to accomplish. This includes not only individual job requirements, but also who must share data with whom. Are there groups of users who regularly share files for editing or approval? If so, you need a system for allowing easy access to the shared information, while ensuring that people who don't need this data or who aren't authorized for it can't get to it. Perhaps even more important, you need a system that reduces the possibility that the incorrect version of a file is used.

We've seen the "'wrong file" problem crop up in a number of networked businesses. For example, consider the bidding/contract cycle that occurs among a sales staff. The person who made the initial contact with a client writes the first draft of a proposal and asks a supervisor or another team member to review it. The review is completed and the changed file saved to a networked drive, but in a different location from the original. (You will find that computer users are habit-driven. It can sometimes be extremely difficult to persuade them to store files where you want them to instead of where they want to store them!) An E-mail message is sent to the first salesperson saying the proposal is ready to send. The original writer opens the original file—the one without the supervisor's changes—and prints the proposal for the client.

This problem results from the assumption that because you are in a networked environment, data is shared. It also results from the narrow-sighted view that the individual's directory and storage scheme is the correct one or the only one. Even in a small network of three or four people—and particularly if their computers are not physically close to each other so that over-the-partition conversation is possible—you need a workable design of shared disks and directories coupled with an agreed-upon procedure for managing such shared file problems.

One procedure that can reduce this type of problem is for everyone on the network to develop the habit of adding a footer—with the file name and path—on every document. Word processors, spreadsheet programs, presentation packages, and most other software will support some type of page footer. If this information is included with all documents, you can see easily where the file is stored. And, if you include the date and time so that it changes with each new load or print of the file (again, a feature supported by most of today's software) then you can determine when the version of the file you are viewing was last printed. Many software packages also include a document properties, statistics, or summary section where information about the last edit, the person who created the file, and so on is stored. Some of this information is automatically inserted, and there usually is room for custom data as well (see Figure 8.18).

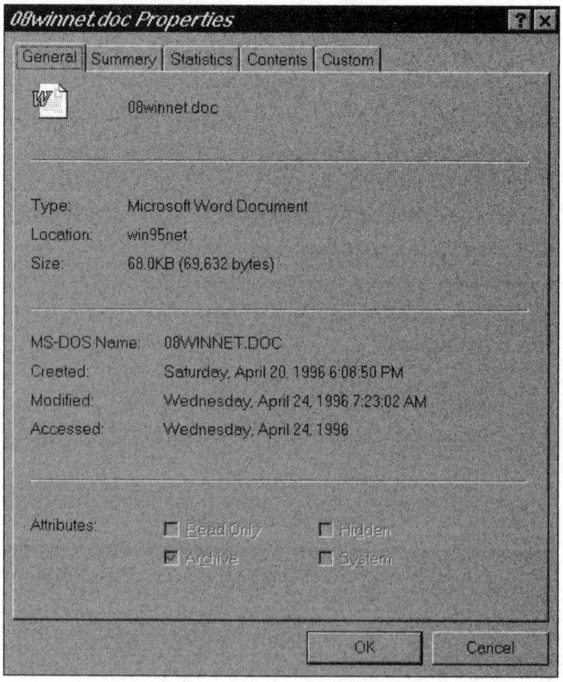

FIGURE 8.18 Microsoft Word Document Properties dialog box.

Again, the key to successful use of this kind of information is procedure and training. Users must be instructed to include the proper information on document footers, to habitually view the properties information, and to store documents in an agreed-upon location.

This problem is one where a logical directory and sharing structure for your network can help. You'll have to design a system that works for you, of course, but the following guidelines can help:

Consider a *server-based design*, even for a peer-to-peer network. That means: don't share everyone's disk drive with the network. Rather, establish a single computer as the data server, install enough storage to accommodate the storage needs of the network, and share only the server drives. This procedure channels all shared data through a single computer, making version tracking, updates, backups, and security easier to manage.

Use a *directory structure* that fits your data management needs. Just as a server-based network structure helps make data management easier, creating directories that help individual users track their files and makes it easy to share information will facilitate network use. In general, you need to separate data types. How you do this depends to a great degree on the number of users, the type of information you manage, and your own habits of use.

Here's one approach. Create separate directory branches for shared programs and shared data. We have used this structure successfully in small to medium-size networks. One directory off the root is named **prog** or **programs**; another directory off the root is named **data**.

Under the programs directory, create separate subdirectories for each class of application you are using: WP (for word processing), SS (for spreadsheets), Util (for utilities), DB (for database), and so on. Under the WP directory you might create directories for WinWord and WordPerfect, or whatever word processing software you are using. In the SS directory, create directories for Excel and 1-2-3. Of course, if you are using only one word processor and one spreadsheet on the network, you can simplify the structure by cutting out the WP and SS directories and create WinWord and Excel directories under the program directory. In the WinWord or Excel directory, you install the shared applications. Create similar directories for other networked applications.

Now for the data side. Again, if you use multiple word processing packages, create a general directory for WP under the data directory, then additional subdirectories for each word processing package beneath that. If you only use one word processor, then create a WP or WinWord directory under data to hold your word processing files. Also create an SS or Excel directory to hold spreadsheet information, and so on.

Then you can get creative to support the data needs of your individual or departmental users. We like to create individual directories for different types of data. In your word processing subdirectory, for example, you might have other directories for letters, proposals, contracts, technical, training, and so on. Depending on your work habits, you may also want additional subdirectories beneath some of these. For example, under proposals you might want a directory named originals, one named edited, and another named accepted. Then as you move a proposal through the entire process, you have a record of each proposal along its development path.

How do you ensure that each person along a document's development path adheres to the proper directory structure? Password-protect each directory and provide each user the password only to the directory or directories you want them to use. If one department or one person within a department always writes the original proposal, and then a supervisor or second-level sales staff reviews and edits it, then you give the person who creates the original read/write access to Originals, but read-only access to Edited. Likewise, the person or group who does the editing has read-only access to Originals and read/write access to Edited.

Use forms (boilerplate) to reduce redundant development and to reduce the possibilities of errors. Most modern software includes facilities for creating documents with fixed information and variable fields for individualized data for particular applications. Store the blank forms in one directory and the completed forms in one or more additional directories according to the type of data, the client, or the department that created the form.

Use *access management techniques* to control individual access to networked devices, directories, and information. We showed you earlier in this chapter how to password-protect access to networked components. You can't actually create user groups in a stand-alone Windows 95 network— not as you can with Windows NT or NetWare—but you can create some group access simply by controlling carefully who gets the passwords to which resources.

Software Licensing

We have mentioned in passing the importance of understanding the software licensing requirements of the applications you use on a network. It frequently is extremely easy to allow multiple users access to a single software application. But in most cases your purchase of a piece of software for a single user does not allow the application to be shared by multiple users.

Several national associations, including the Software Publishers Association, conduct programs seeking to find and prosecute major violators of licenses. In truth, your small company's chances of falling into their trap is remote, but nevertheless we want to encourage you to stay on the right side of the law.

Different companies license their software in different ways. Many companies let you install as many copies of a particular package as you like, but you can only use one copy at a time. Here's an easy way to think of one popular class of software licenses: when you bought this book, you received the right to use it as often as you like, to move it around from place to place, and even to lend it, give it, or resell it to another user. What you cannot do with this book, though, is make copies of it to give to others or appropriate it in whole or in part in a product of your own.

For other companies, more than one installation is a violation. And, if you have purchased a software package licensed for network installation, then it is licensed for a certain number of concurrent users, usually two, five, ten, twenty-five, and so on.

And the rules are changing. Microsoft, for one, has changed its previous policy of allowing multiple people to use an application as long as they don't use it concurrently. The Microsoft move requires businesses to purchase additional licenses if more than one user of a given application will ever access it, even if no more than one user at a time will use the software.

As you might expect, this move has created a lot of discussion and disagreement in the industry, and there is a slight chance that the policy could be modified. Read carefully the license that came with your software to understand precisely what your rights and responsibilities are with each package. If in doubt, contact the software manufacturer for information and ask for a ruling in writing. Then make sure you abide by what you learn.

Remote Administration

Remote administration tools built into Windows 95 are designed to let you assess and perhaps solve problems at individual user workstations without having to physically go to the user's location. Remote administration gives you access to the System Policy Editor (see the System Policy section later in this chapter), the Registry Editor, System Monitor, and Net Watcher.

To use these facilities remotely you must first enable **Remote Administration** on each workstation. Here's how to do that:

1. Open the Control Panel.
2. Double-click the **Passwords** icon to open the Password Properties dialog box.
3. Click the **Remote Administration** tab to bring it to the top of the display.
4. Click on the button beside **Enable Remote Administration**.
5. Type a password in the PASSWORD field and confirm it by typing it again in the CONFIRM PASSWORD field. Your display should now look like the one in Figure 8.19.

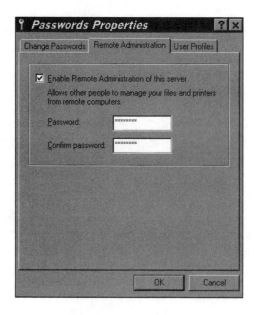

FIGURE 8.19 Remote Administration tab of Password Properties dialog box.

N O T E   If you are using a network that supports user-level security, your display will look slightly different. You will be allowed to enter a list of administrators who can access the remote administration facilities you just enabled. In addition, the range of remote administration duties you are able to perform may change with the type of network or networks you have installed.

If you are using a network that supports user-level security, you may want to enable **Remote Registry Services** to allow you to use the Remote Registry Editor facilities. Here's how to install remote registry services:

1. Open the Control Panel.
2. Double-click the **Network** icon.
3. Click on **Add**.
4. Double-click **Service** in the Select Network Component Type dialog box.
5. Click **Have Disk** in the Select Network Service dialog box.
6. Use **Browse** to enter the path to the utility you want to install on the Windows 95 distribution CD-ROM: **admin\nettools\remotreg**.
7. Click **OK**.
8. Click **Microsoft Remote Registry** in the Select Network Service dialog box (this should be selected by default).
9. Click **OK** to complete the installation. You should see Remote Registry in the Network Components list.

N O T E   You may be asked for the location of additional files during this installation. Enter the path to the Windows 95 source files on your CD-ROM (**win95**) or to the networked drive that contains the Windows 95 files if you have set up a network program server for these files.

You must install the Remote Registry utility on all computers with which it will be used, including the administrator's workstation.

Using System Monitor

The System Monitor is a network utility that lets you monitor the real-time performance of some networked components.

NOTE You can use System Monitor on a local machine with all networks. However, to monitor performance of a remote computer you must be using a network that supports user-level security and user-level security must be enabled. In addition, you must enable the **Remote Registry Service** as described earlier in this chapter.

You can display performance information in graphs and charts. As with many of the management tools, you probably won't concern yourself with too many performance issues in a small network. In a network with five, ten, or more users and especially one in a production environment where overall performance is important, then this tool may help you identify bottlenecks in data flow.

If you made a full installation of Windows 95, then the System Monitor will appear in the System Tools area under Accessories in your pop-up Programs list on the Start menu:

1. Click on **Start**.
2. Point to **Programs**, then to **Accessories**.
3. Point to **System Tools**. You should see the display in Figure 8.20.

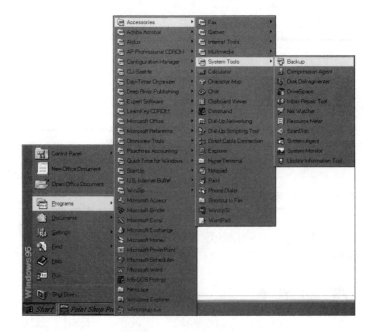

FIGURE 8.20 System Tools list.

4.   Click on **System Monitor** to launch the program.

If you don't see System Monitor listed here, you can install it from your distribution CD-ROM or diskettes:

1.   Open the Control Panel.
2.   Double-click **Add/Remove Programs**.
3.   Click the **Windows Setup** tab.
4.   Make sure **Accessories** is checked, then click **Details**.
5.   Make sure **System Monitor** is checked.

N O T E   If System Monitor was not installed originally, chances are other network tools were not installed. Now is a good time to check Net Watcher and the other tools shown in the Accessories list. In fact, why not install everything under Accessories so that you have access to the full range of accessories supplied with Windows 95?

6.   Click on **OK**.
7.   Click **OK** again to begin the installation.

To use this utility, click on **System Monitor** in the Accessories list, or use **Start**, **Run**, type **sysmon**, and click on **OK**. You will see a display like the one in Figure 8.21.

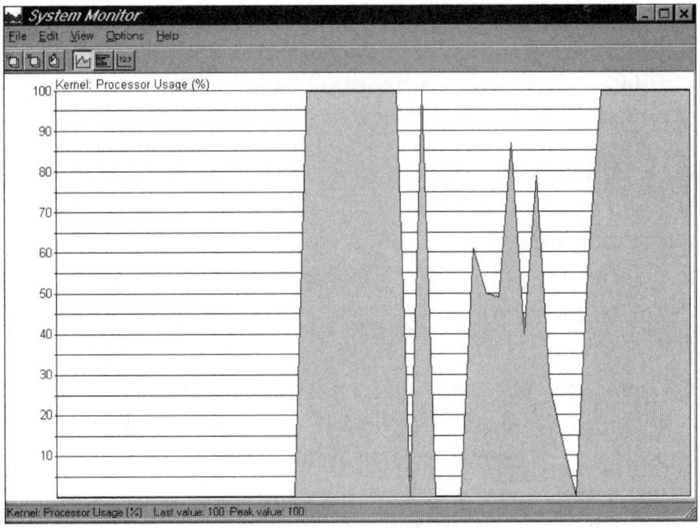

FIGURE 8.21 System Monitor display.

This display changes as the activity on your local machine changes. If you are using user-level security, click **File** and choose **Connect** to specify a remote machine you would like to monitor.

In addition, with user-level security enabled (which, remember, requires a network protocol other than Windows 95), you can specify other features to monitor. Click on **Edit** and choose **Add Item...** to display the dialog box shown in Figure 8.22.

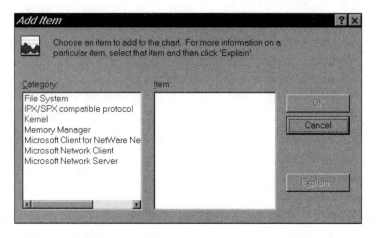

FIGURE 8.22 Add Item dialog box in System Monitor.

Choose an item to add to the monitoring, then click on **Explain** if you want more information about this item. You can also choose different types of information display (the type of chart, for example) by using the tool bar or the View menu.

Using Net Watcher

The Net Watcher utility is interesting and fun to use on any size Windows 95 network and it can become indispensable on a larger network, particularly when you want stronger administrative controls and when other users are not network-savvy.

With this program you can view connections to remote computers (those networked machines physically connected to the specified remote computer), you can display a list of open files on a remote computer, view what resources are shared, turn on sharing for devices on remote machines, and more. This is an excellent tool to help you understand how machines on your network are being used. If you allow individual users to determine what resources they are sharing on their own machines and what remote resources they access, then Net Watcher is especially important for an administrator. In fact, it is about the only way you can determine what resources are available and what is being used across the network.

In general, these are the services supported by this utility:

○ Show all shared resources on a specified machine.

○ Add a shared resource.

○ Stop sharing a shared resource.

○ Show all users connected to a remote machine.

○ Show all open files on a remote machine.

○ Close files other users have opened.

○ Disconnect a user.

If Net Watcher is not already installed (look in the Accessories list from Programs on the Start menu), you can install it with the **Add/Remove Programs** option in the Control Panel. Use the same process described under installation of the System Monitor in the previous section of this chapter.

To launch Net Watcher and connect to a remote machine:

1. Click on **Start** on the Task Bar.

2. Choose **Run** and type **netwatch** in the RUN field of this dialog box.

3. Click on **Administer** and choose **Select Server**.

4. Type the name of the computer to which you want to connect and observe using Net Watcher.

5. Type the password for remote administration on the remote computer. You will see the dialog box shown in Figure 8.23.

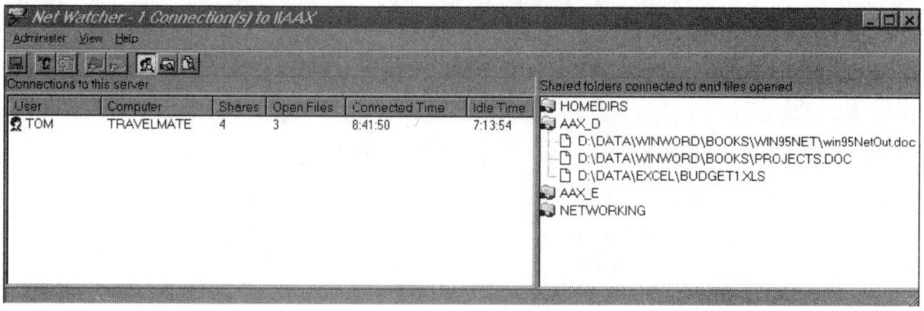

FIGURE 8.23 Net Watcher screen with remote server open.

NOTE This password varies with the type of security enabled on the remote computer. If the remote machine is running share-level security, then the password is the one you specified when you turned on **Remote Administration** (see a description of this process earlier in this chapter). If the remote machine is running user-level security (on a network other than or in addition to Windows 95), then the password is the one assigned to the Administrator account on this network.

This screen provides a lot of information about the specified server. You can see what computer or computers are currently connected to it, and what files are open (see the right side of the display). The larger the network and the more users, the more information and activity you will see with this utility.

Now change the view. Click **View** on the menu and choose **Shared Folders**. The display now looks like the one in Figure 8.24. The screen is reversed and the emphasis is changed to files instead of server.

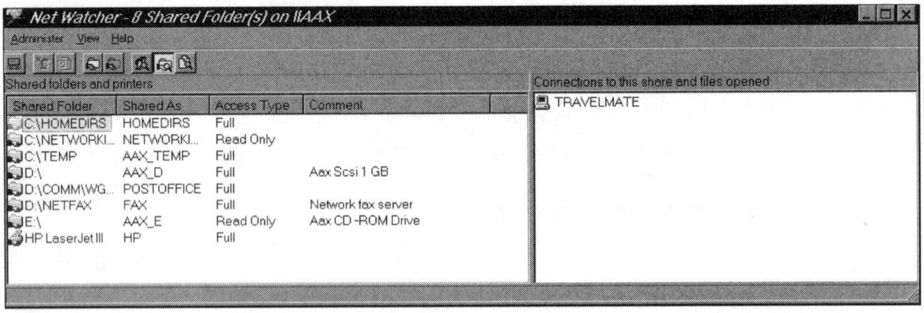

![Net Watcher window titled "Net Watcher - 8 Shared Folder(s) on IIAAX" with menu items Administer, View, Help. The left pane "Shared folders and printers" lists shared folders with columns Shared Folder, Shared As, Access Type, Comment. Entries include C:\HOMEDIRS (HOMEDIRS, Full), C:\NETWORKI... (NETWORKI..., Read Only), C:\TEMP (AAX_TEMP, Full), D:\ (AAX_D, Full, Aax Scsi 1 GB), D:\COMM\WG... (POSTOFFICE, Full), D:\NETFAX (FAX, Full, Network fax server), E:\ (AAX_E, Read Only, Aax CD-ROM Drive), HP LaserJet III (HP, Full). The right pane "Connections to this share and files opened" shows TRAVELMATE.]

FIGURE 8.24 View shared folders in Net Watcher.

Why is this view important? Suppose you are ready to run a backup utility on that server. Many backup routines won't copy open files (some force the file closed before trying to back them up; some don't). Thus, if you run a backup, the open files won't get copied. For a letter or proposal the damage is minimal. But suppose one of the open files is the corporate general ledger from your accounting system? If you make a backup and this file is missed, what will you do in the event of a server crash that destroys this file?

You also may want to study this view of a server just to determine who is doing what so as to get an idea of load, file location, and so on.

Now change the view again. Click **View** and choose **By Open Files**. The display now looks like the one in Figure 8.25.

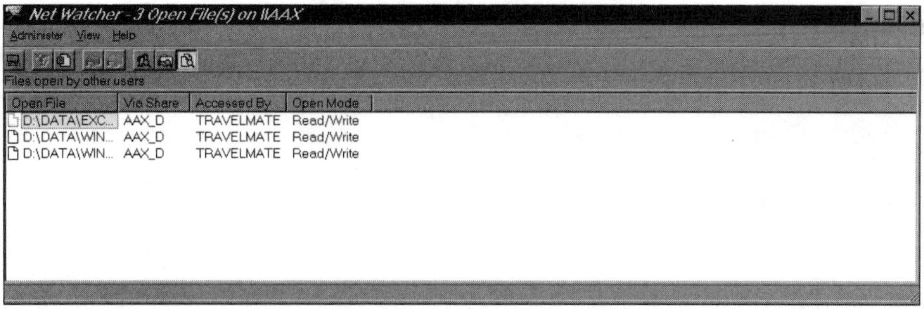

FIGURE 8.25 View By Open Files in Net Watcher.

This is just one more way to view and analyze activity on the specified server. Of course, if you want to see what is going on with another machine on the network, simply click **Administer** and choose another computer.

There's more to this useful utility. In addition to watching server activity, you can actually control remote machines over the network. Suppose you have Net Watcher set for the Open Files view shown in Figure 8.25. Now click on **Administer** and view your choices (see Figure 8.26).

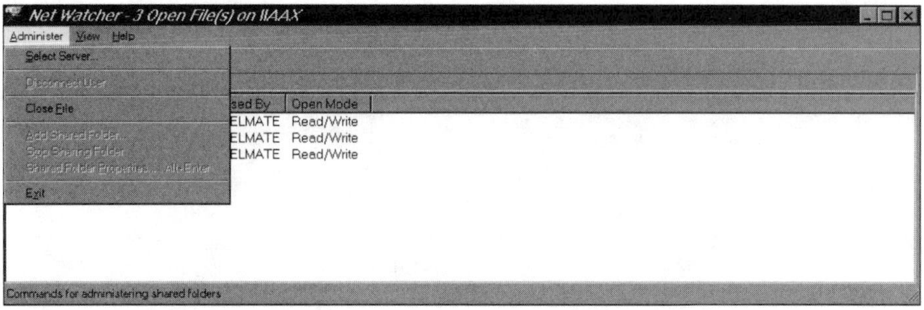

FIGURE 8.26 Administer menu with Net Watcher set for Open Files view.

You can select a server, of course, since this option is available in all views. But you also can close a selected file. Again, you might want to do this to conduct a backup or to free up a file opened by someone who then went home or out to lunch.

Change the view back to the one shown in Figure 8.24, Shared Folders. The Administer menu changes again, as shown in Figure 8.27.

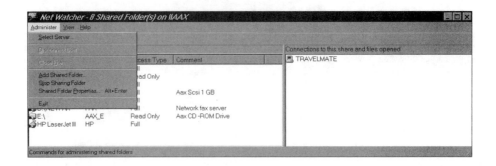

FIGURE 8.27   Administer menu with Net Watcher set for Shared Folders view.

Now you can add a shared folder, stop sharing a folder, or view the properties of one of the existing shared folders. Are you beginning to see the value of this remote administration facility? Even if the computers on your network are in different offices or behind locked doors, you can reconfigure the network as long as you have administrator privileges.

When you select a shared folder and choose **Shared Folder Properties** from the Administer menu (or press **Alt+Enter**), you will see the dialog box shown in Figure 8.28.

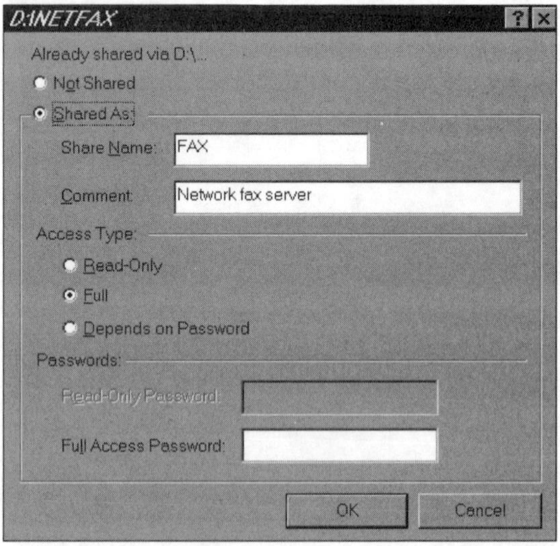

FIGURE 8.28 Share Folder Properties dialog box in Net Watcher.

This is a familiar dialog box. It is the one you use to establish a shared resource. The difference is that you are now viewing the properties of a folder on a remote computer, not the computer you are using. You can use this dialog box simply to view how a folder is shared (read-only, read/write, password-protected) or to change the properties. Suppose you want to add a password to a folder that currently is shared without one. Use this dialog box from Net Watcher.

Notice that printers and other devices show up in this Shared Folders display. You can view their share properties as well.

Finally, change back to the Connections-oriented view shown in Figure 8.23. When you click on **Administer**, the menu choices now look like Figure 8.29.

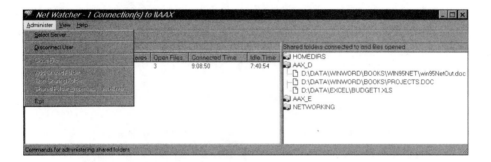

FIGURE 8.29 Net Watcher Administer menu in Connections view.

Now you have the option of disconnecting a user from the displayed server. Again, this is a useful capability when you want to conduct backups or when someone walks away from a computer without logging off the network.

Using the Registry Editor

The System Registry is an extremely important part of Windows 95. It is a database that keeps track of your system configuration, including what applications are installed. The registry is actually composed of several files that are updated as you change configuration.

Each computer on a Windows 95 network has its own registry, stored on the local hard drive. Under normal circumstances, most of us don't need to be concerned with the registry and, in fact, we don't really want to be. One false move in changing the registry, and you can make some or all of your Windows 95 or associated applications unusable. The registry is updated and maintained automatically by Windows 95 as it relates to the applications you install and use and as you manipulate the operating system itself through other utilities.

However, Windows 95 does include a Registry Editor for those times when you want to view the current configuration or make necessary changes. A full discussion of the Registry and the Registry Editor is beyond the scope of this book and should be considered an activity for system-savvy folk who really want to delve into the inner workings of their machines. However, we want to introduce the concept of the Registry and of editing this database so that you at least understand that it exists and you can use it if you need to. For example, there may be times when Microsoft Technical Support will ask you to open the Registry Editor and tell them about some settings or to change a configuration. Having experimented with the process will make your technical support tasks easier.

To launch the Registry Editor on a local machine, use the following steps:

1. Click **Start** on the Task Bar and choose **Run**.

2. Type **regedit** in the RUN field of this dialog box and click on **OK**. You will see the dialog box shown in Figure 8.30.

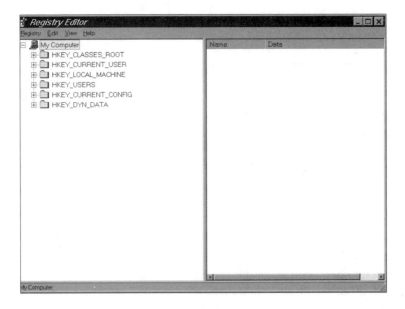

FIGURE 8.30 Regedit opening screen.

You can use this dialog box to browse your system. For example, notice that the Registry is segmented into different types of data, including information about the local machine, current configuration, and current user. This data is presented like the directory and drive structure of your computer in Microsoft Explorer. Notice that a folder symbol appears beside each major entry and that a plus sign (+) indicates that this particular folder can be opened to display additional information.

To see how this works, click on the + beside **Current User**. The display opens to show the list in Figure 8.31 (your display may be different, depending on your configuration).

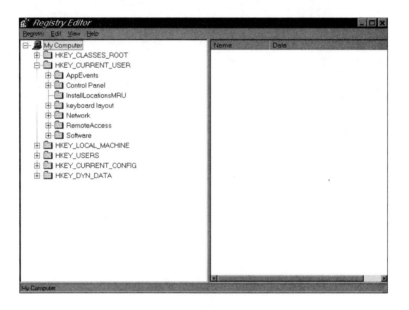

FIGURE 8.31 Current User display in Registry Editor.

Now click on the + beside **Network** to further expand the display. You should see other folders, including **persistent** and **recent**. This shows what network connections are established each time you log onto the network (**persistent**) and what connections you have most recently made (**recent**). Open up both of these folders to see a display similar to the one in Figure 8.32 (your display depends on how your network is configured).

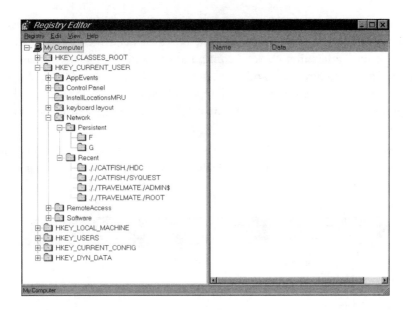

FIGURE 8.32 Persistent and Recent network folders in Registry Editor.

Try the same thing with **Local Machine**. You will see several folders that can be expanded to provide information about how your local machine (the one you are using right now) is configured. Notice that when you have opened the last folder in any hierarchical link (when a folder appears that does not have a plus sign beside it), you can select this folder and additional information appears in the right side of this dialog box. For example, if you open the **Local Machine** folder, choose **Network**, and then click on **Logon**, you will see information similar to (but not the same as) that shown in Figure 8.33.

FIGURE 8.33 Local Machine Network log-on display from Registry Editor.

This shows the primary network protocol in use, the file name for shared profiles (if any), the current user name, and so on. Obviously some of this data—such as user name—is quite dynamic, changing with each log-on or other change. The registry is updated automatically to reflect these changes.

NOTE

You can shrink the display by closing open folders. A folder that is displayed with a minus sign beside it (-) is open. A folder with a plus sign (+) is closed. Click on the - beside any folder to close it and shrink the display for that section.

You can edit information in the right side of the display (but don't do it!) by double-clicking on the name of any of the entries. When you do, a pop-up Edit dialog box like the one in Figure 8.34 will appear.

FIGURE 8.34 Pop-up Edit dialog box in Registry Editor.

You can make a change and click on **OK** to make the change. Again, you probably don't want to do this because the implications of changing registry information can run wide and deep throughout your system. In the event of a system problem, however, a Microsoft or other vendor's technical support representative may ask you to make some changes.

Now, suppose you need to change registry information on a remote machine. You could walk to that machine, log in, and make the changes right there, of course. Or, if you have enabled **Remote Registry Services**, as described earlier in this chapter in the section on setting up remote administration, then you can connect to the registry of a remote machine over the network.

Here's how to do that:

1. Open the Registry Editor as described above.

2. Click on **Registry** and choose **Connect Network Registry**.

3. Type the name of the remote server you want to access in the Connect Network Registry dialog box.

4. Click on **OK**. You should see the Registry information for the specified machine.

Once the remote registry is opened, you can browse that machine's configuration and make changes as required (careful!) just as we described for the local machine.

You must enable **user-level security** for remote registry operations to work. This means you must be using a network in addition to Windows 95.

N O T E

When you have finished viewing registry information, click on **Registry** and choose **Exit** to close the editor.

USING SYSTEM POLICIES

Windows 95's System Policies facility is either part of the operating system's security system or part of the System Registry system, depending on your orientation. As we mentioned in the previous section, the registry is a database of system data: users, applications, configurations, and so on. The registry is the standard point of reference on how things work and what does what in your system.

What do System Policies have to do with the Registry? A System Policy setting is similar to a Registry setting, except that when you enable policies, you override existing Registry settings for the computer or the local user.

And what does *that* have to do with system security? Well, for example, you can use Policies to enforce certain system configurations to restrict what certain users can do from the desktop and whether they are able to change configurations specified in the Control Panel. And you can use Policies to centrally configure such network settings as File and Printer Sharing services.

Why didn't we discuss Policies in detail in the Security section of this book? Because configuring and using policies is fairly esoteric, certainly more difficult to set up and use than other security features. We mention it here as a way to expand your control of your network as you gain understanding of what is possible and what is desirable in your particular situation.

Like the Registry, System Policies are controlled with a System Policy Editor. (By the way, you can use the System Policy Editor to edit Registry settings as well.)

First, a little technical background. In the Registry are two files that control some of the user-level and computer-level settings: **USER.DAT** and **SYSTEM.DAT**. These are system-level files that are normally hidden. The settings they contain are evoked when you log onto the network.

Now, if you enable System Policies, a third file, **CONFIG.POL**, is created, and the settings it contains overwrites those stored in **USER.DAT** and **SYSTEM.DAT**.

 NOTE Refer to the previous section on the Registry. Notice the `Hkey_Current_User` section of the registry in Figure 8.30. This section defines the contents of the **USER.DAT** file. The `Hkey_Local_Machine` section defines the contents of the **SYSTEM.DAT** file.

You must install some files from your Windows 95 distribution CD-ROM to use the System Policy Editor:

1. Open the Control Panel.
2. Double-click on the **Add/Remove Programs** icon.
3. Click the **Windows Setup** tab.
4. Click the **Have Disk** button.
5. Click **Browse** in the Install From Disk dialog box.
6. Browse to this directory on your Windows 95 CD-ROM: `ADMIN\APPTOOLS\POLEDIT`.
7. Click on **OK**, and then click **OK** again.
8. Make sure **System Policy Editor** and **Group Policies** are checked (click on each name to place a check mark in the box to the left of the name) and then click the **Install** button.

Once the editor is installed, you can run it:

1. Click on **Start** on the Task Bar.
2. Choose **Run**.
3. In the RUN field of this dialog box, type **poledit**. You will see the dialog box shown in Figure 8.35, which is pretty much a blank dialog box, like a text editor without a file loaded.

FIGURE 8.35 System Policy Editor dialog box.

With the editor installed and loaded, you have two choices. You can use the editor in Registry mode, which allows you to edit the local registry file (or a remote registry file, if you have user-level security). Or, you can use the editor in Policy File mode to create and edit the System Policy file on a local or remote machine.

To use the Registry Mode:

1. Click on **File**.
2. Click **Open Registry**. You should see a display similar to the one in Figure 8.36.

FIGURE 8.36 Open Registry in System Policy Editor.

3. Double-click on **Local User** or **Local Computer** to display some registry information about these entities (see Figure 8.37).

FIGURE 8.37 Local User detail from System Policy Editor.

4. Open additional folders to view or edit registry information. Remember to be very careful.

You can also use the following editor for System Policies:

1. Click on **File**.
2. Click **New File** (or **Open File...** if you have previously created a Policy File).

You will see a display very similar to the previous, Registry-mode display, but the title bar at the top of the Editor dialog box will show System Policy rather than Registry. If you clicked on **New**, then the file is untitled.

Notice that when you open a new System Policy file, the system preloads a set of user and computer settings from a default file. The icons are labeled

Default User and **Default Computer**. This way you have basic settings enabled and don't run the risk of enabling policies and leaving out something crucial.

To make changes in this basic default configuration, double-click on **Default User** or **Default Computer** to produce a display like the one in Figure 8.37.

You can add a new user or new computer to the editor display by clicking on **Edit** and choosing the appropriate menu item. A new icon will appear in the Editor display.

As with the Registry Editor, you can use the System Policy Editor to view or change settings on a remote (networked) machine, but you must have user-level security settings enabled on both machines.

N O T E

Again, setting and changing System Policies is an advanced topic, beyond the intended scope of this book. However, we wanted to introduce the concept to give you some room for growth and help you respond to suggestions from technical support personnel. You can get more information on using the System Policy Editor—and on establishing and using System Policies in general—from the Windows 95 Resource Kit included on your Windows 95 distribution CD-ROM.

That said, let's work through one simple example of setting a System Policy, just to give you the idea. Suppose you want to restrict a user's ability to edit Network settings in the Control Panel, a good idea if you are charged with managing a network of more than a few users and you don't want to have to continually troubleshoot connection problems caused by a user's misguided attempt to be helpful.

Here's how to use the System Policy Editor to do that:

1. From the System Policy Editor on the machine you want to configure, click on **Edit** and choose **Add User....**

2. Type a valid network user name when the Add User dialog box asks for it.

3. Double-click on the new icon created for this user to display settings for that user.

4. Click on the **Control Panel** folder to open it.

5. Click on the **Network folder** under Control Panel to open it.

6. Click on **Restrict Network Control Panel** to produce the display in Figure 8.38.

FIGURE 8.38 Restrict Network Control Panel display from System Policy Editor.

7. Choose one or more restrictions from the list at the bottom of the display.

8. Click on **OK** to close the Properties dialog box for this user.

That's the idea. And there are many more features you can control with this useful tool. The best way to become conversant with it is to use it and to read the information available on your Windows 95 distribution CD-ROM.

WHAT'S NEXT?

That's about it. With the information in this chapter we have covered all the major procedures you will ever need associated with Windows 95 networking. Oh, there are other things that you may want to use as you become more advanced in Windows 95 networking, but we've covered the basics.

The rest of this book deals with reference material you may need as you conduct some of the operations we suggest in this book. The next chapter, for example, is a troubleshooting reference, to help you solve potential problems in configuring your network. Later material offers some technical references, points you in the direction of some suppliers of networking products, and provides the obligatory glossary and index.

So what's next from here? Hook up your network, use the expanded features and facilities you get from a network, and expand your knowledge as you work with the system.

CHAPTER NINE

Troubleshooting a Windows 95 Network

W e hope you don't have any problems with your Windows 95 network. And, for the most part, you shouldn't. This network scheme is, according to our experience, easy to configure and use and very reliable.

The reality of using computers, however, is that problems are bound to arise. In this chapter we will discuss some common problems we have observed with networks in general and with Windows 95 in particular; we'll offer some suggestions for locating and correcting problems; and we'll provide information on a few more utilities included with Windows 95 to help you evaluate your network and help you with your own troubleshooting.

CABLE PROBLEMS

You can't say that any one part of the network is more important than any other. Without all network components, the network doesn't function. However, the cable that connects computer to computer is certainly among the more important components, and it is one of the components that frequently causes problems.

Cable problems can be obvious or they can be nearly impossible to find. We have been surprised to learn from bitter experience how difficult it can be to diagnose and then to find a network cable problem. However, a little experience can help.

The problem with most network cable problems is that they are intermittent. Everything may work fine one afternoon, but the next morning one or more machines aren't visible to the rest of the network. You may reboot everything, spend some time worrying over the problem, and things start working again. You naturally assume it was a software or driver problem that was corrected by your actions. That is, until one of your networked servers or clients mysteriously disconnects itself from the network again.

When this starts happening, first suspect a cable problem. While it is true that memory problems or a bad network driver on an individual machine can cause similar symptoms, when whole segments of the network are acting up, or when a machine that worked today doesn't work tomorrow, suspect a cable problem.

If you suspect a cable problem, here are some hints to help you track it down.

10Base2 Networks

Check for loose terminators. Remember that a 10Base2 topology is an end-to-end network that requires cable terminators at each end of the backbone. More times than we want to count, we have brought a network down while adding a cable segment by forgetting to reinstall the terminator at the end or by installing it loosely. When cable problems develop on a 10Base2 network, go first to the ends of the network and make sure the terminators are properly installed.

Downsize the network. If the network ends are properly terminated but you still have a network problem, chances are there is a loose connector at one of the connections to a workstation. And, with a 10Base2 network, one bad connection can cause problems for the whole network. One troubleshooting technique is to remove network components a few at a time until the network functions, then replace connections one at a time to identify the problem.

Do a "binary search" for the problem, if you haven't a clue where it lies. You'll need two more terminators and a "Tee" connector to try this technique. When you have collected the extra hardware, follow these steps to complete the search:

1. Disconnect one side of the network at the Tee connector on the workstation midway in the network.

2. Attach a terminator to the free end of the network cable you removed from the tee. You'll need to place a tee on the cable end, then attach the

terminator to the other end of the tee. This isolates one network segment from another.

3. Test both segments of the network. One segments should work and the other probably won't. Now you have narrowed down the problem to only half of the total network length.

4. Repeat the segmentation process on the section of the network that is not functioning. Again, one of the new segments should work and the other should not.

5. Repeat this process until you have identified the machine causing problems.

Once you know where the problem is, you can try these steps to correct it:

1. Replace the cable segment that runs from the Tee connector on this machine to the section of the network that isn't functioning properly.

2. Replace the tee on this machine. It doesn't happen too often, but sometimes a tee that looks perfectly good is loose or shorted inside.

3. If you can't replace the cable segment, cut off the BNC connector at the end of the cable and replace it. (You'll need special tools to do this. If you don't know how to crimp or solder new BNC connectors, you can get instructions from cable manufacturers or distributors.)

If none of this works, your problem may be a bad network interface card (NIC) instead of a cable problem. Replace the card.

10BaseT Networks

Isolating cable problems on a 10BaseT network is easier than on a coax network because the design of the network itself keeps individual workstations isolated. That's one of the strengths of 10BaseT. When a workstation in a 10BaseT network can't access other network components, the problem must be in one of three places:

❍ On the cable segment that attaches the isolated computer to the nearest hub

❍ In the port on the hub to which this computer is attached

❍ In the NIC that attaches the computer to the network

Test the cable segment by replacing the cable, if that is practical. If, because of cable length or how it is run, this isn't practical, replace the connectors, one at a time, to determine if there is a bad connector.

NOTE We have seen problems with some cables because the RJ45 connectors are slightly too-small for the jack on the NIC or hub. Sometimes just wiggling the cable at the jack will restore network traffic. If this is the case, replace the connector with one that better fits the connector on the other end.

Are the other machines connected to this hub working properly? If so, then the entire hub isn't bad. Test whether the port hub is bad by moving the cable that runs to the computer that isn't working to another port on the same hub.

Test the NIC by swapping it out with one from another computer that is working properly.

Are all of the machines connected to a particular hub off the network? Obviously the problem has to do with the hub. Here are some things you can check:

❍ Is power connected to the hub? Status and power-on lights should appear on the front or rear of the hub.

❍ Is the hub attached to another network segment through a 10Base2 link? Check the coaxial cable, Tee connector, and terminator associated with this segment of the network to make sure the link to the hub is functioning.

❍ Unplug all network segments and reconnect them one at a time. Do some segments work while others do not? A malfunctioning segment shouldn't cause the rest of the hub to go down, but it can happen.

❍ Check the test lamps on your hub; this is one reason to buy a hub that delivers as much information as possible through its own reports.

❍ Replace the hub. This is the best test of the hub. If a replacement hub works properly, then you can begin to troubleshoot the malfunctioning hub.

NETWORK INTERFACE CARD PROBLEMS

Sometimes it is difficult to determine whether a network problem is the cable or the NIC. After you have tried the cable troubleshooting techniques described in the previous section, if you suspect an NIC problem, the best and surest method of troubleshooting it is to replace the card. Even if you are using a fairly high-end card, the cost of replacement is relatively low compared to time lost trying to troubleshoot an existing card and lost productivity caused by a bad network connection.

Some interface cards include indicator lights to show when network traffic is flowing through the card. If these lights are dark, then either the card is bad or you have a bad cable. Try replacing the cable or its connectors first. If you still can't get the indicator lights on your card to light, then proceed to troubleshoot the card.

In fact, with even a relatively small network, it is a good idea to have in stock at least one spare NIC of the same type and configuration. This is the best insurance against possible interface card problems. After a faulty card is replaced, you can send that card to a repair facility if you wish or (a more sensible move, given the cost of these devices) throw it away and buy another replacement.

Even if you replace a suspect card, there are some things you may have to check or change:

○ Make sure the card is set for the proper I/O address and interrupt. Check the documentation that came with your card for information on how to do this. Most NICs are configured with software and Windows 95 can probably do this for you. Read the documentation to be sure.

○ Ensure that the proper card is specified in the Windows 95 Network section (double-click on the **Network** icon in the Control Panel).

GENERAL CONNECT AND SOFTWARE PROBLEMS

Sometimes you may experience connection problems on your network that can't be traced to a bad cable or NIC. Here are some general starting points to give you a few more places to look for problems:

○ Remember the basic question of troubleshooting: What changes have you made since the last time the system worked properly? Undo the changes and see if the problem is fixed.

○ Open the Network dialog box (double-click on the **Network** icon in the Control Panel) on a machine that is not visible to the rest of the network. Click on **File and Printer Sharing**. Does this machine have sharing enabled?

If not, that explains why no one else on the network can access it. This can happen with new network machines if you forget to turn on sharing.

❑ Check for drive or other device mappings on machines that can't attach to a specific machine on the network. We have occasionally installed a new network machine, then forgotten to map its drives on remote computers.

❑ Check and then double-check the configuration for your network in the Network dialog box. Follow these steps:

○ You must have a network protocol installed that is compatible with the rest of the network.

○ You must be using the proper network client.

○ If you are using TCP/IP, you must have the proper configuration settings for all machines.

○ You must make sure that the proper network interface card is selected.

WINDOWS 95 TCP/IP TROUBLESHOOTING TOOLS

Whether or not you have hardware problems, you may want to use some of the intrinsic Windows 95 tools and utilities for TCP/IP network research, tuning, and so forth. As with most software products, the best way to become proficient with these utilities is to use them. In this section, we'll show you how to launch these programs and examine their general operation. Then we'll leave it up to you to get the most out of them.

Ping

If part of your network connections are over TCP/IP—and they probably are if there is a UNIX machine somewhere on your net, perhaps as part of an Internet connection—then you will find the Ping utility helpful. Ping is used to verify a physical connection between your local machine and a specified remote host. We like to think of Ping as network sonar. You send out a signal for your machine and "bounce" it off of a specific machine somewhere else on the network. If a physical connection exists, the Ping utility tells you how long it took for your message to reach the remote machine.

Ping is built into Windows 95 and should be available to you whenever you have enabled the TCP/IP networking protocol. The syntax for using Ping is:

```
ping <IP Address>
```

The <IP Address> part of this command is the Internet Protocol address of the machine you want to ping. You can run Ping from the MS DOS prompt (recommended) or by clicking on **Start** on the Task Bar, choosing **Run**, and typing **Ping <IP Address>** in the RUN field of this dialog box. However, when the program is launched from the Run menu, the MS DOS window is closed when the program ends.

Type ping without an argument to display this command help:

N O T E

```
Usage: ping [-t] [-a] [-n count] [-l size] [-f] [-i TTL] [-v TOS]

            [-r count] [-s count] [[-j host-list] | [-k host-list]]

            [-w timeout] destination-list
Options:

    -t              Ping the specified host until interrupted.

    -a              Resolve addresses to hostnames.

    -n count        Number of echo requests to send.

    -l size         Send buffer size.

    -f              Set Don't Fragment flag in packet.

    -i TTL          Time To Live.

    -v TOS          Type Of Service.

    -r count        Record route for count hops.

    -s count        Timestamp for count hops.

    -j host-list    Loose source route along host-list.

    -k host-list    Strict source route along host-list.

    -w timeout      Timeout in milliseconds to wait for each reply.
```

If you use Ping with just an IP address to a valid machine that your computer can reach, you will see output similar to what you see in Figure 9.1.

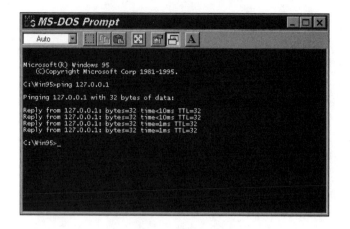

FIGURE 9.1 Sample Ping output.

This standard output shows how many bytes of data were returned by the specified remote computer and how long (in milliseconds) the response required. By studying these return times you get an idea of the quality of your network connection and of the distance from your local machine to the remote computer. If you are attached with a dial-up modem connection the return times will obviously be longer than if you are on a 10 Mbps network link.

NOTE The IP Address `127.0.0.1` is a built-in loop-back address that will show you how the **Ping** command works. If you have configured your machine for TCP/IP and it has been assigned its own IP address, then use that address instead of the loop-back address. If you are attached to a local or remote network (such as the Internet) with other machines that have IP addresses, then you can use Ping to test the link to one or more of the remote computers.

If you enter an invalid IP address for the current network, you will see an error message. Ping will either say that the address is invalid or that the specified host cannot be reached. If you know that the specified IP address is correct but Ping can't locate it, there is something amiss with your network connection. If you are on a dial-up connection, check your modem and phone line. Sometimes a dial-up connection will spontaneously drop because of difficulties on one end of the link or the other. The solution is to redial the remote host, log in again, and try your Ping test again.

If Ping can't find a specified host on a permanent network connection, the machine you are trying to reach may be turned off or disconnected from the network. Also, make sure the IP address you specify is a valid address for the machine you are trying to Ping.

You can send the output of the **Ping** command to a file or to your printer by redirecting the output with the > symbol after the command. To print the output, for example, use the command like this:

```
Ping 127.0.0.1 >prn
```

You can send the output to a file in the same way:

```
Ping 127.0.0.1 >pingoutput.txt
```

You can use whatever file name you want. We have suggested **pingoutput.txt** as one possibility.

Notice that by default the **Ping** command sends five packets to the specified remote computer. This is usually enough if you just want to verify that a particular computer is online and responding to network packets. If you are trying to pinpoint a network problem—particularly an intermittent one—then you might want to increase the number of transmissions so you can watch for changes.

For example, use Ping 127.0.0.1 -t to have Ping send packets to the specified address (again, substitute the IP address for a machine on your network for the loop-back address we have used in this example) until it is interrupted. If you use this command switch, stop Ping execution by holding down the **Ctrl** key and pressing **C** (**Ctrl+C**).

You can specify the precise number of packets to send to the remote host with the -n switch on the **Ping** command. For example, to send 20 packets instead of the default 5, use the command this way:

```
Ping 127.0.0.1 -n 20
```

And you can use Ping to learn something about the route across the network from your machine to the remote host and back again. Use the -r (route) switch:

```
Ping 127.0.0.1 -r 5
```

The number after the -r switch tells Ping how many hops to report along the route. You can enter a number from 1 to 9 after the -r switch to report up to nine hops along the way from your local machine to the specified remote host.

Tracert

The **Tracert** command is a standalone utility that traces the route from your local machine to a specified remote host. (See the discussion of Ping with the -r switch in the previous section.) Like the **Ping** command, Tracert uses the IP address of a remote host as the main argument, as shown here:

```
Tracert <IP Address>
```

You are shown the route from your machine to the remote host. The more computers between you and the remote machine, the more information you will see as the result of this command.

NOTE

Enter the **Tracert** command without an argument to view the command help shown here:

```
Usage: tracert [-d] [-h maximum_hops] [-j host-list] [-w timeout]
target_name
Options:
-d                 Do not resolve addresses to hostnames.
-h maximum_hops Maximum number of hops to search for target.
-j host-list    Loose source route along host-list.
-w timeout      Wait timeout milliseconds for each reply.
```

Tracert isn't particularly smart. If you use the command with an invalid IP address, the utility will wait indefinitely for a reply. You can use **Ctrl+C** to stop Tracert execution if it seems to "hang" waiting for a response from an invalid host.

Netstat

The Netstat utility is yet another routine you can use to study the state of your TCP/IP network. What you see in the display after starting Netstat depends on the configuration of your network, of course, but in general you should see a display of active network connections that includes information about the protocol in use, the local address, the remote address, and the state of the connection.

Use the **netstat** /? command to display a command reference like the one shown in Figure 9.2.

N O T E

```
C:\Win95>netstat /?

Displays protocol statistics and current TCP/IP network connections.

NETSTAT [-a] [-e] [-n] [-s] [-p proto] [-r] [interval]

  -a           Displays all connections and listening ports.  (Server-side
               connections are normally not shown).
  -e           Displays Ethernet statistics.  This may be combined with the -s
               option.
  -n           Displays addresses and port numbers in numerical form.
  -p proto     Shows connections for the protocol specified by proto; proto
               may be tcp or udp.  If used with the -s option to display
               per-protocol statistics, proto may be tcp, udp, or ip.
  -r           Displays the contents of the routing table.
  -s           Displays per-protocol statistics.  By default, statistics are
               shown for TCP, UDP and IP; the -p option may be used to specify
               a subset of the default.
  interval     Redisplays selected statistics, pausing interval seconds
               between each display.  Press CTRL+C to stop redisplaying
               statistics.  If omitted, netstat will print the current
               configuration information once.
```

FIGURE 9.2 Netstat command reference.

Net Diag

The Net Diag utility lets you establish a diagnostic host on one network computer and then test the network links to this server from other computers on the network. This is a command-line (MS DOS) utility like the others we have discussed in this chapter. To use Net Diag:

1. Type **Net Diag** at the command line of the machine you want to configure as a diagnostic server. The utility will display a list of network protocols in use.

2. Press the number that represents the protocol you want to test.

3. Press **N** (for no) when you are asked if another machine on the network is serving as a diagnostic server. The network diagnostic server starts on the local machine.

4. Go to another machine on the network and type **Net Diag** on the command line. A message is displayed that shows the protocols in use.

5. Press the number that represents the protocol you want to test. You will see a message that indicates the diagnostic server has been detected, and the test begins.

WinIPcfg

You can use the WinIPcfg utility to view or edit TCP/IP values. Launch WinIPcfg from the Start menu by choosing **Run** and typing `winipcfg` on the Run line of this dialog box. You will see a display similar to the one in Figure 9.3.

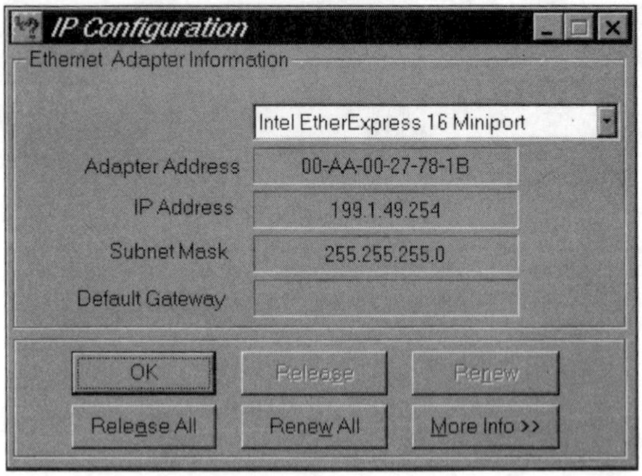

FIGURE 9.3 WinIPcfg opening dialog box.

Click on the **More Info>>** button to expand the display, like the sample in Figure 9.4.

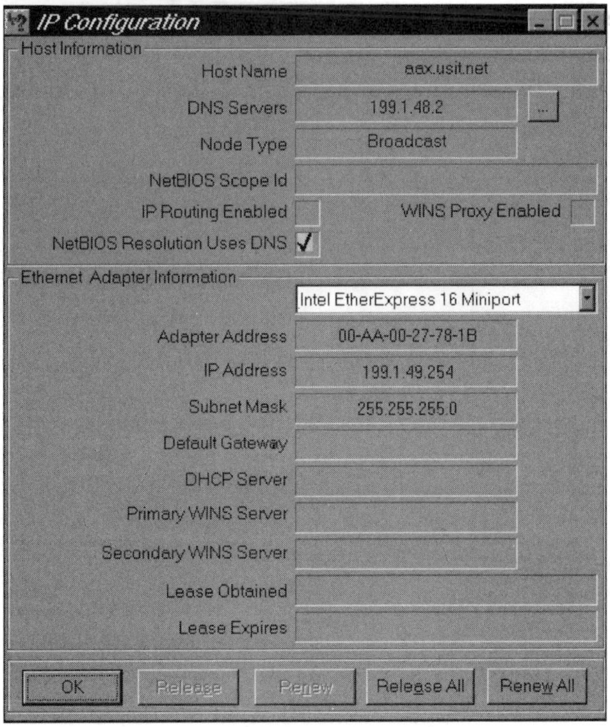

FIGURE 9.4 More Info>> display from WinIPcfg.

Of course, the information in your display will be different from this sample, because it depends on how your network is configured, what IP addresses are in use, and so on. If you are using dynamic IP addressing (an IP address assigned by the host) and you have the **PPP Adapter** selected, you will see zeros in the IP address fields.

If you have more than one value specified for a field, a button appears to let you toggle among the values (notice the button beside the Dns servers field in Figure 9.4).

WHAT'S NEXT?

Use the information in this chapter to help you set right a network problem. Following this information is a brief reference on technical aspects of Windows 95 networking, plus some information on where you can find networking-related hardware and software.

In fact, if you have read at least parts of this book, you are ready to relegate the whole thing to a deskside reference to help you expand an existing network, troubleshoot a network, or guide you through setting up a second network at home or at the office.

Technical Reference

We said in the beginning we didn't want this book to be too technical. We still don't. However, you may find the information in this chapter useful as you learn your way around Windows 95, set up your network, and use it.

We'll offer some suggestions for sources for some of the hardware and other stuff you may need in building a network. We can't really endorse any particular vendor; different companies are better at different things. However, the sources we list here are among the prominent and popular companies and, at the very least, offer you a starting point for price and feature comparison.

Enjoy!

EXPLORING WINDOWS 95

We've spent most of the space in this book discussing Windows 95 networking. Occasionally we offered a general Windows 95 tip, but there is much, much more in this operating system that you may find useful as you start Windows 95 networking. A good place to start learning your way around is in the Operating System itself.

Particularly if you have the CD-ROM version, you can find a lot of information and utilities that aren't documented or are hardly documented anywhere. To get started exploring Windows 95, insert the distribution CD and wait a few seconds. You should see the display in Figure A.1.

FIGURE A.1 Windows 95 CD-ROM AutoStart screen.

This display demonstrates the autostart features of Windows 95. When Windows detects an autostart file on a CD-ROM, it launches that file automatically as soon as the disk is inserted.

You can learn something about what is on the disk by clicking on the buttons on this browser display. The Windows 95 Tour, for example, will show you some of the main features of Windows 95. You can click the **Add/Remove Software** button to install new applications or remove existing ones. This is the same routine you can access from the Control Panel.

The HoverCraft game is nice, if you like that sort of thing, and the Cool Video selection shows you some of the power of the CD-ROM and Windows 95 combination. This is truly a multimedia environment that is strong in video and sound.

Now try this. Click on the **Browse This CD** button. You will see a display similar to the one in Figure A.2.

FIGURE A.2 The Browse This CD dialog box.

For information on custom drivers for selected computers:

○ Double-click on the **Drivers** folder on this display.

○ Choose **Network** from the next folder list. You will see another collection of folders with computer names: Compaq, IBM, and so on. These are special files that can help you solve networking problems with specific machines.

○ To find out more about these drives, choose **HCL Help** or **HCL.RTF**. *HCL* stands for Hardware Compatibility List. The Help version gives you details on special drivers in Windows 95 Help format. The **HCL.RTF** file is in Rich Text Format and will load Microsoft Word automatically to provide a text display you can read or print.

Using the MSD Utility

From the Browse This CD dialog box, double-click on **Other** to display another folder list. Choose **MSD** and you will see a dialog box with a single folder labeled **msd**. This is an older Microsoft System Diagnostic utility that shipped with previous versions of DOS and Windows.

Double-click on the **msd** icon to run the program. You will see a warning screen saying that Windows was detected and suggesting that you exit Windows to DOS and run the program again. Click on **OK** to continue with the program anyway, since you can't really exit to DOS without Windows in Windows 95 (you can choose the **MS-DOS** icon to enter a DOS window, but you can't run DOS without Windows 95). You will see a display similar to the one in Figure A.3.

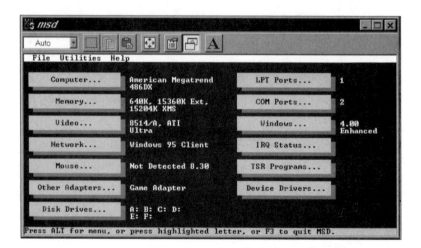

FIGURE A.3 MSD main screen.

As you can see, this utility provides general information about the configuration of your computer, including which network client you are running, the type of CPU, and so on. Click on any of the displayed buttons for additional information about any of these topics.

For example, if you click on the **Network** button, you will see a display similar to the one in Figure A.4.

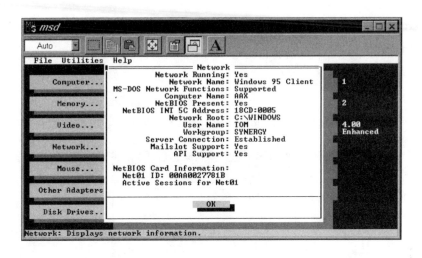

FIGURE A.4 The Network Information dialog windows from MSD.

Click on the **Disk Drives** button for information about all of the drives available to your system. This includes the local drives as well as any active network drives. This display will tell you what type of drive is assigned to each drive letter, including capacity and other information. However, you may not see full information about remote drives.

SNMP and System Management Information

What else can you find of interest on your distribution CD-ROM?

Double-click on the **Admin** folder for a dialog box with some useful options. Choose **nettools** and then **snmp**. The **SNMP.TXT** file in this folder will describe how to install the Simple Network Management Protocol (SNMP) on networks that support this useful network-monitoring tool.

On a network with two or three computers you may not want to try snmp monitoring, but in even a small office with a couple of printers and half a dozen or more computers, the ability to remotely monitor the status of your network hardware could be useful.

Windows 95 Resource Kit

One of the other folders inside the Admin folder is the mother load of Windows 95 information. Here's how to get to it:

1. From inside the Admin folder, double-click on **Reskit**.
2. Double-click on **Helpfile** to produce the display in Figure A.5.

FIGURE A.5 Helpfile folder display.

3. Double-click on **Win95rk.hlp** and you will load the Windows 95 Resource Kit in Windows Help File format (see Figure A.6).

FIGURE A.6 Win95rk.hlp opening display.

4. Choose a topic, any topic. You can browse the topic list by working with the Default tab in this Help file, or you can search for topics using the Index or Find tabs.

NOTE Double-click the **Samples** folder inside the Resource Kit folder and select policies or scripts for a number of sample files to help you get started with autologin scripts, policy settings, and more.

Suppose you want more information about remote administration, including SNMP, the topic we just barely introduced in the previous section. Here's how to get it:

1. Click on the **Index** tab to give it *focus* (bring it to the front of the display).

2. In the "Type the first few letters of the word you are looking for" field of this display, type **snmp**. As you type each letter, the Help routine will jump to the first location in the file that matches this letter combination. After you finish entering **snmp**, your display should look like the one in Figure A.7.

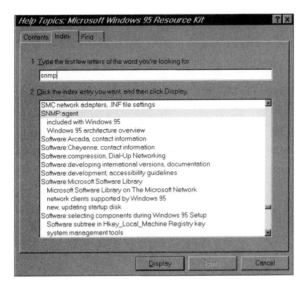

FIGURE A.7 Resource Kit Index with snmp search.

3. Double-click on **snmp agent**, the first entry highlighted. You will see a display with additional topics. Choose **Sources for Windows 95 System Management Tools** to display the dialog box shown in Figure A.8.

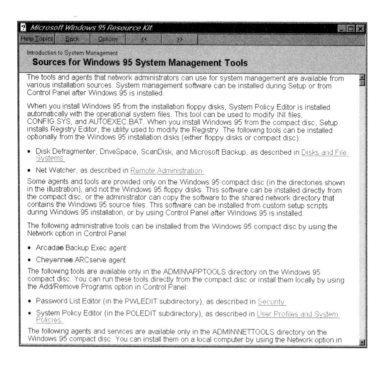

FIGURE A.8 Remote Administration dialog box.

4. Use the vertical scroll bar to display the bottom of this dialog box. There you will see additional sources of information on system management tools.

You can locate virtually any Windows 95 topic this way. As with all Windows 95 Help files, some topics are covered in more detail than others; some searches will turn up many subtopics, others only one or two. But this file contains a wealth of information about using Windows 95 and about Windows 95 networking topics.

Do you have some Macintosh users on your network who are moving to Windows 95? There's help in this folder for them as well. In the Helpfile folder, double-click on the **MACUSERS.HLP** file for some hints on making the switch.

An additional useful Help file is **TOUR4ADMIN.HLP**. This file offers a guided tour of Windows 95 for system administrators. Expand each of the topics and read as desired. This Help file is basically an introduction to the Windows 95 concept, showing, for example, how the user interface works, how the system is designed, and so on. It is a good starting place for new users or for administrators who have installed one or two systems and who are contemplating migrating the entire network to Windows 95. This file will help you evaluate Windows 95 in terms of your system needs and conventions and will show you some cost comparisons and other data that might be useful.

Well, you get the idea. The Windows 95 Resource Kit (which is actually a huge Windows Help file) is an invaluable resource. Remember, too, that you can print these Help topics a page at a time or several pages together. You'll probably get into the habit of referring to the Resource Kit regularly as you work with Windows 95 and Windows 95 networking.

Using Serial Line Internet Protocol

Earlier in this book we showed you how to connect to the Internet and to other Windows 95 machines using the Point to Point protocol (PPP). An older protocol, and one that is still used by many host computers, is the Serial Line Internet Protocol (SLIP). Although the Windows 95 installer doesn't automatically make SLIP available to you, you can use it by accessing it off of the distribution CD (SLIP facilities are not supplied with the diskette version of Windows 95).

Here's how to access the SLIP tools on your Windows 95 CD:

1. Click on the **Browse** button on the Autorun dialog box.
2. Double-click the **Admin** folder on the next display.
3. Double-click the **Apptools** folder on the next dialog box.
4. Double-click on the folder labeled **descript**.
5. Double-click on the **DESCRIPT.TXT** folder to launch Notepad. There you can read how to use the remaining folders in this group, including SLIP and the scripting tool to automate remote computer login.

Use the Windows 95 Resource Kit to search for SLIP to get more information about using these facilities.

T I P

Using Batch Setup

If you are installing Windows 95 and networking on one or two machines, you'll probably do it in the normal way, by running **Setup** and answering the required questions one at a time. If you are managing a larger network and you want to be able to install Windows 95 and networking so that it is the same on all machines, you might decide to do it with a batch script.

A *batch script* is like an automatic input routine for the Setup program. You first create an **MSBATCH.INF** file that contains as many parameters as you want to preconfigure, then you run **Setup** to use these parameters.

T I P   The Windows 95 Resource Kit (available on your distribution CD-ROM, remember?) has two sections to help you use batch setup. Look first in chapter 5 of the kit "Custom, Automated, and Push Installations." Also, check out the kit's appendix D for a reference on batch file parameters.

To locate batch setup facilities:

1. From the Admin folder, double-click on **Nettools**.
2. Double-click on **NetSetup** to display the files shown in Figure A.9.

FIGURE A.9 NetSetup folder contents.

3. Double-click BATCH.TXT to launch Notepad and open this text file that describes the basic batch process and points you to additional resources.

In this same folder you can find information about other useful tools to help you manage a relatively large and/or growing network. For example, the NETSETUP.EXE file runs a Wizard to help you place the Windows 95 software on a network server so that users can install files form a remote location. To get more information on this facility, double-click on NETSETUP.TXT to launch Notepad and display the text of this description file.

Buying or Making Cables

One of the crucial components of any network is the wire you use to connect one machine to another. Your computer dealer can probably sell you preconfigured cables to build your network. For a relatively small network, simply purchasing cables in precut lengths with the required connectors already installed on each end is the cheapest and easiest approach.

As your network grows and the wiring becomes more complex, however, you may want to consider buying bulk cable and wiring your own. Remember that two types of cable are possible with Windows 95 networks: coaxial and twisted pair. You must purchase the proper cable to build or expand your network. Also remember that the connector and tool requirements for each of these cable plans are different. In this section we will introduce you to the tools and techniques of cable construction and offer some suggestions on sources for supplies. Use this information as a starting point and, whenever possible, purchase your network supplies from a local source. This will help ensure that you buy the right product, and you probably will be able to get faster support before and after the sale from a local supplier.

Whether you purchase preconfigured cables or make your own, here are the general specifications you should look for:

Coaxial (10Base2) Networks: RG-58 A/U or equivalent cable

Twisted Pair (10BaseT) Networks: Category 5, 4-Pair (8 wires) cable

You can buy—from most sources—either of these cables with connectors in lengths starting at 3 feet. And you can buy bulk cable in lengths from 100 feet to 1,000 feet. There are numerous sources for these cables (look under "Wire and Cable" in your telephone directory yellow pages), including The DataCom Mall (see the name and address list under "Sources" later in this appendix).

For coaxial cable, you will need the DataCom Mall's "Coaxial Thinwire Ethernet" cable or equivalent (Part Number 75333 for 500-feet, or Black Box No. LCN300A-0500). The DataCom twisted pair cable is listed as "4-pair, Category 5" cable (Part number 78685 for 1000-feet, or Black Box No. EYN739A-B). Many of the other suppliers in the "Sources" section of this appendix also offer these cables.

When you buy bulk cable you will also need connectors, of course. For twisted pair cables, you need RJ-45 connectors that you crimp onto the cable (you'll need a special tool for this, too—see the next section). The DataCom part number for an RJ-45 stranded wire connector is 67095, or Black Box No. FM010.

T I P Most crimp-on connectors are designed for either solid wire or stranded wire. Although you can usually get by using either type of connector with either type of wire, don't depend on it. You may find that you don't get reliable connections if you use the wrong connector. Stranded cables are generally packaged in a flat cover while the solid cables are usually round. In general, you should use stranded wire for short runs to individual workstations, such as the cable that connects a wall connector to your PC. The solid cable is used for in-wall or plenum runs. This is because the stranded cable can withstand more flexing without breaking than the solid wires can.

For coaxial cable, look for BNC connectors in twist-on or crimp-on style. DataCom lists these connectors as No. 75347 for Crimp-on style (Black Box No. FC055).

Once you have collected the proper cables and connectors, you'll need a way to put them together. A variety of tools with varying levels of features and performance is available. That's the good news. The bad news is, these things aren't inexpensive. Expect to spend between $100 and $250 for a quality tool! However, if you are interested in network building and need custom lengths, you'll use these tools over and over again. If you don't plan to do much network building, cheaper (and less functional tools) can be found for less than $50.

Look for the DataCom RJ-45 tool number 75961 (Black Box No. FT150) or the Coax Crimp Tool, Number 75960 (Black Box No. FT046A).

T I P Many suppliers of networking cable products offer free documentation on cable designs, connector styles, how to attach connectors, how to use the crimping tools, and so on. Just ask.

Wall Plates and Patch Panels

Once you go beyond a few computers connected in a network, you may want to consider some additional hardware to make things a little easier.

For example, when you wire for a 10BaseT network, we like to use termination wall plates to make it easier to connect individual workstations. You run cable from the wiring closet (maybe not a closet in the strictest sense of the word, but the central terminating point for your network) to the workstation location where you attach an RJ-45 jack mounted in a wall plate. Then to connect a computer to the network you run a short piece of cable from the wall plate to the network interface card on the computer. Look for the DataCom No. 75167 wall plate in conjunction with the No. 75194 jack (Black Box No. WP504, which includes the wall plate and one 8-conductor jack).

To facilitate the central connections of a 10BaseT network, you'll want to use RJ-45 patch panels. These panels contain a series of RJ-45 jacks on the front with punch-down connectors or other attachments for the individual network cables. When you have run the network cables (the ones that attach to individual workstations) through the walls and attached to wall plates, you can connect the other end at a common point inside a patch panel. Now to connect a particular workstation to a hub or server, you connect a short RJ-45 cable between two jacks.

You can buy patch panels that contain only a few connections or those that contain dozens. DataCom, for example, offers a 24-port panel (No. 75112) for about $160 as this book is written. These panels are designed to mount inside a standard, 19-inch rack, or on the wall with an integral cover. The Black Box offers an interesting 24-port model for wall mounting that lets you make all Category 5 connections from the front of the unit (Model JPM085A).

Sources

There is an almost unbelievable variety of suppliers for the hardware you need to configure a Windows 95 network. Again, we recommend local suppliers in general because this lets you see and touch the products you are buying, and it lets you benefit from personal advice. However, you can sometimes find more variety and better prices from national, mail order sources. Besides, just as browsing a hardware store can show you items you perhaps didn't know about before, browsing network supply catalogues can help you find solutions you didn't know about previously.

Here are a few sources you can consult to help you get started. These companies have offered mail order service for quite some time and they offer a wide variety of computer and network supplies. We can't list everyone here, of course, just the ones we know about and can recommend as a starting place for your research. Request catalogues or study World Wide Web sites for additional information.

Allied Electronics
7410 Pebble Drive
Fort Worth, TX 76118-6997
Phone: (817) 595-3500
www.allied.avnet.com/allied/index.html

Black Box Corporation
PO Box 12800
Pittsburgh, PA 15241
800-552-6816
412-746-5500
www.blackbox.com

CDW Computer Centers, Inc.
1020 E. Lake Cook Road
Buffalo Grove, IL 60089
800-216-4239
www.cdw.com

DataCom Mall
2645 Maricopa Street
Torrance, CA 90503-5144
800-898-3242
www.datacom-mall.com

Digi-Key Corporation
701 Brooks Avenue South
Thief River Falls, MN 56701-0677
800-344-4539
www.digikey.com

Micro Warehouse
1720 Oak Street
Lakewood, NJ 08701-5926
800-367-7080
www.warehouse.com

PC Connection
6 Mill Street
Marlow, NH 03456
800-800-1111
206.170.160.2:80/PC_CONNECT/

The PC Zone
15815 SE 37th Street
Bellevue, WA 98006-1800
800-258-2088
www2.pcy.mci.net/marketplace/mzone/html/2300.html

Glossary

batch program	A text file that contains one or more commands to control a computer process. Batch files can be executed like program files. They in turn call other programs or processes as if the commands were typed from the keyboard. Batch files can be used to automate software setup or installation, to run a series of programs, and other tasks.
binding	A process that establishes a relationship between a protocol driver and a network adapter driver. Binding controls the operation of a Windows 95 network.
browse	Scanning lists of directories or other online information. Browsing usually involves using one or more computer utilities. If you browse a directory list, for example, you will use an intrinsic directory tool in Windows 95. You can also browse online information, such as World Wide Web data, using a browser such as Netscape or the Microsoft Internet Explorer.
cascading menu	See *hierarchical menu*.
client	A computer on a network that accesses shared data, programs, and other resources on a central computer called a *server*. Also a program that runs over a network and access program and data resources from a central server.

coaxial network cable	A network interconnect cable that consists of a central wire, encased in a dielectric sheath, which is in turn covered with a woven shield. The entire cable is bound with a protective covering.
computer name	A unique name that identifies a computer on a network. In Windows 95, computer names can be up to 15 characters long but cannot contain any spaces.
device driver	Software that permits a computer or computer application to work with specific devices. Driver software is required for printers and to support network interface cards. Software drivers may also be required for some software applications.
dial-up networking	A process of sharing resources on a remote network via a dial-up link on a telephone line. Windows 95 contains built-in support for dial-up networking. Dial-up networking permits users with laptop or desktop machines at remote locations to log into a Windows 95 network to run applications and share data and other resources as if they were connected to the network from a local position.
directory tree	A hierarchical structure of files and directories on a computer disk. The tree structure is so called because of the similarity of the structure to a tree trunk with multiple branches off the central structure. This design helps users track and maintain files in a logical manner.
DNS	See *Domain Name System*.
domain	A collection of computers on a network. Domains are usually given names to facilitate intra- and Internet access.
Domain Name System (DNS)	A name service for a TCP/IP network. A DNS maintains a database of device names and associated IP addresses. A DNS permits users and applications to query a TCP/IP network,

including the Internet, by device name instead of IP address.

file sharing

Enabling multiuser access to a single file over a network. Shared files reside on a server workstation and are accessed over the network from one or more client machines. Networking and application software must protect shared files from damage and enable multiple users to update information. Any Windows 95 Network workstation can share files (act as a *server*) and access shared files (act as a *client*) if the proper settings are enabled in the Network dialog box.

File Transfer Protocol (FTP)

A networking protocol to enable remote users to download (copy) files from a server to a client over the network. Windows 95 includes an FTP client that you can access from the Run dialog box by typing **ftp** and clicking on **OK**.

folder

A logical container for computer objects. A folder is usually the same as a subdirectory and is named to allow easy access to the information it contains. Folders in Windows 95 are represented by small icons that look like conventional office file folders. Folders contain files.

font

A set of character attributes. Fonts are named so that you can apply the set of characteristics easily to a selected group of characters or to a whole file.

free space

The amount of storage space available for use on a disk drive.

FTP

See *File Transfer Protocol.*

Gateway

A computer on a network that serves as a conduit or port to external resources. An electronic mail gateway, for example, enables multiple users on a local area network to access remote mail services through one workstation configured as a gateway. In Windows 95, you can use a

	fax gateway to permit multiple users access to incoming and outgoing faxes across the network.
hierarchical directory	A subordinate directory structure. Hierarchical directories contain one or more subdirectories that contain files associated in some logical way with the directories above them.
hierarchical menu	A menu that is a submenu of another menu item. It is sometimes called a *cascade* or *stairstep* menu.
home directory	A network user's personal directory. It contains configuration files, data, and programs for that particular user. A home directory also can be shared among groups of users.
host	In a TCP/IP network, any device connected to the network. The term host also is frequently used interchangeably for *server* on some networks.
hub	A hardware device that permits interconnection of computers in a twisted pair network.
INF file	A data file that contains information used by Windows 95 Setup to configure a device. An INF file usually is provided by the manufacturer of the product, such as a printer, that is being configured by Setup. Special INF files also can be created to help automate the setup process.
INI file	Initialization file used by Windows-based applications to control start-up configuration. Windows 95 doesn't use INI files, but it can support *legacy* applications that require them.
interrupt request lines (IRQ)	Hardware lines used by computer devices to request services from applications or other devices. IRQs are numbered and generally each device in the computer is assigned a unique IRQ ID.
I/O device	An Input/Output device. Any device that controls, manages, or passes information going into or coming out of a computer or computer

	subsystem. A disk drive, for example, is an I/O device, as is a keyboard or a display adapter.
IP address	Internet protocol address, used to provide a unique identity for all devices on a TCP/IP network.
IP router	A hardware device used to control the routing and destination of TCP/IP information over a network and among networks.
IPX/SPX	Transport protocols used in Novell networks.
IRQ	See *interrupt request lines*.
ISA	Industry Standard Architecture, the name for the original IBM PC/AT system bus.
legacy	Older hardware and software that doesn't support some of the advanced features of Windows 95, particularly devices that do not conform to the Plug and Play standard.
local printer	A printer connected directly to a computer's parallel or serial port instead of accessed over the network. A local printer may be shared with the network to become a remote printer for other workstations on the network.
logical drive	A subpartition or extended partition on a local or remote hard drive.
login script	A command file that automates the log-in process to a Windows 95 or other network.
MS-DOS-based application	A software application that is designed to run in MS-DOS instead of the Windows or Windows 95 environment. Such an application cannot take full advantage of the extended features available in Windows 95.
NetBEUI transport	NetBIOS Extended User interface. NetBEUI is the network transport protocol supplied with Windows 95.
NetBIOS interface	Network Basic Input/Output System Interface. A programming interface that facilitates input/output requests from a remote computer. A

software interface such as this makes the hardware associated with the network transparent to applications that are exchanging data across the network.

network basic Input/Output system (NetBIOS)
Software that allows communication across the the network through other applications.

NIC
See *network interface card*.

network interface card (NIC)
A hardware device that interfaces a computer workstation to a network. NICs are available for *ISA* and other bus architectures to support connection to *twisted pair* (10BaseT) or *coaxial* (10Base2) networks.

Password
A unique series of characters to allow individual users to log into a network. Proper password management prevents unauthorized persons from accessing accounts.

Path
Specifies the precise location of a file within a directory tree by showing each directory and subdirectory in order.

PCI
Peripheral Component Interconnect. A local bus architecture that is gaining popularity with PC hardware and is expected to become the successor of the VESA local bus. A local bus is used for high-speed data transfer between a computer's processor and memory as well as among peripheral devices such as a display adapter.

PCMCIA
Personal Computer memory Card International Association. An interface card standard used to connect external devices such as disk drives or modems to a personal computer. Currently the reference is mostly shortened to *PC card*.

Plug and Play BIOS
A BIOS that configures Plug and Play cards and other system devices during configuration or during computer power-up operations.

Point to Point Protocol (PPP)	A dial-up networking protocol used to connect remote computers to a local host or local network. PPP software is supplied as part of Windows 95 and is most frequently used to connect a Windows 95 computer to an Internet host or to another Windows 95 machine.
printer sharing	The process of making a computer's local printer available for use by other computers on a local area network.
protocol	A set of software rules or conventions that allows computers and other devices to communicate across a network.
Registry	A Windows 95 database that stores information about hardware and software available on an individual machine. The Registry supersedes the *.INI files used by previous versions of Windows.
Registry Editor	An editing utility that permits you to change entries in the Windows 95 Registry.
remote administration	The administration and configuration of one computer by a user working on a remote machine over a network.
RJ-45	A twisted pair cable connector commonly used for networks. This connector is similar to the RJ-11 connector used on most telephones.
router	A hardware device that tracks the location of individual network components and manages traffic moving to and from these devices.
routing	The process of forwarding packets of information to other network devices.
SCSI	Small Computer System Interface. An Input/Output standard for connecting a variety of devices to a computer system. A SCSI interface can mix printers, disk drives, plotters, and other devices on the same bus. Each SCSI device has a unique number and ID.

Serial Line Internet Protocol (SLIP)	A dial-up networking interconnect standard. Windows 95 includes SLIP software that can be used to connect two Windows 95 computers, or to connect a computer running Windows 95 with an Internet host. See also *PPP*.
server	A computer that stores shared data or applications. Client computers access server facilities over a network.
session	The interconnection of two applications over a network. When a user logs into a network host to conduct some operations, the user is said to be *participating in a session*. Users in general can open multiple sessions to conduct simultaneous operations.
share	To make resources on a local computer available for use by other users across the network.
shared directory	A directory on a local computer that is *shared*—made available for use by others over the network.
simple network management protocol (SNMP)	A protocol used by SNMP-compliant software to communicate over a network. SNMP applications perform a variety of functions, including monitoring device status of network components.
SLIP	See *Serial Line Internet Protocol*.
SNMP	See *simple network management protocol*.
socket	A logical (software) Input/Output facility that permits networked computers to communicate.
spooler	A software facility that stores information destined for a printer or other device on a network disk drive. Once stored, the data can be managed by the spooler software, freeing the source application for other duties.
TCP/IP	Transfer Control Protocol/Internet Protocol. A networking protocol that is the primary transport protocol for wide area networks such as the Internet.

Telnet	A software facility that allows a local computer to communicate over a network with a remote system.
twisted pair cable	A network interconnect cable that uses multiple wires twisted together inside an outer covering. High-speed networking cable uses 8 twisted wires (4 pair).
user name	An unique name that identifies an individual user to Windows 95 or another network.
VESA bus	Video Electronic Standards Association bus. A local bus standard that permits high speed communication between a computer's central processor and memory or other devices. See also *PCI*.
workgroup	A collection of computers on a network. A workgroup can be a physical or logical grouping of machines to make management easier and to facilitate the work habits of individual machine users.
workstation	A powerful computer system. However, today the term is used generally to refer to any networked computer system.

INDEX